Home Economics and Food Technology

Elaine Prisk, Lynn Rogers and Miriam Staddon

CollinsEducational
An Imprint of HarperCollins*Publishers*

Published in 1991 by CollinsEducational
An imprint of HarperCollins*Publishers*
77–85 Fulham Palace Road
Hammersmith
London W6 8JB

First published 1991
Reprinted 1992

British Library Cataloguing in Publication Data
Prisk, Elaine
   Home economics and food technology.
   1. Home economics
   I. Title   II. Rogers, Lynn   III. Staddon, Miriam
   640

ISBN 0 00 329486 2

Illustrated by Paul Allingham, Jenny Mumford and
Angela Lumley
Cover illustration from Zefa Picture Library
Typeset by Cambridge Photosetting Services
Printed and bound in Great Britain by
Butler & Tanner Ltd, Frome and London

CONTENTS

Welcome!

This book will help you to succeed in GCSE or Standard Grade Home Economics. Each topic is presented in a self-contained unit, and covers a necessary part of your syllabus. If you do not know about the subject content of your syllabus, ask your teacher to explain this to you and to show you the syllabus. It is not intended that you work your way through this book in any order – just pick out the topics as and when you need them. Answering the workshop questions will help you to understand each topic. Some workshop questions also suggest further research and some suggest practical investigations and assignments for you to carry out. Read the pages about the assignments and investigations to help you to plan these.

What's in it for me?

Succeeding in Home Economics will not only give you a useful qualification, it will also help you to learn many skills which will be useful in your everyday life in the future.

How does this happen?

All the examination boards have **objectives**. The objectives set out the skills you will develop through learning about Home Economics. The written work you do, the practical work and the assignments will all help in developing these skills. You will learn how to:

- Analyse, to decide what is most important
- Find and use information
- Find out in a practical way, to investigate things
- Make plans
- Carry out plans using practical skills
- Evaluate, to make conclusions

How can these skills be useful in the future?

Suppose you want to buy a new fan oven.

a **Analyse, decide what is most important** You ask yourself some questions: Who will use the fan oven? How much money do you have to spend? How much space is available in the kitchen?

b **Find and use information** You go to the library, look up *Which?* reports and make a list of reliable makes.

c **Investigate** You visit several shops, compare prices and examine fan ovens.

d **Make plans** You decide which fan oven to buy and how to pay for it.

e **Carry out plans** You return to the shop and order the fan oven.

f **Evaluate** You use the fan oven at home and decide how to get the best out of it.

You could also use your skills to:
- Plan and prepare meals suitable for various types of people
- Use a variety of appliances
- Manage money well
- Judge new foods and food products

Studying Home Economics helps you to solve problems and make decisions. This is important in our rapidly-changing world.

Practical assignments

The number of marks you get for coursework varies, but can be as much as 65% of your final mark. These marks are based on two or three practical assignments. There are two main types of assignment, Problem-solving and Investigation. The following information will help you with these.

Problem-solving assignments

This is an example of a problem-solving assignment:

Suggest some healthy dishes which could be served as school lunches. In a practical session, prepare a selection of these dishes. Evaluate the whole assignment.

Let's see how this assignment could be planned by following objectives.

---

a Analyse

Read the question carefully, pick out the most important points: recipes chosen must be healthy, dishes must be suitable for school meals, dishes must appeal to school pupils, dishes must be economical.

b Recall, seek out, select, record, apply knowledge

Ask pupils about likes and dislikes. Which foods would they like for school meals? *Talk* to school meals staff about the type of meals they serve, the amount of time for preparation and cooking, the costs and equipment available.
Look at recipe books for ideas. *Read* about healthy eating, follow dietary guidelines. *Find out* about the dietary needs of school pupils. *Make notes* about the most important things you have found out.

c Make choices, justify choices

Write a list of suitable dishes. Give reasons for your choice. Select the dishes you are going to prepare in the practical session.

d Plan a course of action

Make a time plan for the practical session. This does not have to be too detailed. Include brief notes of the methods used, oven times and temperatures.

e Carry out your course of action

Cook the dishes in the practical session. Try to follow your time plan. Be tidy, hygienic and well organised. Use equipment well, carry out methods skilfully and correctly.

f Evaluate

Evaluate the whole assignment, the planning and the practical work as well as the finished results.

You may be given headings under which to write each part of the written explanation. Study the marks allocated to each part of the assignment. This will help you to decide how much time should be given to each section, and how detailed you should be.

Your assignments will not spell out how many dishes you should make. It is up to you to decide what you are capable of doing and to use your time as well as you can.

Your guide to investigation assignments

In an investigation there is no one right answer. Your own opinion matters. Your results might be different from your friend's results, and you might come to different conclusions. Each investigation is a piece of original work, and that is one reason why they are interesting to do.

Home Economics investigations can take many forms. Here are some examples:

Test or compare appliances
Compare two similar food mixers, processors or blenders. Decide which performs best, is best value for money. Compare a food mixer with a processor for making cakes or pastry.

Compare methods of preparation and cooking
Compare quick methods of cake making with traditional methods.

Adapt recipes
Adapt recipes to reduce sugar, reduce fat and increase fibre.

Investigate ways of saving fuel
Investigate ways of saving fuel by using small appliances. Investigate ways of using fuel more efficiently by using the oven only or the hob only.

Compare ingredients
Compare wholemeal with white flour, polyunsaturated fat with saturated fat, low-fat products (e.g. cheeses) with full-fat varieties.

These are just some examples of investigations, many of which can be found in the workshop sections throughout the book.

You do not have to cook anything to carry out an investigation. You could learn a great deal about saving energy by just boiling water in different ways. In an investigation it is not the finished dishes which are important but the way in which you carried out your investigation and the results you obtained.

Planning an investigation

Investigations need to be carefully planned. You must have a clear idea in your mind of what you are hoping to achieve. For example, suppose your investigation is to find out whether half-fat Cheddar gives a good result in cooking. You decide to make cheese scones, using two types of cheese: Cheddar and half-fat Cheddar. Cheese is your *variable*. Everything else must be *constant* (stay the same) so you must use the same recipe, the same ingredients, the same amounts, the same method, roll scones to exactly the same size, put on the same oven shelf, cook for the same length of time. Why is this important? It is very important because when you draw up your results you must be sure that any differences you can see or taste in the scones are the result of using different cheeses.

Let's look at another example: *Investigate types of yeast for breadmaking.* You make two batches of bread rolls, one with easyblend dried yeast and one with fresh yeast.

Variable   Easyblend yeast, fresh yeast

Constants   Use the same recipe, the same quantities, the same method, leave to rise for the same length of time, weigh rolls before shaping to make sure they are the same size, bake on the same shelf for the same length of time.

Apart from deciding which are variables and which are constants, you can plan investigations in a similar way to other assignments.

Investigate the use of a low-sodium salt substitute in cooking

a Analyse

A recipe must be chosen which can be made with salt and a salt substitute. The recipe needs to be one which can be finished and tasted in the time.

b Recall, seek out, select, record, apply knowledge

Find out about the salt substitute. How is it used? How much does it cost? It is easily obtained? Read information about salt in the diet, look up recipes. Write about the salt substitute and about the need to reduce salt in the diet.

c Make choices, justify choices

Make a list of suitable dishes in which the salt substitute could be used. Give reasons for choosing these dishes. Select dishes to prepare.

d Plan a course of action

Make a time plan for the practical session. Remember that you have only one variable (the salt). Make sure everything else remains constant. Decide how to present your results.

e Carry out your course of action

Carry out the investigation, arrange for three testers to take part in comparison tasting.

f Evaluate

Using the results of the tasting session, write about the use of salt substitutes in cooking. Remember to give your own opinion.

Presenting your results

Having well-recorded and clearly-presented results is important because it will help you to evaluate your investigation and make conclusions. Here are some ways you might record and present results.

A comparison chart

	Pressure Cooker	Steamer	Microwave
Cooking time			
Colour			
Flavour			
Texture			
Fuel cost			

A bar graph

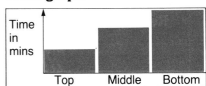

Investigation of heat distribution in gas oven. Time scones took to cook on each shelf.

A line graph

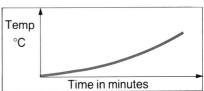

Investigation of frozen food temperatures during shopping and carrying home.

7

Your guide to evaluations

You will probably find writing evaluations difficult – most people do! So, what is the point of an evaluation? Why can't you be given a mark for your finished work and leave it at that?

Evaluation can serve many useful purposes. It can help you to

- learn about your own strengths and weaknesses
- look at your own work critically and pick out your mistakes
- analyse your mistakes so that you can improve your work
- appreciate what you have learned
- have a sense of achievement when you have done well.

If you check your mark scheme you will see that evaluations have quite a high mark allocation and so you can improve your total marks a lot by making a good and detailed evaluation. Most assignments ask you to evaluate the whole assignment. This means you need to write about your planning and the way you worked in the practical session as well as your finished results. You may find it helpful to make some notes as you go along. When you are ready to write your evaluation:

Read the assignment question again
Read your notes
Think about your work
Ask yourself some questions

These are questions you should ask yourself about your work:

Introduction   Did I start by writing a sentence of introduction?

My assignment was about healthy school meals.

Written   How good was my written plan?

I think my plan was good, but I found it difficult to decide the most important points to write about.

Research   Was my research good?

My research was good because I talked to pupils and school meals staff.

Information   Did I find out all the information I needed to know?

I found out a lot about healthy eating from books and leaflets.

Choice   Was my choice of dishes good?

After talking to pupils and reading about healthy eating, I found it easy to make a list of suitable dishes. I think my choice was good.

Use of time   Did I set myself the right amount of work?

I set myself a lot of work. I was very busy for the whole hour but I just managed to finish on time, apart from washing up.

Time plan

Was my time plan good? Was I able to follow it?

I was not able to follow my plan. I had not allocated my time very well. A better plan would have helped.

Preparation time

Did I use the preparation time sensibly?

I did all my weighing-out and collected all my equipment in the preparation time. I don't think I would have finished if I had not done this.

Equipment

What equipment did I use? Did I use it well?

Cooking the potatoes in the microwave and using the processor for the pizza base saved a lot of time

Methods

Did I show skill in the methods I used?

I didn't make any mistakes in the methods I used but I think I could have kneaded and shaped the pizza dough better.

Organisation

Was I well organised in the way I worked? Was I tidy and hygienic?

One of my main faults in the practical was that I was untidy. This was because I was short of time and I panicked a bit.

Results

What was the appearance, taste and texture of the finished dishes?

I was pleased with my finished results. The pizza was colourful because of the red and green peppers on top and it tasted very nice, with just enough herbs, but the base could have been better shaped.

Conclusion

How well did I carry out this assignment? Could I have done anything differently or better? What have I learned?

I thought this was an interesting assignment. I learned a lot about healthy eating and about what pupils would like for school meals. If I did the assignment again the main thing I would change would be my plan. If I had done a better plan I might have been better organised in the practical session. Otherwise I think I did a good assignment.

Some important dos and don'ts

Don't be vague. If you make a statement, try to give a reason for what you are saying. This is just a statement:

The dough was heavy and not well risen

But it could be improved:

The dough was heavy and not well risen because I did not leave it to rise for long enough before I put it in the oven.

This is better because a reason has been given for what happened. This shows you are able to analyse what happened.

Don't give vague descriptions of your finished results, such as "looked nice", "tasted all right" or "was quite good". Try to explain why it looked good or what it was about the taste that you liked.

This is too vague:

The pie looked all right.

This is better:

The pie was evenly browned and shiny on top. It looked very appetising.

Do admit your mistakes. You need not be afraid of being critical of yourself. If you made mistakes during the practical session you will have lost some marks, but you can not lose any more marks for saying what your mistakes were. In fact, you can gain marks in an evaluation by saying what went wrong and how it could be avoided in the future.

The proof of the pudding is in the sensory evaluation!

You will gain more marks in evaluations if you are able to describe your results well. Sensory evaluation means that you judge your results by using your senses.

The chart below gives some ideas for describing results. In groups, draw up your own descriptions chart. You can then use it to help you evaluate your results.

Appearance:	Colourful, attractive, well risen, well shaped.
Taste:	Sweet, salty, sour, any distinctive flavour, herbs, spices, garlic, strong flavour, bland.
Aroma:	Pleasant, unpleasant, garlic, herbs, spices.
Texture:	Crunchy, smooth, light, heavy, floury, dry, moist, greasy, chewy, tender.

Appearance   Aroma

Taste   Texture

Comparison tests

This descriptive way of evaluating your results is suitable for assignments in which you need to judge how good your results are, but you may need to compare results. Many investigations lead you to make comparisons:

> salt *versus* a low-sodium
> salt substitute
> sugar *versus* reduced sugar
> fat *versus* reduced fat
> home-made *versus* convenience food
> microwave *versus* oven-baked

If you carry out one of these investigations you will have two dishes which need to be compared and evaluated. Is there any difference? Which is the best?

How to carry out comparison tests

1 Put small samples of each dish on saucers. Label saucers ○ and □. Keep a note of which is which, but do not tell the tasters.
2 Ask two or three people to taste your samples.
3 Ask your tasters if they can detect any difference between ○ and □. If so, ask them which one they prefer.

The triangle test

This is a comparison test similar to the previous one.
1 Put out three samples for tasting, labelled ○, □, ×. (Two samples will be the same.) Make sure you know which is which but do not tell the tasters.
2 Ask the tasters if they can pick the odd one out.
3 Ask them which they prefer.

These comparison tests will help you to write about the results of your investigations and to make conclusions. For example, your assignment could be to investigate the possibility of using less sugar in cooking. You might make two versions of a fruit cake, one with less sugar. The tasters say one sample of cake tastes less sweet but they still like both of them. You are then able to conclude that people can tell the difference if you reduce sugar but this does not spoil their enjoyment of the cake. You have proved that it is possible to use less sugar in cooking and still get an acceptable result.

A rating scale

Another way of making a sensory evaluation of your results is to ask people to taste a sample and to give it a rating depending on how much they liked it. You might do this if you were trying out a new recipe. This is an example of a rating scale:

5	4	3	2	1
I really like this food	I quite like this food	I neither like nor dislike this food	I rather dislike this food	I strongly dislike this food

Healthy eating

Over the last decade many people have become very concerned about the amounts and kinds of foods they are eating. They are realising that the British diet contains:

TOO MUCH fat.   TOO MUCH salt.
TOO MUCH sugar. NOT ENOUGH fibre.

To help people eat more healthily and choose food more wisely, experts have published guidelines in reports. The main reports about the British diet have been published by NACNE[*] in 1983 and COMA[†] in 1984. This is what the reports recommended:

NACNE		COMA
Reduce to 30% of total energy.	**FAT**	Reduce to 30% of total energy.
Only 10% from saturated fats.		Only 15% from saturated fats.
Reduce by 50%.	**SUGAR**	There should be no increase.
Reduce to 3 g per day.	**SALT**	There should be no increase and we should try to find ways of decreasing the amount used.
Increase from 20 g to 30 g per day.	**FIBRE**	Increase from 20 g to 30 g per day.

What is the percentage of total energy from food?

Energy from food is obtained from carbohydrate, fat, protein and alcohol.

1 g of carbohydrate	provides 4 kcal or 16 kJ of energy
1 g of fat	provides 9 kcal or 37 kJ of energy
1 g of protein	provides 4 kcal or 16 kJ of energy
1 g of alcohol	provides 7 kcal or 29 kJ of energy

If we look up the amounts of these nutrients in food composition tables we can calculate the amount of energy they would provide. For example, 100 g of chocolate biscuits contains 67.4 g carbohydrate, 27.6 g fat, 5.7 g protein, so the energy content is:

67.4 × 4 =	269.6 kcal from carbohydrate
27.6 × 9 =	248.4 kcal from fat
5.7 × 4 =	22.8 kcal from protein
Total	540.8 kcal

[*] The National Advisory Committee on Nutrition Education.
[†] Committee on Medical Aspects of Food Policy.

To calculate the percentage of energy from fat, we need to know the energy from fat and the total energy. For chocolate biscuits the energy from fat is 248.4 kcal and the total energy 540.8 kcal.

$$\% \text{ energy from fat} = \frac{248.4}{540.8} \times 100 = 45.93 \text{ or } 46\%$$

Is this a healthy food?

In the same way, we can calculate the percentage of energy from any nutrient in either a food, a meal or a day's meals, so long as we know the amount of energy from the nutrient and the total energy of the food, meal or day's meals.

Heart disease

One in eleven men and one in forty women will die of this disease before the age of 65. Death rates from heart disease in the UK are among the highest in the world.

Death rates from diseases of the circulatory system for the twenty highest ranking countries in 1987 (age standardized) per 100 000 of standard population.

Males		Females	
Bulgaria	826	Romania	708
Romania	823	Bulgaria	636
Hungary	820	Yugoslavia	559
Czechoslovakia	812	Hungary	549
Poland	774	Czechoslovakia	536
German Democratic Republic	752	Malta	536
Malta	729	German Democratic Republic	535
Yugoslavia	714	Poland	477
Republic of Ireland	656	Argentina	410
Scotland	644	Republic of Ireland	401
N. Ireland	641	N. Ireland	394
Finland	620	Scotland	378
Argentina	581	Austria	377
Bahamas	566	Italy	355
Austria	565	Luxemburg	353
Luxemburg	564	New Zealand	337
England and Wales	556	Israel	336
New Zealand	542	England and Wales	327
German Federal Republic	529	German Federal Republic	327
Sweden	527	Australia	325

How can you beat heart disease?

Eat healthily
Avoid becoming overweight

Exercise regularly

Don't smoke

Workshop

1 Which foods contain high amounts of sugar?

2 In what kinds of foods will you find fibre?

3 Carry out a survey in your class to find out what the favourite foods are, then decide if your class could eat more healthily.

4 a Calculate the percentage of energy from fat in a day's meals that contain 180 g carbohydrate, 105 g fats, and 90 g protein.
   b Was the percentage of energy from fat in this day's meals higher or lower than the NACNE and COMA recommendations?

5 a Using the table above, write down the five countries where the risk of heart disease is the greatest for males and females.
   b Do these countries have anything in common which may explain why there is such a high rate of heart disease?

6 List four rules for healthy eating.

7 a Plan a day's meals for yourself and three friends, one of whom is trying to lose weight. Make sure that you follow the dietary guidelines. Explain why you have chosen these foods.
   b If you have a computer program available (e.g. MICRODIET), find out the amounts of fat, sugar and dietary fibre which are present and evaluate your day's meals.

How do you measure up?

There is plenty of advice available about healthy eating, and the eating habits you develop as a teenager may stay with you for the rest of your life. Your diet will not only influence your health now but also in the future. Therefore *you* have to decide:

- How you measure up to the targets set
- What changes you need to make, and how you are going to make them.

Is your weight OK?

Use the chart below to assess whether you are a healthy weight for your height.

Mark the point where the straight line across from your height meets the line up from your weight

Measure your height without shoes and your weight without clothes

What is a healthy weight?

Underweight   Try to eat more, but choose healthy foods.
OK   You are eating the right amount of food – but is it healthy food?
Overweight   Try to lose weight – eat less and exercise more.
Fat   It's very important that you lose weight.
Very Fat   You need to lose weight urgently. See your doctor.

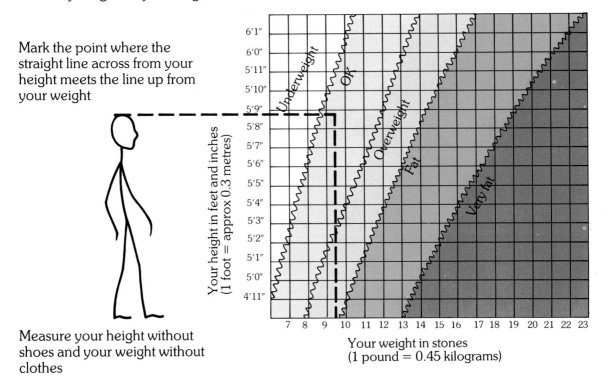

Your height in feet and inches
(1 foot = approx 0.3 metres)

Your weight in stones
(1 pound = 0.45 kilograms)

How many fillings do you have?

Eating too many foods containing high amounts of sugar leads to tooth decay, especially if these foods or drinks are eaten as snacks between meals.

Almost one in four adults have no teeth of their own, and nearly half the under fives in England and Wales show some signs of tooth decay. On average, fifteen-year-olds have 8.4 decayed, missing or filled teeth.

Is your diet OK?

Try the quiz on this page and overleaf to help you find out the answer.
The sections are related to the dietary guidelines for the average person.
Remember, be honest!

§§§ **Quiz** §§§

A Fat

1 Which type of fat do you usually spread on bread or savoury biscuits?
   a Butter or hard margarine
   b Soft margarine
   c Polyunsaturated margarine
   d Low-fat spread
   e No fat

2 Which type of fat do you usually use for cooking and baking?
   a Butter/margarine/dripping/lard/white cooking fat
   b Blended vegetable oil
   c Pure vegetable oil, e.g. soya or sunflower oil

3 How many times a week do you eat chips?
   a Every day
   b 3–4 times a week
   c Once a week
   d Very rarely or never

4 How many times a week do you eat crisps?
   a Every day
   b 3–4 times a week
   c Once a week
   d Very rarely or never

5 Which method of cooking do you use for bacon, sausages and burgers?
   a Frying
   b Grilling
   c You rarely eat these foods

6 How frequently do you eat sausages, meat pies or burgers?
   a Most days
   b 3–4 times a week
   c Once a week
   d Very rarely or never

7 Which type of cheese do you usually eat?
   a Full-fat, e.g. Cheddar, Cheshire
   b Medium-fat, e.g. Camembert, Edam, cheese spread
   c Low-fat, e.g. Cottage cheese, low-fat cheese such as Shape or Tendale.

8 Which type of milk do you use?
   a Channel Island
   b Full-cream
   c Semi-skimmed
   d Skimmed

§§

B Sugar

9 How much sugar do you have in a cup of tea or coffee?
   a 3 tsps
   b 2 tsps
   c 1 tsp
   d No sugar

10 How frequently do you eat sweets or chocolate?
   a 3–4 times a day
   b 1–2 times a day
   c Occasionally
   d Rarely or never

11 How often do you eat cakes or biscuits?
   a 3–4 times a day
   b 1–2 times a day
   c Occasionally
   d Rarely or never

12 How often do you have soft drinks?
   a 3–4 times a day
   b 1–2 times a day
   c Occasionally
   d Rarely or never

§§

(continues on next page)   15

§§§

C Salt

13 Do you add salt to your food at table?
  a Always, before tasting it
  b Sometimes, only after tasting
  c Rarely or never

14 How much salt do you add when cooking vegetables?
  a 1 tsp
  b ½ tsp
  c A pinch
  d None or a salt substitute

15 How often do you eat crisps and/or salted nuts?
  a More than once a day
  b Once a day
  c 2–3 times a week
  d Once a week
  e Rarely or never

§§§

Look at page 17 for the scores to each question.
Total your score for each of the sections A–D.
What was your score and how can you improve it?

D Fibre

16 What type of bread do you eat?
  a Wholemeal
  b Brown
  c White
  d Mixture

17 What type of rice or pasta do you eat?
  a Whole-grain
  b White
  c Mixture

18 How do you prepare fruit and vegetables?
  a Wash thoroughly and leave skins on when possible
  b Wash thoroughly but always peel
  c When possible eat raw after thorough washing

19 How often do you eat pulse vegetables? (dried peas, beans and lentils)
  a 4–5 times a week
  b 2–3 times a week
  c Once a week
  d Rarely or never

20 How often do you eat jacket potatoes?
  a 4–5 times a week
  b 2–3 times a week
  c Once a week
  d Rarely or never

§§§

Workshop

1 With the help of a partner find out
  (a) How many of your teeth are missing?
  (b) How many fillings have you got?
2 Collect all the class information on
  (a) teeth missing
  (b) number of fillings.
  Use this data to produce two bar charts.
3 What is the average number of
  (a) teeth missing?
  (b) filled teeth?
4 How could you cut down on the amount of fat which you eat?

Scoring for Quiz

A Fat

1	a	4		5	a	2
	b	3			b	1
	c	2			c	0
	d	1				
	e	0		6	a	3
					b	2
2	a	3			c	1
	b	2			d	0
	c	1				
				7	a	3
3	a	3			b	2
	b	2			c	1
	c	1				
	d	0		8	a	3
					b	2
4	a	3			c	1
	b	2			d	0
	c	1				
	d	0				

B Sugar

9	a	3
	b	2
	c	1
	d	0
10	a	3
	b	2
	c	1
	d	0
11	a	3
	b	2
	c	1
	d	0
12	a	3
	b	2
	c	1
	d	0

C Salt

13	a	2
	b	1
	c	0
14	a	3
	b	2
	c	1
	d	0
15	a	4
	b	3
	c	2
	d	1
	e	0

D Fibre

16	a	4		19	a	3
	b	3			b	2
	c	2			c	1
	d	1			d	0
17	a	3		20	a	3
	b	2			b	2
	c	1			c	1
					d	0
18	a	2				
	b	1				
	c	3				

In sections **A, B** and **C** the lower the score, the closer you are to following the healthy eating guidelines.

If your score for section A is over 10 you should try to find ways of reducing the amount of fat you eat. Perhaps you could start by reducing the number of convenience foods you eat, reducing the number of times per week that you eat chips, or by changing to a milk or cheese with a lower fat content.

If you scored more than 5 in sections B and C you should try to reduce the amount of sugar and/or salt you are using. **For section D** the higher your score the better. If you scored 10 or above you choose your food and methods of preparation wisely to ensure that your diet contains sufficient fibre.

Having completed these sections you should have a better picture of how you measure up. However, it is important to realise that there are many other factors which influence your health which we have not looked at. Such things as your living conditions, whether or not you have an active lifestyle, whether you smoke or drink alcohol, whether you have had accidents or infections, and hereditary conditions you may have inherited. All of these help to determine how healthy you are. You cannot alter some of these things, but you can control others.

The healthy diet pyramid should help you to choose foods wisely so that you are following the guidelines for healthy eating.

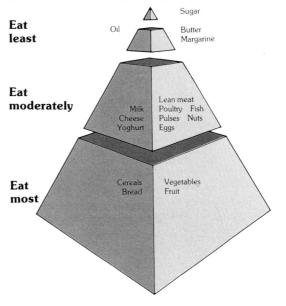

Know your nutrients (1)

Most food is a complex mixture of chemical compounds in the form of nutrients. Nutrients supply the material for the body to:

- provide energy to carry out the body's functions
- form or renew all parts of the body

The main nutrients are carbohydrates, fats and proteins. As these nutrients are needed in fairly large amounts, they are known as the **Macronutrients**. They are usually measured in grams (g).

The human body requires far smaller amounts of vitamins and minerals. These are the **Micronutrients** and they are either measured in milligrams (mg) or micrograms (µg). As well as macronutrients and micronutrients, the body also requires water to function properly.

Macronutrients

Nutrient	Source	Function in body	Recommended daily amount
Carbohydrate	Cereals, vegetables and fruits are best sources. Foods such as cakes, sweets, biscuits, cordials, syrups, sugars, honey and jam contain large amounts but little of other nutrients in proportion to their sugar content, and little or no fibre	Major source of energy Essential for normal cells – necessary for protein to be used properly Excess will be converted to body fat	No specific recommendation but NACNE suggests that in the long term carbohydrates should supply 54% of the total energy intake
1 Monosaccharides (simple sugars)			
Glucose	Fruit, plant juices	Provides energy	
Fructose	Some fruit and vegetables, honey	Provides energy	
Galactose	Present in milk combined with glucose	Provides energy	
2 Disaccharides			
Sucrose	Sugar beet, sugar cane	Provides energy	NACNE recommends that sucrose consumption should be no more than 20 kg per person per year (less than 10% of total energy intake)
Maltose	Germinating cereals, malt products	Provides energy	
Lactose (milk sugar)	Milk of all mammals	Provides energy	
3 Polysaccharides			
Starch	Cereals, bread, flour, rice, yams, bananas, potatoes	Provides energy	
Cellulose (an indigestible polysaccharide)	Cereals, vegetables, fruit, pectin in fruit	Acts as dietary fibre: provides bulk, by absorbing water, aiding the passage of waste products through the digestive tract	NACNE recommends a daily intake of 30 g of dietary fibre per person

Protein	High quality: meat, milk, cheese, yoghurt, fish, eggs, soya beans low quality: nuts, cereals, vegetables	Necessary to build all new cells (synthesis) – life depends on protein Enzymes are proteins Hormones (body regulators) are usually proteins Forms antibodies in the blood to defend the body against infection Can be used for energy production. Excess converted to body fat	Great variation depending on sex, age, occupation Girls under 1 year 27 g Boys under 1 year 30 g Girls 12–14 years 53 g Boys 12–14 years 66 g Girls 15–17 years 53 g Boys 15–17 years 72 g Women 18–54 years 54 g (most occupations) Men 18–34 (moderately active) 72 g Men 35–64 69 g Women 55–74 47 g Women 75+ 42 g Men 65–74 60 g Men 75+ 54 g
Fat	Large amounts: butter, margarine, dripping, lard, oils, cream Average amounts: egg yolk, meat, dairy foods (except butter and cream), fish, nuts Small amounts: some fruits, vegetables, cereals	Provide the body with fat-soluble vitamins A, D, E, K A very rich supply of energy Forms a protective pad around vital organs. Pads pressure points of the body, e.g. heels, buttocks, fingertips. Some hormones are fatty substances. Helps in cell functions	No specific recommendation but NACNE recommends that in the long term fat should provide 30% of total energy intake. COMA suggests 35% total energy intake
Saturated fats	Found in all animal fats in varying amounts and in some vegetable oils such as coconut and palm oil	Provide energy	NACNE suggests that in the long term these fats should supply about 10% of total energy intake COMA suggests 15%
Monounsaturated fats	Most foods which contain fat	Provide energy	No specific recommendation
Polyunsaturated fats	Corn oil, sunflower oil, soya oil, polyunsaturated margarines, oily fish	Help with cell function Required for proper growth and development of brain Production of some hormones	Should provide about 5% of total energy intake
Water (not a nutrient but an essential substance for life – second only to air in importance)	All drinks, fruit, vegetables, meat, dairy foods, cooked cereal products	Essential for all body fluids Essential for hormonal activity Essential for digestion and absorption of nutrients Solvent for waste products	

Workshop

1 What are the macronutrients and in what units are they usually measured?
2 What substance which is neither a macronutrient nor a micronutrient is necessary for the correct functioning of the body?
3 Name two monosaccharides and state in which foods you would find them.
4 What percentage of the energy in your diet should you get from carbohydrates?
5 Why is dietary fibre important in the diet?
6 Explain why proteins are important in the diet.
7 How much protein do you require per day?
8 Name the different groups of fat.
9 How much energy should fats supply in the diet?
10 State two functions of polyunsaturated fats.

Know your nutrients (2)

Micronutrients

Vitamins are a group of organic substances with a wide variety of uses in the body. They are required in very small amounts and must be obtained from the diet, as the body either cannot make them itself or in some cases cannot make sufficient to meet its needs. Vitamins are usually put into two groups:

(a) fat-soluble vitamins A, D, E and K, which, as their name suggests, are found mainly in foods rich in fat.
(b) water-soluble vitamins B complex and C.

Micronutrients: vitamins

Nutrient	Source	Function in body	Recommended daily amount
Vitamin A (retinol & β carotene) 6 μg β carotene produces 1 μg retinol	Cod-liver oil, cheese, liver, carrots, green leafy vegetables, apricots, mango. (On a normal varied diet deficiencies are rare) Excess may be toxic	For normal vision To keep nasal passages moist Helps prevent respiratory infections Involved in growth	Depends on age: babies under 1 year 450 μg, boys and girls 12–14 years 725 μg, boys and girls 15–17 years 750 μg, pregnant women 750 μg Women who are breast-feeding 1200 μg
Vitamin D	Major source is the action of sunlight on the skin. Dietary sources are less significant but best sources are oily fish and cod-liver oil. Excess is toxic	Is needed for the absorption of calcium and phosphorus in the bones and teeth	Varies depending on exposure of skin to sunlight and rate of growth. Most people and babies under 1 year 7.5 μg, pregnant and breast-feeding women 10 μg
Vitamin E	Fairly widely distributed in food. Most important sources: wholegrain cereals, wheatgerm, most vegetable oils and margarine made from vegetable oils, eggs	Is an antioxidant. In some animals necessary for reproduction. Use in human diet still being investigated	No specific recommendation
Vitamin K	Widespread in vegetable foods, particularly green leafy vegetables Also present in liver	Needed for blood clotting	No specific recommendation

Vitamin B Complex			
Thiamin	Marmite, yeast, legumes, green leafy vegetables, wholegrain cereals	Involved in energy release from carbohydrates. Necessary for a healthy nervous system	Depends on amount of carbohydrate in the diet. babies under 1 year 0.3 mg girls 12–14 0.9 mg boys 12–14 1.1 mg girls 15–17 0.9 mg boys 15–17 1.2 mg
Riboflavin	Milk, liver, Marmite, yeast, nuts, green vegetables	Involved in energy usage and cell respiration	Varies with age: babies under 1 year 0.4 mg boys and girls 12–14 years 1.4 mg boys and girls 15–17 years 1.7 mg
Nicotinic acid (Niacin)	Marmite, yeast, legumes, peanuts, liver, kidney	Essential for a continual supply of energy to the cells. Helps the body to use carbohydrate, protein and fat	Varies with age: babies under 1 year 5 mg boys and girls 12–14 years 16 mg boys and girls 15–17 years 19 mg
Vitamin B_6	Widespread in foods (deficiencies are rare)	Vital for the body's use of protein, and formation of haemoglobin Important for brain function Involved in energy usage	No specific recommendation
Biotin	Egg yolk, liver, kidney, yeast, nuts. Produced in the intestine.	Essential for use of food in the body. Necessary for normal metabolism	No specific recommendation
Pantothenic acid	Widespread in foods (deficiencies are rare)	Essential for the body's use of carbohydrate and fat, and therefore the release of energy	No specific recommendation
Folic acid (Folates)	Yeast, meat, liver, green leafy vegetables, bananas and a wide variety of foods	Essential for normal cells Helps in usage of protein For the production of red blood cells	babies under 1 year 50 µg boys and girls 12–17 years 300 µg pregnant women 500 µg
Vitamin B_{12}	Offal (e.g. kidneys, heart, tongue, liver), eggs, seafoods, dairy foods, yeast	Works with folic acid to produce red blood cells Essential for normal cells	
Vitamin C (Ascorbic acid)	Fruits, green peppers, brussels sprouts, potatoes, cabbage	Helps wounds to heal Helps prevent infection Essential for the formation of connective tissue between body cells (collagen) Must be present for the body to use folic acid Increases absorption of iron Protects vitamins A and E Important in hormone production	babies under 1 year 20 mg boys and girls 12–14 years 25 mg boys and girls 15–17 years 30 mg pregnant and breast-feeding women 60 mg

Micronutrients: minerals
Major elements

Nutrient	Source	Function in body	Recommended daily amount
Calcium	Dairy foods, fish, green vegetables	For bone and teeth formation and hardening For muscle contraction Necessary for blood clotting Transmission of nerve impulses	Varies with age: children 1–8 years 600 mg boys and girls 12–14 700 mg boys and girls 15–17 600 mg pregnant women 750 mg women breast-feeding 1200 mg
Phosphorus	In most foods	Essential in all cells Essential in formation of hard tissue Essential in energy release	No specific recommendation
Iron	Prunes, red meat, green vegetables, bread, eggs, liver, wheatgerm, baby cereal	Transports oxygen to all body tissues Necessary for healthy blood	babies under 1 year 6 mg boys and girls 12–17 years 12 mg pregnant women 13 mg women breast-feeding 15 mg
Sodium	Common salt, take-away foods, packet-mix soups and sauces, soya sauce, soup cubes, cured meats. Average intake of sodium is too high. This may encourage high blood pressure	Maintains osmotic pressure For nerve impulses Helps maintain the internal environment of body Helps transport glucose into cells for energy	No specific recommendation but NACNE suggests that salt intake should be about 3–6 g/day in the long term
Potassium	Wheatgerm, branflakes, dried figs, prunes, sultanas, baked beans, haricot beans, milk, whitefish	Helps maintain the internal environment of the body Regulates heart beat Regulates nerve impulses Helps to get glucose into the cells for energy	No specific recommendation but a diet containing a wide variety of foods should provide sufficient for the needs of the body

Micronutrients: minerals
Trace elements

Iodine	Seafood, vegetables, iodised salt	Essential in fluids outside cells (extra-cellular fluid) Essential part of the hormones produced by the thyroid gland	
Fluoride	Seafood, tea, some plant foods	Maintains hard bones and teeth	No specific recommendation but a diet containing a wide variety of foods should provide sufficient for the needs of the body
Magnesium	Peanuts, legumes, green vegetables	Important for enzyme activity Works with calcium and potassium Involved with nerve and muscular activity	
Zinc	Eggs, wheatgerm, roast beef, cheddar cheese, poultry, wholegrain cereals	For normal foetal and infant growth For normal reproduction For wound healing	

Other minerals required in trace amounts are cobalt, copper, chromium, manganese, selenium and molybdenum.

There are 15–20 **minerals** known to be essential for life. It is usual to group them into major and trace elements, depending on the amount required, but both groups are equally necessary.

Workshop

1 Why must vitamins be obtained from the diet?
2 Explain why some vitamins are known as fat-soluble.
3 What is the recommended daily amount of Vitamin D for pregnant women?
4 How much β carotene would you need to eat to get $500\,\mu g$ of retinol?
5 State three ways in which the body uses ascorbic acid.
6 Why is calcium important in the diet of pregnant women?
7 Name three trace minerals.

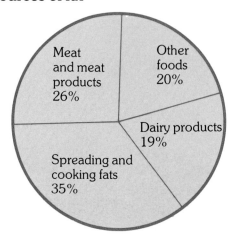

Less fat, more fit

Most of the fat we eat comes from four sources:
a *Meat and meat products* e.g. red meat, chicken, meat pies, sausages.
b *Spreading and cooking fats* e.g. butter, margarine, low-fat spreads, white cooking fats and oils.
c *Dairy products* e.g. milk, cheese, cream, yoghurt.
d *Other foods* e.g. eggs, fish, cakes, pastries, biscuits, cereal, and nuts.

Sources of fat

Hidden fat

The fats we eat in cakes, pastries, biscuits, chocolate and convenience foods are often forgotten, but they are still part of the total.

Facts about fat

1 Fats can be solid at room temperature (called "fats"), or liquid at room temperature (called "oils").
2 Foods contain a mixture of two main types of fat, *saturated fat* and *unsaturated fat* (which includes *polyunsaturated fat*). The chemical structure of these two types of fat differs in one small but crucial way. All fats or triglycerides are made up of three fatty acids attached to glycerol (an alcohol):

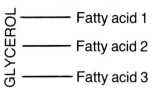

The fatty acids, which are long chains of carbon and hydrogen atoms, affect the way the fat behaves in the food, and therefore in the body. The carbon atoms are linked to one another by a single bond which is very stable.

$$C - C - C - C - $$

In a saturated fatty acid, on either side of the carbon atom is a hydrogen atom:

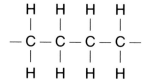

The chain is *saturated* with hydrogen. A diet containing a lot of this type of fat seems to increase the risk of heart disease.

In unsaturated fatty acids there are hydrogen atoms missing, and the spare bond is linked to the next carbon atom, forming a double bond which is not very stable.

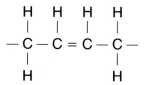

This chain is *unsaturated* – it is not saturated with hydrogen atoms. A fatty acid with one double bond is a *mono-unsaturated fatty acid*. A fatty acid with two or more double bonds is a *polyunsaturated fatty acid*.

3 The body needs some fat to:
a provide energy
b make food palatable
c give a feeling of fullness, which occurs as fat is digested slowly
d provide fat-soluble vitamins A, D, E, K (only found in fat from animal sources)
e insulate the body and protect vital organs
f help in the building and repair of some cells
g produce some hormones

Too much fat?

Both the NACNE and COMA reports reveal that the British diet contains too much fat. We should reduce the amount of fat we eat in order to try to reduce the very high death rate from heart disease. Too much fat may cause the coronary arteries to become blocked.

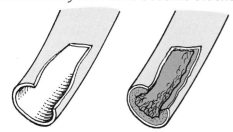

Normal artery   Artery with build-up of fatty material

Fat is also a very high energy food and eating too much may result in becoming overweight.

Reducing fat in the diet

- Use low-fat products, for example low-fat spreads instead of butter, skimmed or semi-skimmed milk instead of full-cream milk, low-fat cheeses. Use yoghurt or fromage frais in place of cream.

- Eat less meat, particularly red meat, and choose lean cuts. Use vegetables, particularly pulse vegetables, to replace meat.

- Grill rather than fry but if you must fry, use a non-stick pan.

- Drain off excess fat, or use kitchen paper to absorb fat.

- Omit browning in fat when making stews and casseroles.

- Reduce fat in recipes or find low-fat recipes.

- Spread butter or margarine more thinly – soft margarine will help. Cutting thicker slices of bread also helps in using less fat.

- Don't add margarine or butter to hot cooked vegetables.

- We all like chips occasionally, but if you cut them thicker they will absorb less fat.

Workshop

1 Which main groups of food provide the largest percentage of fat in the diet? What is the percentage?
2 Make a list of all the foods which you ate yesterday which contained fat.
3 Which of the following foods contain fat? Sausages, biscuits, cabbage, cheese, wholemeal flour, oranges, crisps, coffee, chicken, nuts.
4 Carry out a class survey to find out how many times a week chips are eaten.
5 Give five reasons why some fat is necessary in the diet.
6 Explain why too much fat may be harmful.
7 How could cooking methods be changed to reduce the fat in the diet?
8 Which of the following foods are high in fat? Cottage cheese, sausages, baked beans, wholemeal bread, cream, beefburgers.
9 Investigate low-fat cheese by making two pizzas or two batches of cheese scones, one using low-fat Cheddar cheese and one using full-fat Cheddar cheese. Compare flavour, texture and colour. Calculate the total fat content of both.
10 Prepare a low-fat meal and calculate the total fat content.

Slash the sugar

In Britain each person eats 38 kg (84 lbs) of sugar each year. The NACNE report recommends that we should halve this amount by the year 2000. More than half the sugar we eat has been added to foods such as sweets, cakes and biscuits during their manufacture, and the remainder we add ourselves during cooking or at table. The amount of sugar we purchase has been gradually decreasing over the past 25 years, as shown in the table below. In fact, we still eat almost the same amount of sugar, but it is found in manufactured foods like cereals, pies and canned fruits.

Average amount of household sugar purchased

Year	Sugar (g/person/week)	Year	Sugar (g/person/week)
1952	312*	1981	314
1956	510	1982	292
1961	513	1983	279
1966	483	1984	259
1970	479	1985	238
1976	346	1986	228

* Sugar was still rationed

Facts about sugar

1 Sugars are the simplest form of carbohydrate.
2 Each sugar is made up of units, the simplest of which are glucose (sometimes called dextrose) and fructose. Both are **monosaccharides**.
3 Sucrose is a sugar formed from one unit of glucose and one of fructose and is therefore a **disaccharide**.
4 Lactose, a sugar found in milk, and maltose are also disaccharides.
5 You will find sugar listed on packaged foods in all these forms. It is even found in savoury foods such as soups, tomato sauce and baked beans.

3 tsps contain 1 tsp sugar

Small tin contains 2–3 tsps sugar

Small tin contains 2 tsps sugar

6 There are many forms of sugar:
White sugars: granulated, caster, lump, icing, preserving and coffee crystals – all refined and chemically pure.
Brown sugars: demerara, soft brown, muscovado – slightly less refined and therefore containing small amounts of minerals.
Syrups, treacle, molasses are all concentrated sugar solutions but may contain iron and calcium.
Honey is made up of about 75% glucose and fructose and 20% water, plus small amounts of vitamins and minerals.

7 Sugar will provide energy but very few other nutrients so gives "empty calories".

Why should we eat less sugar?

- If each person is going to reach the NACNE target of 20 kg (42 lb) of sugar a year from all sources, then we should all consume less than 50 g (about 10 tsp) per day – about half from main meals and the rest from drinks, cakes, sweets etc.

- Eating too many sweet foods can lead to tooth decay, especially if eaten as snacks or drinks between meals.

- It is easy to become overweight if you eat a lot of foods containing large amounts of sugar.

How should we cut down on sugar?

- Try reducing the amount of sugar you have in tea or coffee. You could use an artificial sweetener, but if possible do not add any sugar.

- Choose low-sugar drinks such as low-calorie ones, unsweetened fruit juice or mineral water.

- Choose fruit canned in natural juice, which contains about one-third less sugar than fruit canned in syrup.

- Eat fresh fruit or unsalted nuts as snacks instead of sweets, cakes or biscuits.

- Reduce the amount of sugar in recipes by at least one-third.

- Look at the label before buying, and select brands with no added sugar. Cut down on high-sugar foods and avoid eating them between meals.

- Avoid breakfast cereals with added sugar.

Workshop

1 List the different types of sugar which you can find in the shops. Write a brief description of each and explain how you would use each one.
2 About how much sugar does the average person consume in a year?
3 Work out the percentage of sugar we obtain from manufactured foods.
4 Name three foods in which you were surprised to find sugar.
5 Look at the table of sugar-consumption figures. In which of the years 1981–1986 was the reduction in the amount of sugar used a) the greatest? b) the least?
6 What is the percentage reduction in sugar consumption between the years 1956 and 1986?
7 Give two reasons why eating too much sugar may be harmful.
8 Give four ways in which you could reduce the sugar in *your* diet.
9 Just under 50% of five-year-olds in England and Wales show signs of tooth decay. Show how you could discourage a young child from developing a "sweet tooth" by preparing a selection of dishes which are low in sugar. Explain how these dishes could be used in a child's diet.
10 Look at the labels on the following foods and list the names of the ingredients which would indicate the presence of sugar: sweet biscuits, jam, yoghurt, sugar-coated breakfast cereals, muesli.
11 Many schools have tuck shops which sell foods high in sugar. Suggest alternatives which would do less damage to teeth.
12 Investigate the possibility of using less sugar in recipes by making two batches of cakes or biscuits. The first time, follow the recipe as given; the second time, reduce the amount of sugar by a quarter. Compare the flavour, texture and colour of the two batches.

Spare the salt

Everybody needs some salt in their diet, but many people consume too much. It is estimated that most adults have a salt intake of 9–12 g per day, yet our bodies can function properly if we consume as little as 0.3–1.9 g of salt per day.

What contains salt?

Most of the salt in our diet comes from the food we eat. (We get a very small amount of salt, less than 1%, from drinking water.) About half the salt we consume has been added to such products as crisps, salted nuts, bacon and cheese by food manufacturers.

About a quarter we add during cooking or at table, and the remainder is naturally present in food. There is more salt in food from animal sources than from vegetable sources.

Sources of salt

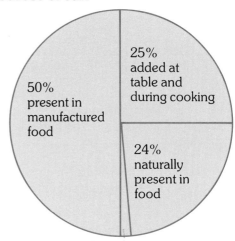

50% present in manufactured food

25% added at table and during cooking

24% naturally present in food

1% in water

Comparison chart of sodium content in fresh and processed foods

Fresh food (uncooked)	(mg sodium/100 g)	Manufactured food	(mg sodium/100 g)
Stewing steak	72	Stewed steak in gravy	380
Minced beef	86	Beefburger, frozen	600
Herring	67	Kipper	540
Milk, cows'	50	Butter	870
		Cheese, cheddar	610
Potatoes, old	7	Crisps	550
		Instant potato (made up)	260
Peas, frozen	3	Canned peas	230
Flour, white	2	Bread, white	540
		Shredded Wheat	8
Bran	28	All-bran	1670
Cornflour	52	Cornflakes	1160

Facts about salt

1 Its chemical name is sodium chloride, and when added to water salt splits into two parts: sodium ions and chloride ions.
2 We get about 95% of the sodium in our diet from salt. One teaspoon (5 g) of salt contains 2 g (2000 mg) of sodium. Food tables or computer programs will give amounts of sodium (Na) in food as milligrams (mg) of Na per 100 g of food.
3 Salt adds flavour to food.
4 Salt can be used as a preservative to prevent or slow down the growth of undesirable micro-organisms.
5 Salt adds texture to processed foods, e.g. bread manufacture

Hypertension

NACNE recommends that everyone reduces their salt intake by 3 g per day. A high salt intake may cause high blood pressure (hypertension) in some people. High blood pressure is one of the main risk factors for coronary heart disease. It is also linked to strokes and kidney failure. So if we all reduce our salt intake, it may reduce the number of deaths from these diseases.

How to reduce salt intake

- Use less salt in cooking, and don't put the salt cellar on the table.
- Herbs, spices and other flavourings can be used instead of salt.
- Use high-salt foods such as bacon, smoked fish, cheese and convenience foods sparingly.
- Cut down on salty snack foods such as crisps, salted nuts etc.
- Look for "low salt" foods or "no salt added" foods when shopping.
- Eat more fresh food.

Workshop

1 What is the present salt intake for the average adult?
2 How much salt is needed for the body to function satisfactorily?
3 List the main sources of salt in the diet and state the percentage of salt gained from each source.
4 The comparison chart shows that there are 550 mg of sodium (Na) in 100 g of crisps. How much salt would be present?
5 Give three reasons why salt is added to food.
6 Suggest four ways in which you could reduce the amount of salt in *your* diet.
7 a Using food tables or a computer program, list the amount of salt in 100 g of the following foods:
    Carrots (raw), canned spaghetti in tomato sauce, oranges, cooking apples, shrimps, luncheon meat, margarine, Oxo cubes, cottage cheese, jacket potatoes.
  b Arrange these foods in order, with the food containing the highest amount of salt at the top of the list and the food with the lowest amount at the bottom.
  c Place an asterisk against those foods which have been manufactured.
  d Are the foods you have asterisked in the upper or lower part of the list?
8 Using the comparison chart, answer the following questions:
  a Which food contains the highest amount of sodium?
  b Which food contains the lowest amount of sodium?
  c For which two foods is the difference in sodium content between the fresh and manufactured product the greatest?
  d What is the percentage increase of salt in the manufactured product?
9 Prepare two casseroles or two shepherd's pies or two batches of soup, one containing salt and the other without salt. Compare the flavour.
10 Evaluate the use of a low-sodium salt substitute in a variety of recipes.

Fill up with fibre

Fibre is only found in plant foods such as fruit, vegetables (including pulses), cereals and nuts. The parts of plants which supply us with fibre are the cell walls and the other structures which support the plant, but the form in which fibre is found will differ in the different parts of the plant.

During the preparation and manufacture of foods the parts which contain fibre are often removed. For example, peeling the skin from some vegetables and fruit removes fibre, and bran is removed when white flour is produced.

Sources of dietary fibre

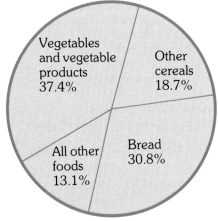

Facts about fibre

1 Fibre is made up of several substances, the main one being **cellulose**. Cellulose is a complex carbohydrate formed from many glucose units linked together.

2 We are unable to digest and absorb cellulose. This means that no cellulose is lost during digestion, so foods containing cellulose help to provide the bulk in the digestive tract, enabling waste material to pass along the tract more quickly.

3 Foods containing dietary fibre require more chewing. Think about how long it takes to eat an apple compared with drinking a glass of apple juice!

4 Chewing encourages saliva to be produced and this will help prevent dental caries.

5 The different forms of fibre work in slightly different ways. Some fibre, like that in bran, holds water whereas some of the fibre in oats is water soluble. It is therefore important to eat a variety of foods rich in fibre, such as unrefined cereal grains, fruit, and leafy, root and pulse vegetables.

Dietary fibre content of some foods

Food	Fibre per 100 g g	Food	Fibre per 100 g g
White flour	3.4	Prunes (stewed)	8.1
Wholemeal flour	9.6	Dates	8.7
White bread	2.7	Baked beans in tomato sauce	7.3
Wholemeal bread	8.5	Brussels sprouts (boiled)	2.9
Rice polished (raw)	2.4	Cabbage (boiled)	2.8
Rice brown (raw)	4.2	Carrots (boiled)	3.1
Cornflakes	11.0	Chick peas (cooked)	6.0
Weetabix	12.7	Lentils (cooked)	3.7
Shredded Wheat	12.3	Potatoes (jacket)	2.5
All-bran	26.7	Potatoes (peeled and boiled)	1.0
Bananas	3.4	Peanuts (roasted)	8.1
Apples	2.0	Lettuce	1.5
Oranges	2.0	Tomatoes	1.5
Raisins/sultanas	6.9	Peas (frozen, boiled)	12.0

Why should we eat more fibre?

The NACNE report suggests that we should increase the amount of fibre in our diets by 50%. At present it is estimated that many people eat less than 20 g of fibre per day. We should aim to eat 30 g of fibre per day.

- A fibre-rich diet is lower in sugar and fat and will therefore help us to eat less of these substances.
- The fibre from cereals, **bran**, helps to prevent constipation and other bowel disorders such as diverticular disease, when, as a result of straining to pass hard stools, pouches form in the wall of the large intestine (colon).

Waste passing along the large intestine

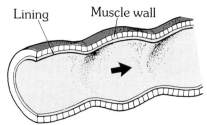

Large volume soft faeces

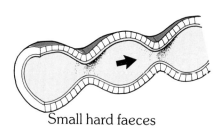

Small hard faeces

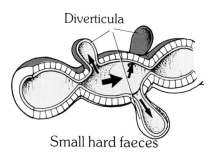

Small hard faeces

- As high-fibre foods give a feeling of fullness more quickly, and you are therefore likely to eat less, these foods are useful in a slimming diet.
- As a fibre-rich diet will pass more quickly along the digestive tract, it may help to protect against cancer of the colon.

How should we increase fibre in our diet?

It is not difficult to eat more fibre, as it will only involve slight changes in the diet.

- Try to eat at least one fibre-rich food at each meal.
- Eat more wholegrain foods, e.g. wholemeal bread, brown rice, wholemeal pasta.
- Use pulse vegetables (peas, beans and lentils) together with vegetables and cereals – costs will be reduced as well as fibre increased.
- Try not to peel fruit and vegetables, just scrub them well and cook them with the skin in place, or eat them fresh.
- Look for the breakfast cereals which are rich in fibre – but check that they do not contain added sugar and salt.
- Remember that bran is an excellent source of fibre, but you should eat wholegrain cereals to get your supply rather than adding bran to food. This will ensure that you get vitamins and minerals from food as well as fibre.
- Replace sugar with dried fruit in fruit pies and crumbles.

Workshop

1 Foods containing complex carbohydrates are good for us. Name four foods which contain complex carbohydrates.

2 Name two parts of plants which contain dietary fibre.

3 What is the main substance which makes up dietary fibre?

4 We cannot digest and absorb dietary fibre. Give three reasons why it is still important in the diet.

5 Why is it better to eat wholegrain foods rather than adding bran to foods?

6 With the aid of diagrams, explain how diverticular disease is caused.

7 a How could the dietary fibre content be increased in the following recipe for Apple Crumble?
   100 g flour
   25 g sugar
   50 g margarine
   500 g peeled, sliced cooking apples
   25 g sugar

   b Prepare two Apple Crumbles, one using the above recipe and one using your adapted recipe.

   c Compare the two dishes for colour, flavour and texture. Work out the fibre content of each.

8 Using the table showing the dietary fibre content of some foods:
   a Arrange the foods in order, with those containing the highest amount of fibre at the top of your list and the food with the lowest amount at the bottom.

   b Calculate the weight of the following foods which you would have to eat to obtain one third of the day's recommended intake (10 g):
   wholemeal bread, Shredded Wheat, apples, raisins, boiled potatoes, frozen peas.

9 a Plan a day's meals for yourself and three friends, ensuring that you include at least one food high in fibre in each meal. Use the table to help you identify foods rich in fibre.

   b Give reasons for your choice of foods and calculate the approximate weight of fibre in the day's meals.

   c Prepare the main meal from the day's menu.

   d Using either food tables or a computer program, calculate the exact amount of fibre in this meal. Give the final figure in grams per person.

10 Investigate wholemeal pasta compared with white pasta by making two dishes, one using wholemeal pasta and the other white pasta. Compare colour, flavour and texture and calculate the dietary fibre content of each.

Adapt it!

Most recipes can be adapted to become healthier and to fit in with the healthy eating guidelines. *Adapt* means to modify or alter a little, but not to change beyond recognition. It is important that adapted recipes are still aesthetically pleasing, in other words still look and taste good.

Don't adapt recipes out of existence!

I WAS GOING TO HAVE PIZZA AND SALAD BUT I'VE ADAPTED IT TO A CHEESE AND TOMATO SANDWICH

There are three main ways of adapting recipes: *Reduction, Substitution* and *Change of cooking method.* Sometimes a combination of these methods can be used. Let's look at each method of adapting recipes in detail.

1. Reduction

In most cases ingredients to be reduced should only be reduced a little, otherwise the balance of the recipe may be upset and the result will be unacceptable.

Adapting a Victoria sandwich cake recipe by reducing sugar.

Basic Recipe	Adapted Recipe
2 eggs	2 eggs
100 g S.R. flour	100 g S.R. flour
100 g margarine	100 g margarine
100 g sugar	75 g sugar
50 g jam	50 g jam

Try reducing sugar, fat, and salt in recipes. Remember – every little helps! In many recipes for sweet things such as cakes, puddings and biscuits the fat and sugar can be reduced a little. Sugar can be reduced to taste in cooking fruit and making custard and sweet sauces. It is easy to reduce or omit salt in recipes because salt is just a flavouring and not a main ingredient.

2. Substitution

This is perhaps the most successful way of adapting recipes. Healthier ingredients can be used without altering the quantities of ingredients. A whole range of healthier ingredients is available in most supermarkets. Some you could try are shown in the table on the next page.

Let's look at the Victoria sandwich cake recipe again and see where we could make some substitutions.

Basic recipe	kcal	Fat (g)	Sugar (g)	Fibre (g)
2 eggs	296	21.8	0	0
100 g S.R. flour	337	0.75	0	3.7
100 g margarine	718	81	0	0
100 g sugar	382	0	100	0
50 g jam	129	0	33	0
Totals	1862	103.5	133	3.7

Adapted recipe	kcal	Fat (g)	Sugar (g)	Fibre (g)
2 eggs	296	21.8	0	0
100 g S.R. Wholemeal flour	342	1	0	9.6
100 g polyunsat. margarine	718	81	0	0
75 g sugar	286	0	75	0
50 g fruit purée	22	0	11	1
Totals	1664	103.8	86	10.6

In place of	Substitute	Benefit
Margarine or butter	Polyunsaturated margarine, reduced-fat spreads (not always suitable for cooking)	Less saturated fat Less fat
Lard, cooking fats	Polyunsaturated oils	Less saturated fat
Cheese	Reduced-fat cheeses	Reduced-fat Cheddar has 50% less fat
Whole milk	Skimmed or semi-skimmed milk	Less fat
Cream	Yoghurt, reduced-fat cream substitutes (e.g. Elmlea, fromage frais)	Less fat
Fatty meat (e.g minced beef)	Lean meat	Less fat
Sausages, paté	Reduced-fat sausages and paté	Less fat
Sugar	Reduced-calorie sweeteners (check if suitable for cooking)	Less sugar
Tinned fruit in syrup	Tinned fruit in juice	Less sugar
Jam	Reduced-sugar jam	Less sugar
Flour	Wholemeal flour	More fibre
Pasta	Wholemeal pasta	More fibre
Rice	Wholegrain or brown rice	More fibre
Salt	Lo salt	Less sodium

As a result of reducing the sugar and substituting wholemeal flour for white flour and fruit purée for jam we have

Reduced the kcal by 198
Reduced the sugar by 47 g
Increased the fibre by 6.9 g

We have not reduced the quantity of fat in the recipe. In fact, we have increased it slightly because there is a little more fat in wholemeal flour than in white flour. However, we have used polyunsaturated margarine. The resulting cake still looks and tastes good.

3. Change of cooking method

Another way of adapting recipes is to change the cooking method. The fat content of a finished dish can be greatly reduced by using methods of cooking which do not add fat. Frying adds fat but grilling does not, and may allow fat in the food to melt and drip away. So grill foods where possible, especially fatty foods such as bacon, sausages and chops.

Fatty foods can also be dry-fried. This means putting foods such as bacon, sausages, chops and minced beef into a frying pan without adding any fat. The fat already in the food melts and drains out of the food.

Some changes in the preparation of food before cooking can also make the finished result healthier. Leave the skins on fruit and vegetables to retain as much fibre as possible. When preparing chips, cut them thick and chunky as these absorb less fat than thin-cut chips.

Workshop

Adapt these recipes and then work out the difference in fat and fibre content, using food tables or a computer program. Draw up two tables to record the differences in fat and fibre content between the basic and the adapted recipe.

Spaghetti Bolognese

Basic recipe

250 g minced beef
1 onion
1 small tin tomato purée
1 tsp mixed herbs
1 stock cube
100 g spaghetti

Fish in cheese sauce

Basic recipe

250 g cod fillet
250 ml milk
15 g cornflour
   (1 rounded tbsp)
100 g Cheddar cheese
pinch salt and pepper
tomato and parsley

Toad in the hole

Basic recipe

250 g sausages
15 g lard
100 g plain flour
½ level tsp salt
1 egg
250 ml milk

Pizza

Basic recipe

For the Dough:
100 g S.R. flour
25 g margarine

For the Filling:
1 rasher bacon
1 onion
1 large tin tomatoes
50 g mushrooms
100 g Cheddar cheese
1 tsp herbs

In a practical session cook both basic and adapted recipes and evaluate for taste, texture and appearance. The same exercise may be completed in pairs, with one person cooking the basic recipe and one person cooking the adapted recipe, then working together to compare the results.

Input v. output

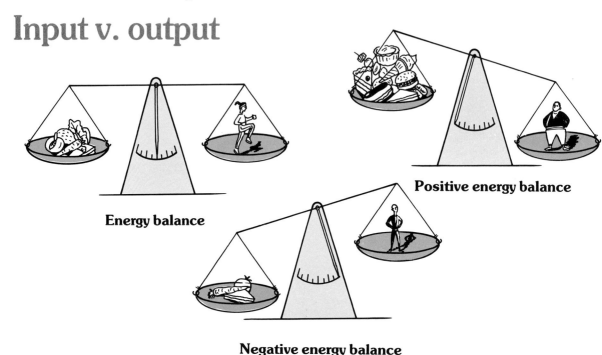

Energy balance

Positive energy balance

Negative energy balance

It is difficult to be precise about how much energy an individual requires. People have different energy needs, and the amount of energy an individual requires varies, depending on what he or she is doing.

We require energy continuously for body activities such as maintaining a constant temperature, digestion, renewing and building tissues, as well as for breathing and pumping blood around the body. The rate at which energy is used for these activities when we are resting is known as the *basal metabolic rate* (BMR). The BMR accounts for more than half our energy needs. A person's BMR is influenced by several factors including

- Body type (the size, shape and weight of an individual)
- Sex – males have a higher BMR than females
- Age – children have a higher BMR than adults
- Rate of growth – more energy is required in relation to body weight during periods of growth (including pregnancy)
- Skin surface area – more energy is required to maintain body temperature in small bodies.

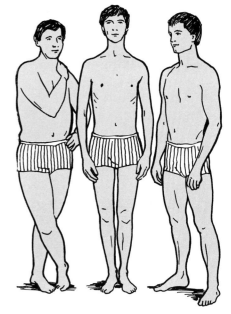

Endomorph (rounded)   Ectomorph (tall and thin)   Mesomorph (muscular)

Skin surface area is often used as a standard for comparing the BMR of different people. For every square metre of body surface the BMR is about 160 kJ (38 kcal) per hour for men and 150 kJ (37 kcal) per hour for women.

Workshop

1 Calculate your skin surface area from the opposite diagram, called a nomogram. Use this figure to calculate your approximate BMR for a day.

In addition to the BMR, energy is required for all activities, for example sitting reading, or dancing at a disco. Obviously you use more energy dancing than sitting. The following chart gives the approximate amount of energy required to carry out a variety of activities.

Activity	Average energy expenditure per minute
Work	
Light work:	
Students, office workers, teachers, doctors, drivers, house workers, shop workers	10.5–20.5 kJ (2.5–4.9 kcal)
Moderate work:	
Nurses, workers in light industry, policemen, workers in the building industry, plumbers, joiners	21–31 kJ (5.0–7.4 kcal)
Heavy work:	
Miners, labourers in the building industry, forestry workers, non-mechanized farm work, foundry workers	Over 30 kJ (7.5 and over kcal)
Leisure activities	
Exercise:	
Walking, gardening, golf	21 kJ (5 kcal)
Tennis, swimming, cycling, jogging	24.5 kJ (6 kcal)
Disco dancing, aerobics, squash, athletics, football	35 kJ (8 kcal)
Relaxation:	
Sitting reading or watching television	6 kJ (1.4 kcal)
Sewing, playing cards, playing a musical instrument	6.5 kJ (1.4 kcal)
Cooking, playing pool	7.5 kJ (1.8 kcal)
Routine activities	
Washing, dressing, meal preparation, shopping	7.5 kJ (1.8 kcal)
Sleeping (basal metabolism)	4.8 kJ (1.2 kcal)

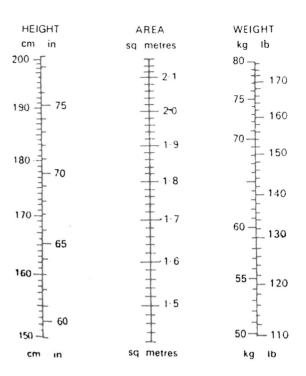

To calculate your surface area, draw a line connecting your height with your weight. It will cross the centre scale at your approximate surface area.

Most people spend about a third of their day asleep, a third at work or school and a third on leisure activities.

2 a Calculate the amount of energy you used yesterday. You may find it helpful to draw up a table with the headings Activity, Time spent (min), Energy used (kJ/kcal). Don't forget the time spent sleeping. When you have filled in the three columns, add up the total energy used.

b How does your energy output compare with your energy RDA? (See chart on page 51.)

3 Explain what is meant by *energy balance*.

4 Suggest two ways in which someone with a positive energy balance could reduce weight.

5 What is the basal metabolic rate?

6 Give three factors which may affect basal metabolic rate.

7 Why is the BMR of a child higher than that of an adult?

Food into fragments

The body makes use of the food you have eaten to:
• form or renew the human body
• provide energy to carry out body functions
However, before the nutrients present in the food can be used in this way, the food must be physically broken down into fragments and then chemically changed into single molecules. The molecules of starches, sugars, fats and proteins are too large to pass through the membrane lining the digestive tract and the walls of the blood vessels.

The teeth and the muscular walls of the digestive tract break the food down physically and help to mix it with the enzymes secreted by the different parts of the tract. The enzymes bring about the chemical changes.

The digestive tract

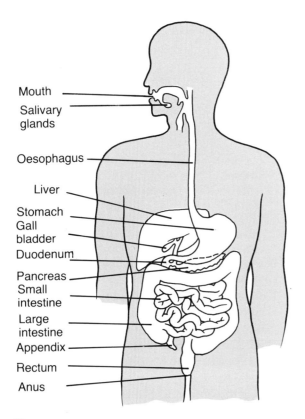

Mouth
Salivary glands
Oesophagus
Liver
Stomach
Gall bladder
Duodenum
Pancreas
Small intestine
Large intestine
Appendix
Rectum
Anus

The process of digestion starts when food enters the mouth.

Mouth   Food is chewed to break up solid particles and mixed with saliva containing the enzyme *salivary amylase* which starts the digestion of starch.

Oesophagus   After swallowing, the food is moved down the tract by contractions, or peristalsis, of the muscular walls. Salivary amylase continues digestion of starch to maltose.

Peristaltic action

Muscles here are circular, they contract

Muscles here are long, they relax

These muscular actions are coordinated to move food to the stomach

Stomach   The food is churned by the muscles of the stomach wall and mixed with gastric juices containing hydrochloric acid and *pepsin* which begin the digestion of proteins.

Duodenum   Muscular contractions continue to move the food along and mix it with bile and pancreatic juices. Bile neutralises the acid and helps emulsify fat. The pancreatic juices contain four enzymes:

Pancreatic amylase (carbohydrate splitting) which converts starch to maltose in the same way as salivary amylase.
Pancreatic lipase (a group of fat-splitting enzymes) which completes the digestion of fat by converting it into fatty acids and glycerol.
Trypsin and *chymotrypsin* (both *proteases* or protein-splitting enzymes) which break down proteins to polypeptides.

Small intestine The enzymes contained in the intestinal juices complete the process of digestion as the food is moved along by muscular contractions:

Maltase converts maltose to glucose and this completes the digestion of starch.
Peptidases complete the digestion of protein by changing polypeptides to amino acids.
Sucrase and *lactase* complete the breakdown of carbohydrates to monosaccharides.

Digestion of food is now complete and the small molecules pass through the wall of the small intestine and into the blood stream.

The wall of the small intestine

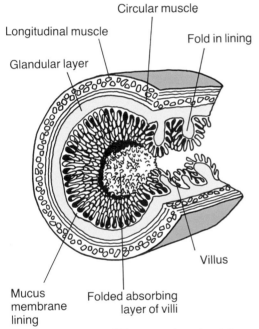

Large intestine Water is absorbed from the remaining undigested food which is passed along the large intestine, and the waste food or faeces is expelled by the anus.

Absorption

The digested proteins, fats and carbohydrates together with vitamins and minerals are absorbed through the wall of the small intestine.

The lining of the small intestine is folded and covered with very tiny projections called villi. This greatly increases the surface area in contact with the digested food. The lining of the villi is very thin so soluble nutrients pass rapidly through into the blood capillaries present in the villi.

Metabolism

This is the process of transporting the soluble nutrients round the body to where they are needed either for building and repairing or for providing energy. If more food is eaten than is needed then some of the nutrients can be stored.

Glucose may be converted to glycogen and stored in the liver and muscles, but this is only a short-term store. The remaining excess glucose is converted to fat and stored beneath the skin in the adipose tissue, along with the products broken down directly from fatty foods. Amino acids cannot be stored and therefore a daily intake of protein is necessary. The digested protein is used for energy production and the excess may be stored as fat.

Other nutrients such as fat-soluble vitamins and some minerals can be stored, mainly in the liver; but water-soluble vitamins are excreted in the urine – so again a daily supply is necessary.

Workshop

1 What are the two main functions of food in the body?
2 Why does food have to be digested?
3 Explain what happens to food in
 a the mouth
 b the small intestine
4 In which part of the digestive tract does the breakdown of fat start?
5 In which part of the digestive tract is the digestion of food complete?
6 Explain how the products of digestion are absorbed in the small intestine.
7 What are the functions of the large intestine?
8 If you eat more food than your body requires, what happens to the excess after digestion?
9 Draw a diagram of the digestive tract and mark the areas where the breakdown of protein takes place.

Food choice

We may think that we are completely free to choose what kind of food we eat, but in fact there are many factors which influence our choice of diet. These are some of the main ones:

Domestic technology
The development of machines such as microwave ovens, freezers, food processors and dishwashers influences the way we eat.

Advertising
In 1988 the food industry spent nearly £500 million on advertising to influence our choice of food

Religion
Some religions have rules about food. Jewish people do not eat pork and Hindus do not eat beef. Food often plays an important part in religious festivals

Peer group pressure
We all have a need to be accepted by our peer group (same age-group), and so we may be influenced by what is fashionable and what people of our own age-group eat and drink

Cost of food
Families on very low incomes may have difficulty achieving a healthy diet

Ethical beliefs
Our beliefs of what is right and wrong can influence our food choice. Many people feel that killing animals for food is wrong and so they choose to become vegetarian

Food industry and food technology
New developments in preserving, preparing, packing and storing foods give us a much wider range of foods to choose from

Taste preferences
We all have our own likes and dislikes based on the colour, texture and flavour of foods

Family influences
In most families, one person (usually the mother) chooses the food for the family and tends to pass on taste preferences

Knowledge about food
What we are taught about food and nutrition may influence our food choice

Availability of food
Government policy, imports, transport and distribution can all affect the availability of food in the shops

Lifestyle
How people live and work and how much time they have to shop and cook can influence food choice

These factors which influence our food choice are sometimes called socio-economic influences.

Some of these influences may make it difficult for us to achieve a healthy diet. If we are influenced by knowledge about food we might consider changing to a healthier diet, but other influences may stand in our way. Much as we appreciate the need for a healthy diet, our food preferences (likes and dislikes based on the flavour, colour and texture of food) often overcome this. We all know that biscuits are not a healthy food but that does not stop us eating over 130 g per person per week! A teenager may decide for ethical reasons to become vegetarian but if the rest of the family continues to eat meat he or she will find it difficult.

Your own food profile

Examine your own food choice and the influences which cause you to choose these foods. Think about the foods you ate yesterday and try to discover the factors affecting your choice. Here is an example:

Zoe (aged 15) gets up too late for breakfast (lifestyle). Drinks a cup of tea and dashes to school. Gets hungry at break, eats the apple Mum gave her but also visits the tuck shop for some chocolate (taste preferences). Has a school dinner and tries to pick a healthy choice: cheese flan, salad and yoghurt (food knowledge). Visits the sweet shop with friends on the way home. Everyone decides to buy ice-creams (peer-group pressure). Dad gets tea: chicken casserole with cook-in sauce, rice and frozen peas (food technology and advertising).

Workshop

1 Study this advertisement for luncheon meat and make an assessment of it, using the following guidelines.
   - Is the advert aimed at mothers, housewives, teenagers, children, husbands, elderly people? Why?
   - Is the food being associated with health, fun, enjoyment, sport and fitness, high-status living, happy family life, labour saving and efficiency? Explain how this association is achieved.

2 Make a study of other food advertisements using these guidelines.

3 Design your own advertisement for low-fat Cheddar cheese, wholemeal bread or oranges.

4 Investigate television advertising of food. In one evening's viewing, note all the advertisements as they appear. What percentage of advertisements are for food (including soft drinks and sweets)? How many advertisements are for fresh foods and how many are for processed foods?

5 Look at the newspaper extract. Explain how dietary guidelines may have influenced these diet trends.

> **Diet trends**
> Quarterly results from the Ministry of Agriculture's National Food Survey, covering the period January–March 1987, largely confirm recent trends in household diets, including the increased consumption of low-fat milks and fruit juices, and a decline in consumption of wholemilk, packet sugar and butter.

Sixty years of cooking and eating

The thirties

The kitchen of a well-off London family in 1937. A cast-iron range has been replaced by an electric cooker, and there is a fridge with an ice-making compartment. Only 200 000 homes had fridges in 1937

There was a severe economic depression in the 1930s. At the height of the depression in 1931, three million or 1 in 5 of the workforce were unemployed. This led to much poverty and a lot of people were unable to afford an adequate diet. Rickets, tuberculosis, anaemia and physical underdevelopment were common among the poor. A survey published in 1936 found that only 50% of the population were able to afford a diet for good health. Undernutrition and malnutrition were causing great concern in the 1930s and infant welfare clinics and free school milk were introduced to combat these problems.

The forties

The Second World War, which began in 1939, caused dramatic changes to people's diets. There was concern that war would bring food shortages because of less imports and also because production of some foods was cut back to enable factories to be used for war work. In 1940 food rationing began. The whole population was registered, given identity numbers and then issued with ration books by the Ministry of Food. The Ministry worked hard to ensure that the rationing was fair and that the population would receive a nutritionally adequate diet. Special groups such as expectant mothers and infants received extra rations. Obtaining a nutritionally adequate diet was not dependent on how much money you had. Everyone was entitled to the same rations, rich or poor.

If you look at the rationed and unrationed foods you will understand why the wartime diet was low in fats and sugars and high in fibre. Advice about nutrition and cooking was given in the papers and on the radio. The wartime diet was nutritionally adequate and the nation's health improved during the war, but people found the diet very dull and boring.

Foods rationed   Rations varied, but for most of the war meat, bacon, ham, cheese, tea, sugar, butter, margarine, sweets and chocolate were rationed.

Foods not rationed   Bread was not rationed (but only national wheatmeal was available – similar to wholemeal) and neither were potatoes, home-grown fruits and vegetables. Imported fruits such as oranges and bananas disappeared during the war.

World War II ration book and coupons

During World War II the Ministry of Food issued guidelines for maintaining a healthy diet during wartime

The fifties

Although the war ended in 1945, rationing was phased out gradually and did not end completely until 1954. As food supplies returned to normal, people began to enjoy the foods they had missed during the war. Consumption of foods like meat, cream cheese, butter and sugar all increased considerably. Chinese restaurants became popular and people began to eat out more.

The sixties

The sixties was a time of increasing prosperity. Home ownership increased, there was very low unemployment, and people were able to afford a nutritionally adequate diet. A typical post-war diet emerged, which was high in fats and sugars. The wartime wheatmeal loaf was unpopular and so people turned to white sliced bread and less potatoes were eaten. Frozen food became popular and families began to buy home freezers. Many housewives worked and did not want to spend long hours in the kitchen.

The seventies

The early seventies was still a prosperous time. Lots of new frozen and convenience foods appeared. Burger bars became popular and there was a growing interest in foreign foods. Health experts began to identify diseases caused by eating too much of certain types of foods. From the mid-seventies rising inflation and high rates of unemployment caused many families to have to economise on food.

The eighties

In the eighties the typical British diet was seen as the cause of many diet-related diseases. Several reports were published (NACNE 1983 and COMA 1984) which emphasised the need to change our diets.

Microwave ovens and freezers became increasingly popular, as did convenience foods and ready-made meals. By the late eighties food surveys began to show some

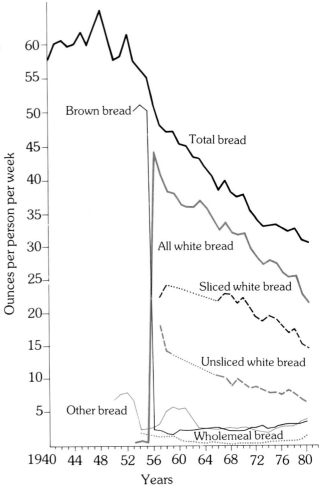

Changes in the consumption of bread in Britain over the past 40 years

changes in our diets, with increased consumption of skimmed milk, low-fat spreads, wholemeal bread and fruit juice. Supermarkets began to stock a wide range of healthier foods and also to provide nutritional information.

Although there are signs that many people are beginning to change their diets, there is still a need for people to be better informed about the way food affects health.

In the sixty years we have looked at, the nutrition problems have changed from undernutrition causing rickets, T.B. and poor physical development to overnutrition associated with tooth decay, obesity and heart disease.

Let's look at how all these changes have affected a typical meal.

1930 – Fish in Breadcrumbs, Mashed Potatoes, Peas, Apple Crumble, Custard.

Time	Method	Skills	Equipment used
11.30	Peel, chop and cook apples	Peeling, chopping, stewing apples	Peeler, knife, chopping board, saucepan
11.40	Make crumble	Rubbing-in method	Scales, bowl, knife
11.50	Put crumble on top of apples in dish		Dish, spoon
11.55	Remove skin from fish, coat in egg and breadcrumbs	Coating fish	Plate, dish, fork
12.00	Put crumble in oven		Cooker
12.01	Peel and chop potatoes	Peeling, chopping	Peeler, knife, chopping board
12.05	Cook potatoes	Boiling	Saucepan, cooker
12.06	Fry fish	Frying	Frying pan, fish slice
12.07	While fish is frying, pod peas and make custard	Sauce blending	Saucepan, spoon
12.20	Take crumble out of oven cook peas		Saucepan
12.25	Mash potatoes		Bowl, potato masher
12.30	Serve meal		

1990 – Fish Fingers, Mashed Potatoes, Peas, Apple Crumble, Custard.

Time	Method	Skills	Equipment used
12.00	Open tin of apple pie filling, put in dish, cover with packet crumble mix		Dish, spoon
12.05	Put crumble in oven		Cooker
12.06	Put fish fingers under grill, cook for 10 mins then leave under low grill to keep hot	Grilling	Grill
12.16	Make instant mashed potato, put in oven to keep hot		Kettle, bowl
12.20	Put frozen peas in microwave oven for 5 mins	Use of microwave	Bowl, microwave oven
12.25	Take crumble out of oven, put instant custard into jug, heat in microwave	Microwave	Jug, microwave oven
12.30	Serve meal		

Workshop

1 Compare the 1930 and 1990 meals. What differences are there in:
   a Time to prepare and cook?
   b Skills needed?
   c Equipment needed?
   d Washing up required?
   e Foods used?

2 Name two things that have affected the British diet in each decade, from 1930 onwards. Write a sentence on each change, explaining whether it resulted in a better or worse diet.

3 Talk to a grandparent or elderly neighbour about how the foods they eat have changed over the years. Ask them if they can remember the foods they ate as a child, and rationing during the war.

4 Look at the 1930s kitchen and explain in what ways it differs from a modern kitchen. How have the differences in the kitchens changed the way we shop, cook and eat?

5 Do you think there will be as many changes in cooking and eating in the next 60 years? Write an essay with the title "Cooking and Eating in the 21st Century".

The world inside Britain

Food and culture in Britain

We have looked at the influences which affect food choice, and we have also seen how foods eaten in Britain have changed considerably, especially since the Second World War. Now let's consider how the type of Britain we live in today has influenced the way we eat.

The foods and meals eaten in Britain today contain influences from all over the world.

Britain is a multiracial, multicultural society

Television programmes teach us about cuisine from all over the world

Increased imports give us a wide variety of foods from all over the world

Many people travel and experience new foods

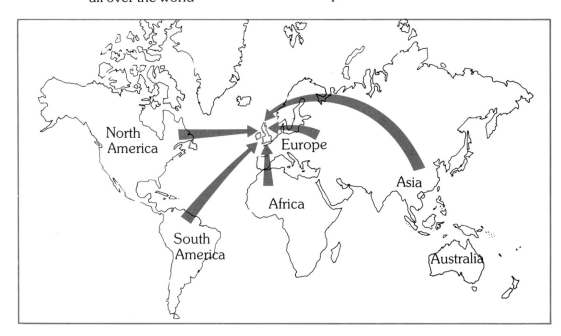

Eating out in Indian, Chinese, Italian, Greek and Caribbean restaurants is popular

Many of us live in large towns and cities and have friends and neighbours with cultural backgrounds different from our own

Many Britons born in this country have ethnic and cultural origins in other parts of the world

---

What type of Briton are you?

What is your cultural and ethnic origin?

Are you . . . ?

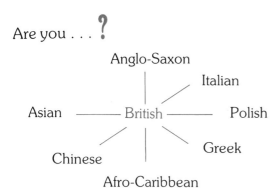

Whatever your ethnic and cultural origins, you have the opportunity to enjoy a great variety of foods and to learn about foods originally from other lands. One of the most interesting aspects of studying food is finding out about foods from around the world, and sampling new foods and recipes. There are so many foods and cuisines (ways of preparing and cooking food) that even if you ate a different recipe every day of your life you would not be able to try all the foods in the world. Next time you visit a large supermarket, look at the cheeses. How many have you tasted? Look at the herbs and spices. How many have you tried? What about the fruits and vegetables? Have you tried them all?

Why do people in different countries eat different foods?

We are now far more adventurous about foods than we used to be, and we have access to a wide variety of foods. However, before travel was as easy, people in different parts of the world could only prepare and cook the foods which were available locally. This gave rise to very different patterns of eating. Even when it is easy to travel and food is imported, basic patterns of eating may remain because people acquire a taste for traditional foods which are part of their culture. Foods eaten in a country are dependent on many factors (see page 40). These are some of the main influences on a nation's diet.

Availability
Before increased travel and imports, people had to rely on food which could be grown in their part of the world. This in turn depended on the climate and type of soil found there. The type of animals which could be raised also varied. The staple carbohydrate foods which form the basis of a diet vary, depending on what can be grown locally:

Asia and parts of India	Rice
Europe and USA	Wheat
Africa and West Indies	Cassava root
Central and Southern America	Maize
Europe, USA, South America	Potato

The type of fruits and vegetables which can be grown is also dependent on climate.

Religion
The religions of a country influence the foods eaten. Many religions have rules about the types of foods which can be eaten. Some religions forbid the eating of meat or of some types of meat. Food is an important part of many religious festivals.

Lifestyle
Where people live and work affects the way people eat. The type of houses and cooking facilities also vary.

Money
The wealth of a country has a great influence on the foods eaten. Wealthy western nations can afford to import a lot of their food. Many countries in the world are too poor to import food and have to rely on the food they can grow. If harvests are poor, starvation can be the result.

Healthy diets

Many diets from other parts of the world are very healthy. Some rely more on fresh fruits and vegetables and in some diets more staple foods are eaten. In some countries a lot of pulses are eaten and in many there is less reliance on meat and fatty foods. We could improve our own diets by studying healthy foods from other lands.

Stir-fried chicken and vegetables with rice
Low in fat, high in fibre

Lentil curry, vegetable curry, chapatis
A healthy high-fibre meal

Healthy meals from around the world

Chow Mein
A good mixture of starches, vegetables and meat

Kebabs with rice
Small amounts of meat with lots of rice and vegetables

Pasta with tomato sauce, green salad
High in starch and vegetables, low in fat

Pizza
Healthy if thick bread base, low-fat cheese and served with salad

Chicken tacos
Small amount of meat, lots of vegetables

Workshop

1 Explain why there is "a world inside Britain", and how this has affected the way we eat.

2 Why did people from different countries eat different foods in the past?

3 In groups, discuss the ways in which the British diet has been influenced by cuisine from around the world. As a class, compare the ideas each group came up with.

4 How healthy are the meals shown on this page? Prepare one of the meals and calculate the protein, fat, carbohydrate and fibre content. Evaluate the meal for taste, texture and appearance.

What is a good meal?

School meal

Restaurant meal

Fast-food meal

Family meal

Few people now have three cooked meals a day. Meals today are usually quick and easy to prepare. Often, people eat snacks rather than meals. Eating patterns and the type and number of meals/snacks per day are determined by a person's daily routine. Some people may be suited to eating small meals often, especially the elderly and children.

Other people may prefer more substantial meals every four to six hours. Meal patterns should suit our lifestyles. But all meals, regardless of where and when eaten and by whom should be good meals.

A GOOD
MEAL IS
— Aesthetically pleasing
— Healthy
— Planned to use available resources

Making meals aesthetically pleasing

A meal is aesthetically pleasing if it looks, tastes and smells good. Making food attractive is one of the most important considerations when planning meals. A really healthy high-fibre, low-fat, low-sugar meal is useless if it looks so awful that no one will eat it!

Aesthetically pleasing meals . . .

. . . **are colourful**   Avoid having several foods of the same colour, such as fish in cheese sauce, potatoes and cauliflower. Use fruits and vegetables to add lots of colour to meals.

. . . **vary in texture**   Include foods of different textures in meals, e.g. some smooth, some crunchy and some chewy foods.

. . . **are attractively served**   Garnish or decorate food to make it look attractive. Arrange food nicely on plates and dishes and set the table attractively.

. . . **taste good**   People's tastes differ and so you need to find out about the likes and dislikes of the people you are catering for.

Making meals healthy

It is very important that meals are healthy. For more information about the health aspect of eating, look at pages 12–13 and the dietary guides on pages 24, 26, 28 and 30 about fat, sugar, salt and fibre. You must **follow the guidelines:**

Eat less fat
Eat less sugar
Eat less salt
Eat more fibre

and remember to **suit special needs:**

Consider any special needs of the people eating the meal. Is anyone on a special diet? Is anyone elderly, pregnant or vegetarian?

Using available resources

When you plan a meal, make sure it is

. . . **suitable for the time of year**   Make use of fruits and vegetables when they are in season. They are then of the best quality and at their cheapest.

. . . **suitable for the money available** Many people have to plan meals on a limited budget. This takes considerable skill and also knowledge of cheap sources of nutrients (see the chart on page 68).

. . . **suitable for the time available to shop and cook**   Meals have to be planned to fit in with the time available. If time is short, convenience foods and easily-cooked foods may be used.

. . . **suitable for the equipment available**   Wise use of appliances such as microwave ovens, food mixers, food processors and pressure cookers can help you to plan a wider range of meals and can help to save time and money. For example, a stew using a cheaper cut of meat can be cooked in 20 minutes in a pressure cooker.

How much food? . . . How many nutrients?

It is not possible to say exactly how much food or how many nutrients a person needs. This is because each person is different. People need different amounts of nutrients and energy depending on their age, sex, state of health, the amount of physical activity, the rate at which their body absorbs nutrients.

Recommended daily amounts

Recommended daily amounts of nutrients are not intended to be the exact amounts of nutrients and energy a person needs. They are designed as a guide only. The nutrients quoted are based on average requirements, with a bit extra added on so that for most people the RDAs are a bit higher than they

Recommended daily amounts of nutrients for population groups

Age ranges	Energy		Protein	Calcium	Iron	Vitamin A (retinol equivalent)	Thiamin	Riboflavin	Niacin equivalent	Vitamin C	Vitamin D
	MJ	kcal	g	mg	mg	µg	mg	mg	mg	mg	µg
Boys 15–17	12.0	2,880	72	600	12	750	1.2	1.7	19	30	–
Girls 15–17	9.0	2,150	53	600	12	750	0.9	1.7	19	30	–

need. RDAs are useful for planning meals for groups of people and for looking at any special needs which people may have. Here is an extract from one RDA table. The full table is on p. 188.

Using food tables and RDAs

When using complex tables like food tables and RDAs it is easy to make mistakes when reading figures. To make reading tables easier, use a ruler to read along a line of figures. Be aware of the units of measurement and always quote them with any figures you use. Some nutrients are measured in grams (g), some in milligrams (mg) and some in micrograms (µg). Micronutrients are needed in very small quantities and so are measured in milligrams or micrograms. Macronutrients are needed in larger amounts, and are measured in grams.

$1 \text{ mg} = 1,000 \text{ µg}$
$1 \text{ g} = 1,000 \text{ mg}$
$1 \text{ kg} = 1,000 \text{ g}$

Energy is measured in kilocalories (kcal) and kilojoules (kJ). $1,000 \text{ kJ} = 1 \text{ MJ}$ (megajoule). Food tables list nutrients per 100 g of food. So *never* write "Cheddar cheese contains 33.5 fat", *always* write "Cheddar cheese contains 33.5 g fat."

Workshop

1 Think about a meal you have enjoyed eating recently. Write about the qualities of that meal which made it aesthetically pleasing to you.

2 a Garnishing and decorating food helps to make it attractive and appetising. Copy out and complete this chart to show how each of these foods could be made more attractive.

Food	Garnish/Decoration
Fish in cheese sauce Fishcakes Quiche Lorraine Cheese and potato pie Rice pudding Chocolate mousse Trifle	

b Explain the difference between the terms *garnish* and *decorate*.

3 Look at the four scenes on page 49. Which type of meal do you think would be the most aesthetically pleasing? Give reasons for your choice.

4 Plan a special meal for a family birthday. It should be both aesthetically pleasing and healthy. Cook the main course of the meal. In your evaluation of the meal, write a paragraph about the qualities which made it healthy and appetising.

Start the day the healthy way!

Is breakfast important?

When you wake up in the morning you may have been without food for as long as twelve hours. You need to have breakfast to "break-the-fast". Missing breakfast can lead to loss of concentration and less efficient working during the morning. Those who do not eat breakfast are likely to get very hungry in the morning, which may lead to eating high-fat and sugary snacks such as sweets and crisps mid-morning. If eating breakfast is not possible, a healthy snack such as sandwiches and fruit should be taken to eat mid-morning.

Very few people now eat a cooked breakfast. From a nutritional point of view this is a good thing. A breakfast of fruit juice, cereal and toast is much healthier (see comparison charts). A breakfast of cereal and toast is also a good way of adding fibre to the diet.

Breakfast Ideas

No appetite?
Tea, coffee or fruit juice, a plain biscuit or a sandwich. Take sandwiches or a healthy snack for later.

Not much time?
Tea, coffee, fruit juice, grapefruit, wholemeal cereals, Bran Flakes, Shredded Wheat, Weetabix, muesli, skimmed milk, wholemeal toast, low-fat spread, small amount of jam or marmalade, porridge (microwaved).

More time?
Porridge with skimmed or semi-skimmed milk (fresh or dried fruit could be added), baked beans on toast, boiled egg with toast, poached egg on toast, lean grilled bacon with tomatoes and mushrooms.

Traditional breakfast

	kcals	Protein g	Fat g	Fibre g
2 Fried rashers back bacon	233	12.5	20.3	0
1 Fried egg	116	7.3	5.9	0
Sausage, fried	158	7.0	12.0	0
2 Rounds toast (white)	140	4.7	1.0	1.6
Butter	74	0	8.2	0
Marmalade	26	0	0	0
Milk (whole) in 2 cups of tea	36	1.8	2.2	0
Sugar in 2 cups of tea	39	0	0	0
Totals	822	33.3	49.6	1.6

Percentage energy from fat 54%

Modern breakfast

	kcals	Protein g	Fat g	Fibre g
Half a grapefruit	11	0.3	0	0.3
1 bowl Bran flakes	106	3.6	0.4	5.3
150 ml Milk (semi-skimmed)	75	5.2	2.4	0
2 slices Toast (wholemeal)	130	5.2	1.6	5.1
Low-fat spread	36	0	4	0
Marmalade	26	0	0	0
Milk in a cup of tea	13	1	0.5	0
Totals	397	15.3	8.9	10.7

Percentage energy from fat 20%

Workshop

1 Look at the comparison charts of a traditional and a modern breakfast, and use the information to answer the following questions. You may need to refer to the dietary guides on pages 24–30.

   a How much fibre are we recommended to eat per day? What contribution would the modern breakfast make to this requirement?

   b The traditional breakfast is high in fat. What may be the long-term consequences of a high-fat diet?

   c Look up the RDAs for your age group and comment on the kcal supplied by the modern breakfast.

   d Using RDAs for your age group, comment on the protein content of both breakfasts.

2 Using food tables or a computer program, make your own comparison chart for a simple breakfast.

30 g Sugar Puffs	30 g Weetabix
100 ml whole milk	100 ml skimmed milk
tea with 5 g sugar	tea, no sugar
20 ml whole milk	20 ml skimmed milk

3 Suggest a suitable breakfast for
   a Jonathon who is 14. He gets up early and likes a filling breakfast.
   b Kate who is 15, gets up late and never feels like eating breakfast.

4 Make a list of points you would use to persuade Kate that breakfast is a good idea.

5 In a practical session cook the breakfast for Jonathon. In your evaluation, comment on the nutritional value of the breakfast and the time taken to prepare and cook it.

Main meals

Many people in this country still have one main meal a day, sometimes at midday but more often in the evening after work. At weekends, Sunday lunch is still an important meal for a lot of people. Puddings are eaten less often. A sweet course is more likely to consist of fruit, ice-cream or yoghurt.

Use the healthy diet pyramid when planning main meals. Remember the healthy eating guidelines:

- Eat less sugar
- Eat less fat
- Eat less salt
- Eat more fibre

The healthy diet pyramid

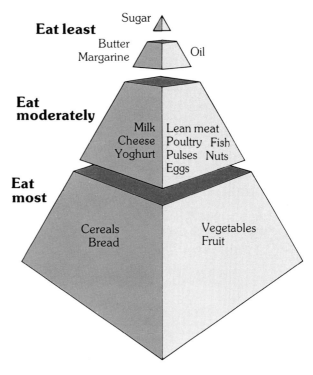

Workshop

1 Copy this chart into your books and complete it by filling it in with a good variety of foods from each group. For ideas see pages on staples, fruit and vegetables, dairy foods, meat and pulses.

Eat most		Eat moderately
(Cereals, bread, potatoes)	(Vegetables)	

2 Meals can be planned by using the meal maker checklist. Use the meal maker checklist to assess the meals below. What is missing? How could each meal be improved?

Fish in batter, chips
Hamburger, french fries
Meat pie, chips
Sausage, mashed potato
Egg, chips

Meal Maker Checklist

1 Select from "eat moderately"
2 Select from "eat most–vegetables"
3 Select from "eat most–cereals"
4 Add any accompaniments needed
5 Decide how to cook
6 Check for "eat least" foods

Some examples

1 chicken
2 onion, peas, sweetcorn, mushrooms
3 rice
4 herbs, stock cube
5 Could be made into either risotto or stir-fry with rice.
6 Low in fat – flavour with stock cube and herbs, do not add extra salt.

1 dahl
2 cauliflower, carrots, onions, mushrooms, tomatoes
3 chapatis
4 spices, chutney or raita
5 vegetable curry
6 Fairly low in fat.

1 beef
2 carrots, cabbage
3 potatoes
4 gravy, horseradish sauce, Yorkshire pudding
5 roast beef, roast potatoes, boiled vegetables
6 Use lean meat. Do not add salt to vegetables.

1 mixed pulses
2 tomatoes, onions, mushrooms, salad vegetables
3 wholemeal spaghetti
4 herbs, garlic
5 spaghetti with bean and tomato sauce, green salad
6 Low in fat.

Packed meals

Many people take packed meals to school or work to eat at lunchtime. Packed meals may also be needed for journeys and picnics. When planning a packed meal consider:

- Who will be eating it? Make the meal suitable for the person's age and occupation.
- Where will it be eaten? It is very important to consider where the food will be eaten and how the food will be eaten. You need to know this before you choose the foods and pack the foods. If the meal is to be eaten on a train or in a car the food must be well packed and easy to eat. If the meal is to be eaten sitting at an office desk or in a school dining hall, food could perhaps be a little more elaborate and cutlery could be included for eating salads and yoghurt etc.

Packed with health

Packed meals can be full of healthy foods. The healthy eating guidelines should be followed when planning packed meals. Unfortunately, many of the foods which are often included in packed meals are high in fats and sugars.

Include bread or crispbread, salad vegetables, lean meats, cheese (especially low-fat or cottage cheese), fresh fruit, yoghurt, unsweetened drinks.

Try to avoid or include only occasionally crisps, chocolate, chocolate biscuits, sweets, fizzy drinks.

Workshop

1 Plan a packed lunch for (a) a manual worker and (b) an office worker. Explain how the meals you have planned take into account the different dietary needs of each of these people.
2 a Plan a packed meal for a school pupil to eat in the dining hall at lunchtime. Explain how you would pack the food you have chosen.
  b Calculate the cost of your packed lunch and compare it to the cost of a school meal.

Packaging

Pack food carefully to ensure food still looks appetising when it is eaten. Use plastic tubs, wrap sandwiches in cling film or plastic bags, use insulated flasks for soup. Plastic cutlery can be used for salads and yoghurt. Include some kitchen paper.

Hygiene

Be aware of food hygiene when packing meals, especially in summer. If there is a few hours' interval between packing and eating the meal and there is nowhere cool to store the food, it might be advisable not to pack highly perishable foods such as cooked meats and patés, sausage rolls and scotch eggs.

Lunchbox Ideas

Wholemeal pitta bread with chicken and salad filling. Orange juice, banana.

Egg and cress sandwiches with granary bread. Nuts and raisins. Apple, fruit juice.

Cheese and onion flan, coleslaw and salad in tub (with fork). Crusty roll, yoghurt, orange.

Crispbread with cheese. Fruit scone, fruit juice.

2 rolls with ham and cucumber. Pear, wholemeal biscuit, fruit juice.

2 vegetable samosas. Apple, fruit juice.

Snacks

Are snacks unhealthy?

The dictionary defines a snack as 'a slight, hurried meal', in other words a small meal which involves little or no preparation or cooking. Eating a lot of snack meals instead of fewer large meals is one of the ways in which our diet has changed in recent years. Sitting down to a meal as a family has become less common. Increasing ownership of freezers and microwave ovens and the greater variety of convenience foods has meant that people can prepare themselves quick snacks as they want them, especially during the week when people come home from school and work at different times.

Eating snacks instead of meals is not necessarily a bad thing; it depends on what types of snack food are eaten. Many snacks such as crisps, chips, sweets, biscuits and cakes are high in fat and sugar. Eating too many of these foods can fill you up. You are then less likely to eat important foods such as fruit and vegetables. This is not good nutrition because your diet may be lacking in fibre and vitamins.

It is possible to plan healthy snacks which are nutritious and quick to prepare. Here are some suggestions.

Ten-minute Snacks

Pizza toast
Thick slice of wholemeal bread, french bread or pitta bread, chopped tomatoes or tomato purée, herbs, cheese.
Toast bread, top with chopped tomato or tomato purée and herbs, cover with grated cheese and grill slowly until cheese melts and begins to go brown.

Baked potatoes
1 medium-sized potato takes about five minutes in a microwave oven. Fill with cheese, ham, sweetcorn, baked beans etc. Use your imagination to invent other fillings.

Toasted sandwiches
Wholemeal bread with various fillings, e.g. ham, cheese, salad, tuna. You could have two or three layers of bread.

Omelette
Quick to make with lots of different fillings: vegetables, cheese, mushrooms, bacon.

Soup
Can be heated very quickly in a microwave oven. Serve with wholemeal bread.

Pitta bread
Split to make a pocket and fill with a variety of fillings such as meat and salad vegetables.

Salads
Salad vegetables with lean meat, tuna, sardines, cottage cheese, coleslaw.

Baked beans on toast
Toast a thick slice of bread, put on a plate, cover with beans and heat in the microwave for two minutes.

Other dishes, such as home-made beefburgers or vegeburgers, savoury flans and pizzas can be frozen in small portions ready to be thawed and served with salads for quick snacks.

Workshop

1 Plan healthy snacks suitable for

   a a twelve-year-old schoolboy who is always hungry when he arrives home from school

   b a seventeen-year-old girl who is trying to lose a few pounds in weight

   c a midday snack for an elderly person

  In each case give reasons for your choice.

2 Suggest some dishes which could be made and frozen in small portions and used to make healthy snack meals. In a practical session, cook a selection of these dishes. In your evaluation explain how the dishes you chose could be used to make meals which would meet healthy eating guidelines.

3 Study the nutrition information for the three different types of crisps and then write down which crisps contain:

   a the most kJ/kcal   d the least protein
   b the least kJ/kcal   e the most fat
   c the most protein   f the most fibre.

Which type of crisps is in your opinion the most healthy? Would you say that these healthiest crisps were useful as part of a healthy diet?

Research: What is meant by *hydrogenated fat?*

4 Study the nutrition information for Fruit and Nut Chewy Bars. Note the carbohydrate content and explain what the main function of Chewy Bars would be in a person's daily diet. What might be the possible consequences of eating several of these bars in place of a meal? Study the ingredients list. How many sugars and sweeteners are listed? Do you agree that Fruit and Nut Chewy Bars are "ideal for people who know what's good for them and live life to the full"?

Research: find out about *sorbitol*.

5 If you have access to food tables or a computer program for dietary analysis, do a snacks investigation. Compare the fat, protein, carbohydrate, energy, and dietary fibre content of 100 g of some common snack foods, e.g. crisps, fruit and nut bars, chocolate biscuits, plain biscuits, currant buns, Mars Bars, chips, baked potatoes, salted peanuts, nuts and raisins. Produce your results in the form of a chart which could be displayed in the classroom. Write an evaluation of your findings to display next to your chart. Use the heading 'What is a Healthy Snack'?

NUTRITION INFORMATION
100 g gives you:

ENERGY	1848 kJ/442 kcal
PROTEIN	6.2 g
CARBOHYDRATES	49 g
(of which sugars 1 g)	
FAT	26 g
(of which saturates plus trans 10.5 g)	
SODIUM	0.6 g
FIBRE	13.5 g

INGREDIENTS. Potatoes, Vegetable Oil and Hydrogenated Vegetable Oil (Total content 26%), Salt.

Lower-fat crisps
Ready salted

INGREDIENTS: potatoes, vegetable oil and hydrogenated vegetable oil, salt.

Typical Nutrition Information

	Per 100 g	Per 28 g pack
Energy	2142 kJ	600 kJ
	520 kcal	146 kcal
Protein	6.5 g	1.8 g
Carbohydrate	40.1 g	11.2 g
Fat	36.8 g	10.3 g

Ready salted crisps

NUTRITION

	TYPICAL VALUES	
	PER 100 g (3½ oz)	PER BAG (50 g)
ENERGY	425 k CALORIES	210 k CALORIES
	1765 k JOULES	885 k JOULES
PROTEIN	11.2 g	5.6 g
CARBOHYDRATE AVAILABLE	37.0 g	18.5 g
TOTAL FAT	26.6 g	13.3 g
of which POLYUNSATURATES	13.3 g	6.7 g
SATURATES	3.5 g	1.8 g
DIETARY FIBRE	17.8 g	8.9 g
ADDED SALTS	1.1 g	0.6 g

INGREDIENTS: STONEGROUND WHOLEMEAL FLOUR, SUNFLOWER OIL, YEAST EXTRACT, SALT

Wholewheat crisps

Fruit and Nut Chewy Bars – "Ideal for people who know what's good for them and live life to the full"?

INGREDIENTS

Rolled Oats, Glucose Syrup, Corn Syrup Solids, Whole Rolled Wheat, Mixed Nuts (8.8%) (Peanut, Almond, Hazelnuts), Raisins (8.5%), Hydrogenated Vegetable Oil, Crisp Rice, Honey, Sunflower Seeds, Glycerol, Brown Sugar, Dried Skimmed Milk, Raisin Juice, Sorbitol, Salt, Dried Unsweetened Coconut, Natural Flavourings.

NUTRITION

This product gives you	per 100 g	per bar
Fat	17.0 g	4.3 g
Protein	7.3 g	1.9 g
Carbohydrates	60.2 g	15.4 g
Energy	1780 kJ/	454 kJ/
	425 kcal	108 kcal
Dietary fibre	3.3 g	0.8 g
Sodium	299 mg	76 mg
VITAMINS		
Thiamine	0.17 mg	0.04 mg
Riboflavin	0.08 mg	0.02 mg
Niacin	2.0 mg	0.5 mg
MINERALS		
Calcium	50 mg	13 mg
Iron	1.7 mg	0.4 mg

FACTS

Fruit and Nut Chewy Bars contain NO artificial flavours, colours or preservatives.

Food for the expectant mother

Planning for a healthy baby should start well before a baby is conceived. Experts advise that the mother should be healthy, fit and well nourished before planning a pregnancy to give the baby the best chance of being born fit.

Eating for two?

Expectant mothers need a diet which is good enough for two in quality, but do not need to eat for two in quantity. In fact, the amount of extra calories required is very small.

Energy The RDA table shows that expectant mothers need an extra 250 kcal per day, which could be met by eating two slices of bread and butter.

Protein There is a need for a slight increase in protein intake, but since most people in this country eat more protein than they require, most expectant mothers would not need to increase the protein content of their diets.

Iron It is important that the expectant mother's diet contains sufficient iron. Good sources include meat, eggs and wholegrain cereals.

Vitamin C Extra Vitamin C is needed during pregnancy for the formation of connective tissue and also to boost the absorption of iron from foods in the diet. Good sources of Vitamin C are fresh fruits and vegetables.

Calcium Extra calcium is required during pregnancy. Calcium is needed for the bone formation of the baby.

Good sources of Calcium	mg per 100 g
Cheese (Cheddar)	800
Sardines	550
Yoghurt (natural low-fat)	200
Milk, skimmed	130
Bread, white	105
Milk, whole	103
Cabbage	57
Bread, wholemeal	54

Good sources of Iron	mg per 100 g
Liver, lamb's	7.5
Cornflakes (fortified)	6.7
Kidney, pig's	6.4
Bread, wholemeal	2.7
Corned beef	2.4
Chocolate, plain	2.4

Recommended daily amounts of nutrients for women aged 18–54

	Energy		Protein	Calcium	Iron	Vitamin A (retinol equivalent)	Thiamin	Riboflavin	Niacin equivalent	Vitamin C	Vitamin D
	MJ	kcal	g	mg	mg	µg	mg	mg	mg	mg	µg
Most occupations	9.0	2,150	54	500	12	750	0.9	1.3	15	30	–
Very active	10.5	2,500	62	500	12	750	1.0	1.3	15	30	–
Pregnant	10.0	2,400	60	1,200	13	750	1.0	1.6	18	60	10
Lactating	11.5	2,750	69	1,200	15	1,200	1.1	1.8	21	60	10

Vitamin D   Extra Vitamin D is needed during pregnancy to help the absorption of calcium from the diet and so to help with bone formation.

Good sources of Vitamin D	µg per 100 g
Herring and kipper	22.4
Salmon, canned	12.5
Margarine	7.9
Sardines, canned	7.5
Cornflakes (fortified)	2.8
Yoghurt	2.0
Eggs	1.6
Liver	0.8
Butter	0.8
Cheese (Cheddar)	0.3

Folic Acid or Folate   Folic acid is needed for the rapid development of a baby's cells, especially in the first few weeks after conception. It is also thought that if a mother's diet contains sufficient folate around the time of conception there is less risk of the baby being born with neural tube defects such as spina bifida. Folic acid is found in liver, oatmeal, oranges, nuts, wholemeal bread, spinach, broccoli, kidneys and brown rice.

Fibre   A diet rich in fibre is needed to prevent constipation, which may occur during pregnancy. Wholemeal cereals, wholemeal bread, fruit and vegetables are all good sources of fibre.

Healthy meals for expectant mothers

Breakfasts   Fruit juice, tea or coffee, wholemeal toast, wholemeal cereals with milk, porridge made with milk, scrambled eggs on wholemeal toast, boiled egg with toast, poached egg with wholemeal toast, grilled bacon and sausages with tomato.
● Avoid greasy fried breakfasts.

Packed Meals/Snacks   Sandwiches made with wholemeal bread filled with cottage cheese, low-fat cream cheese, tinned salmon, tuna or sardines. Salad, vegetables, fruit, yoghurt, soup with wholemeal rolls, baked potatoes with various fillings, omelettes, pizza with salad.
● Avoid too many biscuits and cakes as snacks.

Evening Meals/Main Meals   Liver risotto, liver casserole, potatoes, cabbage. Roast chicken, jacket potatoes, carrots, cabbage, gravy. Spaghetti bolognaise, green salad. Beef and bean casserole, baked potatoes, peas. Fish pie, carrots. Fish in sauce, mashed potatoes, peas, tomatoes. Fish crumble, mixed vegetables. Shepherd's pie, sweetcorn, carrots. Fish bake, pasta. Minced beef cobbler, cabbage, carrots. Cheese and leek flan, mixed salad. Vegetables au gratin, baked potatoes.
● Avoid fatty foods. Spicy or highly seasoned foods could cause indigestion.

Puddings   Yoghurt, fruit, milk puddings.
● Avoid puddings containing lots of fat and sugar.

How the unborn baby (foetus) receives nutrients

All the food eaten by the mother except fibre is digested or broken down into simple component parts which can then be absorbed through the walls of the digestive tract into the blood. The unborn baby receives its nutrients from the mother's blood. The mother's and the baby's blood systems do not mix, but nutrients, oxygen and waste materials are exchanged at the placenta. Unfortunately, harmful substances such as drugs, alcohol and nicotine can also pass through the placenta into the baby's bloodstream.

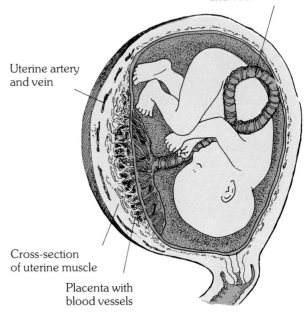

Umbilical arteries and vein

Uterine artery and vein

Cross-section of uterine muscle

Placenta with blood vessels

DON'T SMOKE

DON'T DRINK

DON'T TAKE DRUGS

Breast-feeding mothers

When a new-born baby is fed on breast milk the mother is said to be lactating. During lactation the mother needs to eat a very similar diet to that eaten in pregnancy, but a little more of everything (see RDA table). It is important that mothers eat a good diet when breast-feeding because sufficient nutrients and energy are needed for the production of breast milk.

Workshop

1 As a class exercise or in groups, produce a healthy eating factsheet for expectant mothers that is easy to understand, attractively produced and has lots of advice about foods and meals.

2 Plan a day's healthy meals for an expectant mother who does not have much time for cooking. Cook one of the meals and, using a computer or food tables, work out the calcium content of your meal. Write an evaluation of this meal, commenting on nutritional value, cost, time to prepare and attractiveness.

3 Plan a day's meals for an expectant mother who is on a low income. Cook the main meal and calculate the cost of it. In your evaluation write about the cost and nutritive value of your meal.

4 Many expectant mothers work until the seventh month of pregnancy. Suggest some healthy packed meals that an expectant mother could take to work. Calculate the calcium, iron and Vitamin D content of one packed meal and comment on the contribution it would make to the Recommended Daily Amounts for those nutrients.

5 Compare the Recommended Daily Amounts of nutrients for pregnant women to those for women aged 18–54 (most occupations). Identify the nutrients which need to be increased, and explain why.

From baby to child

Breast-feeding

Doctors, dietitians and midwives all agree that breast-feeding is the best way of feeding babies from birth.

- Breast milk has a good balance of nutrients for the growth of the baby
- Breast milk contains natural agents which protect the baby against disease
- Breast milk is clean and cannot be contaminated by lack of hygiene
- Breast milk cannot be prepared incorrectly

A mother should try to breastfeed her baby for at least two weeks and ideally for 4–6 months after birth

Weaning

Weaning means changing a baby's diet from all milk to a mixture of milk and solids. Babies should not be weaned until they are about four months old because a baby's digestive system has to develop before it can cope with some proteins. It is also thought that if babies are given solid foods too early they may run the risk of developing allergies.

Food for a growing baby

First foods (about 4–6 months) should be smooth and thin and should become thicker gradually as the child gets older. Some experts advise that no wheat products should be given before six months.

Second foods (6–8 months) should gradually be increased and milk feeds decreased. Some chewy foods can be given to help with teething. Rusks should be avoided because they contain a lot of sugar.

Third foods (9–12 months) should introduce a baby to a wide range of tastes and textures.

First foods

Puréed cereal such as rice or oats
Fruit or vegetable purée
Finely mashed banana
Puréed meat such as chicken or liver
Milk feeds

Second foods

Breakfast cereals such as Weetabix or instant oats
Bread or chapatti
Mashed potato with milk
Plain boiled rice
Mashed baked beans
Mashed fish
Natural yoghurt
Pieces of apple or banana
Pieces of tender meat from stews or casseroles

Third foods

Fish, eggs, meat or vegetables, chopped or mashed
Fruit
Breakfast cereals
Baked beans
Bread, rice, pasta or chapatti

Make your own baby foods

Home-made baby foods are easy to make and cheaper than the ready-made baby foods. To make your own baby foods use a liquidiser or food processor to grind up foods from the family meals such as meat, potatoes and vegetables. Home-made baby foods can be frozen in small portions. Be very careful about hygiene.

Never add salt or sugar to baby foods; or give babies foods containing colourings and additives. Avoid sugary drinks, especially in feeding bottles – give water or milk instead.

By about the age of one, babies should be eating much the same sort of food as the rest of the family.

Feeding children aged one to five

Rice Pudding
What is the matter with Mary Jane?
She's crying with all her might and main,
And she won't eat her dinner – rice pudding again –
What *is* the matter with Mary Jane?

A. A. Milne

Small children can be difficult to feed. Their appetites often vary. They may eat a lot one day and not much the next. They may like certain foods and then go off them. Children of this age are growing very fast and are very active. RDA charts show that their need for nutrients is very high in relation to their size. A three-year-old girl is much smaller than a fifteen-year-old girl, but there is not a big difference in the amount of calories they need. Because of her smaller size, the three-year-old cannot eat large bulky meals and will need smaller meals with healthy snacks in-between.

Tips on feeding children

- Give a good selection of nutritious dishes to develop a wide range of tastes
- Give small, attractively served helpings
- Do not make a fuss about food. Children can use food to gain attention and mealtimes can become a battleground
- Let children have their own bowls, mugs and cutlery
- Do not force children to eat
- Do not give children biscuits, cakes and sweets between meals
- Do not use food as a reward or bribe
- Have regular mealtimes
- Allow plenty of time for meals and make meals calm and unhurried. Children need to concentrate on food
- Give drinks *after* meals. Children may feel full if they have drinks before a meal

Recommended daily amounts of nutrients for girls aged 3–17

Age	Energy		Protein	Calcium	Iron	Vitamin A (retinol equivalent)	Thiamin	Riboflavin	Niacin equivalent	Vitamin C
	MJ	kcal	g	mg	mg	µg	mg	mg	mg	mg
3–4	6.25	1,500	37	600	8	300	0.6	0.8	9	20
5–6	7.0	1,680	42	600	10	300	0.7	0.9	10	20
7–8	8.0	1,900	48	600	10	400	0.8	1.0	11	20
9–11	8.5	2,050	51	700	12	575	0.8	1.2	14	25
12–14	9.0	2,150	53	700	12	725	0.9	1.4	16	25
15–17	9.0	2,150	53	600	12	750	0.9	1.7	19	30

Meals for children

Meals for children should be the same or similar to what the family is eating, and children should eat with the family where possible. Foods should be colourful, interesting and easy to chew or eat.

Meal ideas for children

Shepherd's pie or vegetarian shepherd's pie with beans and vegetables
Fish pie, fish-shaped fish cakes or fish fingers with potatoes and vegetables
Bolognaise sauce with pasta shapes
Pasta shapes or macaroni in cheese sauce
Lasagne (meat or vegetable)
Chicken risotto
Natural yoghurt with chopped fruit
Milk puddings such as rice pudding with dried fruit or reduced-sugar jam
Fruit and jelly or fruit and custard

Healthy snacks for children

Crispbread with cheese and Marmite
Sandwiches with wholemeal or white bread and colourful fillings such as cucumber and cream cheese, grated carrot and cheese, ham and tomato
Sticks of raw carrot and celery
Fruit such as bananas, satsumas, pieces of apple and orange
Wholemeal fruit buns or wholemeal fruit or cheese scones

Workshop

1 Explain why breast milk is the ideal food for babies.

2 What is meant by the term *weaning*? Why should babies not be weaned before they are about four months old?

3 What are the advantages of home-made baby foods? In a practical session investigate a commercial baby food and compare it to a similar home-made baby food. In your evaluation, write about the cost, flavour, texture and colour of each food.

4 Suggest ways in which mealtimes for small children can be made interesting and enjoyable so that the children are encouraged to eat healthy meals.

5 Your older sister and five-year-old niece are coming to visit you. Plan a meal which will be suitable for the whole family. Cook the main dish. In your evaluation comment on the finished result and why the dish you chose was suitable for a family including a five-year-old child.

Food for the secondary years

The secondary school years are a time of rapid growth and change. The chart shows how much growth occurs between the ages of 11 and 16. The figures are averages, but there is a wide variety of normal heights in each year group – think of the tallest and smallest girl/boy in your year.

Food needs in the secondary school

Because secondary school pupils grow so rapidly, the need for nutritious food is great. Look at the RDAs on page 188 and compare the figures of boys aged 15–17 to men 18–34, and compare the figures for girls 15–17 to women 18–54. You will see that the kilocalories and protein needed are similar and that for 15–17 year-olds there is a slightly higher need for calcium and some vitamins.

Average height and weight of secondary school pupils

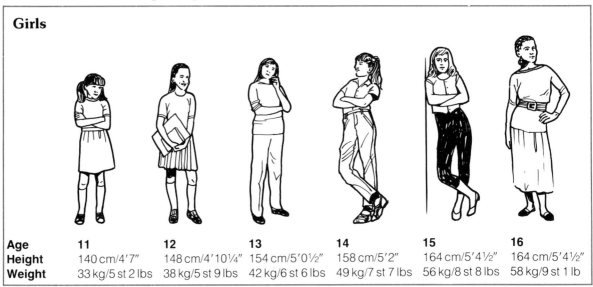

Girls

Age	11	12	13	14	15	16
Height	140 cm/4'7"	148 cm/4'10¼"	154 cm/5'0½"	158 cm/5'2"	164 cm/5'4½"	164 cm/5'4½"
Weight	33 kg/5 st 2 lbs	38 kg/5 st 9 lbs	42 kg/6 st 6 lbs	49 kg/7 st 7 lbs	56 kg/8 st 8 lbs	58 kg/9 st 1 lb

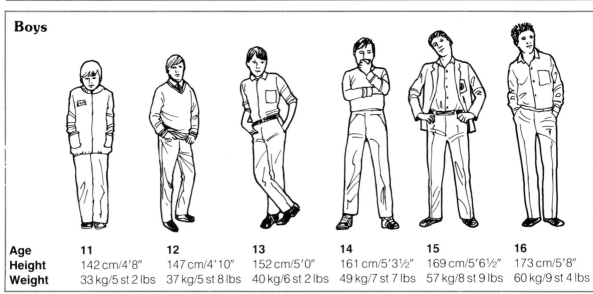

Boys

Age	11	12	13	14	15	16
Height	142 cm/4'8"	147 cm/4'10"	152 cm/5'0"	161 cm/5'3½"	169 cm/5'6½"	173 cm/5'8"
Weight	33 kg/5 st 2 lbs	37 kg/5 st 8 lbs	40 kg/6 st 2 lbs	49 kg/7 st 7 lbs	57 kg/8 st 9 lbs	60 kg/9 st 4 lbs

What do secondary school pupils eat?

Unfortunately, many secondary school pupils do not eat a healthy diet. A survey in 1982 found that 5% had no breakfast and only one meal during the day. A further 3% had a cereal breakfast and only snacks throughout the rest of the day.

Nutritional recommendations for school meals were removed in 1980 and since that time many school canteens have changed to a cafeteria system and serve more convenience foods and more chips. School meals now vary considerably. Some education authorities have healthy eating policies, but many have no nutritional standards at all. Also, many schools have tuck shops and fizzy-drinks machines.

All chips and cola?

All this adds up to many teenagers having an unhealthy diet which is high in fats and sugars and low in fibre. They eat too many cakes, biscuits, sweets, crisps, chips and fizzy drinks. These foods will do you no harm if they are just a small part of an otherwise healthy diet which contains plenty of fruit, vegetables and cereals. Teenagers who eat lots of snacks and do not have any good meals may have a diet which is short of important vitamins and minerals.

Check your diet

To see how healthy your diet is, try the quiz on page 15 (if you have not already done so). Also see the dietary guides for advice. The following points will help you to develop good eating habits:

- Try to pick a healthy school lunch or pack a healthy lunch box (see page 55).
- Keep some healthy snacks with you to prevent you from getting hungry and visiting the tuck shop.
- Try to have at least one meal a day which contains fruit and vegetables.
- Have at least a simple breakfast of toast or cereals.

Weight control

Adolescence is a good time to begin to consider whether you are a healthy weight for your height (see the chart on page 14). Being very overweight (obese) can lead to heart disease, high blood pressure, arthritis, and mature-onset diabetes. The best way to control your weight is to be aware of your energy needs and to eat accordingly so that you never put on weight (see *Input v. Output* on page 36).

If you need to lose weight

If you need to lose a lot of weight (over one stone or 6.5 kg), see a doctor and dietician for advice. If you just need to lose a small amount of weight, changing to a healthier diet may be all you need to do. Follow the healthy eating guidelines.

Slimming tips

- Start by writing down everything you eat for a week before you go on your diet. Work out how you are going to modify your diet by cutting down on fats and sugars.
- Set yourself a target weight.
- Make yourself a graph to monitor your weight.
- Don't weigh yourself too often. Once a week is enough.
- Aim to lose weight very gradually – no more than 2 lbs or 1 kg per week.
- Increase your energy output. Take up a new sport.
- Don't eat between meals.
- Ask your parents to help by not buying biscuits and cakes but buying more fruit instead.

Never
Go on crash diets
Go on severe diets
Go too long without food
Rely on slimming products

Meal ideas for slimmers

Breakfast

Grapefruit or fruit juice, tea or coffee, with one of the following:

Toast, preferably wholemeal, low-fat spread, small amount of marmalade

Bowl of wholemeal cereal with skimmed milk

Scrambled egg on wholemeal toast

Boiled egg with wholemeal toast   Beans on toast

No greasy fried breakfasts or sugary cereals.

Lunch/Snacks

Choose one of the following plus a drink and an apple or orange:

Wholemeal sandwiches with various fillings (e.g. salad vegetables, cottage cheese or low-fat cheese)

Crispbreads with cheese

Salads with small amounts of meat or cheese

Baked potatoes filled with cottage cheese or low-fat cheese or vegetables

Meals

Chicken risotto

Chicken casserole with baked potatoes, peas and sweetcorn

Chicken curry with rice or chapatti

Stir-fry chicken and vegetables with rice

Pizza (made with low-fat cheese), salad

Quiche Lorraine (made with low-fat cheese), salad

White fish with parsley or mushroom sauce (made with skimmed milk), potatoes, peas, carrots

Spaghetti Bolognaise (made with lean mince, wholemeal pasta), salad

Chicken and white fish are good because they are low in fat. Check food tables.

Energy crisis?   If you get hungry eat fruit, raw carrots, a few nuts and raisins, a plain biscuit or a wholemeal scone.

Avoid all foods high in fat and sugar, especially chocolate, cakes, biscuits, crisps, ice-cream, sweets. You should have these for occasional treats only.

SLIMMERS 'IN DANGER'

Big fines urged to beat diet swindlers

TOUGHER penalties are needed to fight conmen who make a fortune out of useless slimming products, says the Consumers' Association.

Many 'slimming' products do not help you lose weight and some might be harmful, says the association's magazine, Which?

It says products claiming to change weight should be reclassified as medicines so that manufacturers have to prove they work. Meanwhile penalties should be as tough as possible under current laws.

Trading standards officers should press for trial by jury, where convictions can carry an unlimited fine or prison sentence of up to two years, says Which?

Appetite suppressants which contain enough bulking agent to make you feel full could impede the body's absorption of minerals, and the Government is concerned that gum-based products could swell in the gullet and cause breathing difficulties, says the magazine.

Some 'magic' slimming products claim to work in pseudo-scientific ways, such as amino acid tablets, while others are marketed as food supplements but have names which suggest they might help weight loss.

'These are all rubbish and a waste of money,' says Which?

'There is only one way to lose weight – you must consume less energy than you are using.'

Workshop

1 Investigate your school meals. Make a list of the food served in one week. Interview pupils and ask them for their opinions about school meals. Could school meals be healthier? Could the choice of food be improved? Could school meals be better organised? Do you have to queue for long?

2 Does your school encourage healthy eating? Is there a tuck shop/a drinks machine? In what ways are pupils encouraged to have a healthy diet? In what ways could they be encouraged to have a healthy diet? Write a short report to answer these questions.

3 Suggest some healthy dishes which could be served as school lunches. In a practical session, prepare a selection of these dishes. In your evaluation discuss the suitability of the dishes you cooked as school meals. Were they appetising, economical and easy to prepare?

4 You would like to lose a few pounds in weight. Plan a day's meals for yourself. Cook the main meal. Work out the fat and sugar content of your meal using food tables or a computer program.

5 Read the article "Slimmers In Danger" and explain the dangers of slimming products. Explain why it is much better to modify your eating habits than to rely on slimming products. You could present your answer as a magazine article entitled "Lose lbs not £s".

How old is old?

We are now living longer due to better health care and improved social conditions. The number of people in the population aged 65 and over is now one and a half times greater than in 1951, and in 1986 represented just over 15% of the population (compared with 11% in 1951). The number has grown by 3.2 million since 1951 and is expected to increase by another 2.6 million by the year 2025.

Many elderly people are very active, and see their time of life as a time to enjoy the freedom they have now that they are relieved of the responsibilities of family and employment.

Eat well, stay well

Elderly people should follow the healthy eating guidelines to stay fit and well. It will be to their advantage if they have always had a well-balanced diet.

Elderly people tend to become less active, especially after the age of 75. Their energy requirements are less and so they should eat less carbohydrates and fats to avoid an increase in weight. This often happens naturally, as elderly people find their appetites become smaller. The recommended daily amounts table below shows that apart from less dietary energy and a little less protein, elderly people need similar nutrients to most adults.

'Marathon Madge', still running in her seventies

Recommended daily amounts of nutrients for the moderately active

Age ranges	Energy		Protein	Calcium	Iron	Vitamin A (retinol equivalent)	Thiamin	Riboflavin	Niacin equivalent	Vitamin C	Vitamin D*
	MJ	kcal	g	mg	mg	µg	mg	mg	mg	mg	µg
Men											
18–34	12.0	2,900	72	500	10	750	1.2	1.6	18	30	–
35–64	11.5	2,750	69	500	10	750	1.1	1.6	18	30	–
65–74	10.0	2,400	60	500	10	750	1.0	1.6	18	30	–
75 and over	9.0	2,150	54	500	10	750	0.9	1.6	18	30	–
Women											
18–54	9.0	2,150	54	500	12	750	0.9	1.3	15	30	–
55–74	8.0	1,900	47	500	10	750	0.8	1.3	15	30	–
75 and over	7.0	1,680	42	500	10	750	0.7	1.3	15	30	–

* Most people who go out in the sun need no dietary source of vitamin D, but children and adolescents in winter, and housebound adults, are recommended to take 10 µg of vitamin D daily.

Factfile

- There are 4,000 centenarians in the UK.
- Britain's oldest man is John Evans of Swansea, born 19th August 1877.
- Britain's oldest woman is Mrs Kate Begbie, born 9th January 1877.
- The Queen Mother, born 4th August 1900, still carries out public engagements.
- The oldest marathon runner is Mr Dimitiron Yordanidis. He completed a marathon in Athens at the age of 96 in October 1976.
- Mrs Thelma Pitt completed a marathon in New Zealand at the age of 82 in August 1985.

Store-cupboard foods for the elderly

Milk (dried, evaporated or longlife).
Tins of meat and fish.
Instant mashed potato (with added vitamin C).
Packets or tins of vegetables and soup.
Breakfast cereals or oats.
Biscuits or crispbread.
Blackcurrant juice or pure fruit juice.
Tins of fruit.
Tins of milk puddings.

Cheap sources of energy and nutrients (in approximate order, cheapest first)

Energy	Lard, margarine, vegetable oil, sugar, white bread, butter, brown or wholemeal bread, old potatoes, pasta, rice, biscuits, breakfast cereals.
Protein	White bread, brown or wholemeal bread, pasta, liver, eggs, baked beans, cheese, milk, chicken, rice, frozen peas, old potatoes.
Carbohydrate	Sugar, white bread, old potatoes, rice, pasta, brown or wholemeal bread, breakfast cereals, new potatoes, biscuits, baked beans, ice-cream.
Calcium	Milk, cheese, white bread, brown bread, wholemeal bread, carrots, ice-cream, biscuits.
Iron	Liver, fortified breakfast cereals, brown or wholemeal bread, white bread, baked beans, new potatoes, old potatoes, eggs, biscuits.
Vitamin A	Liver, carrots, margarine, butter, eggs, milk, cheese.
Thiamin	Fortified breakfast cereals, old potatoes, new potatoes, brown or wholemeal bread, white bread, frozen peas, pork, liver, bacon and ham.
Riboflavin	Liver, fortified breakfast cereals, milk, cheese, brown or wholemeal bread, old potatoes.
Niacin	Liver, breakfast cereals, white bread, old potatoes, new potatoes, chicken, sausages, frozen peas.
Vitamin C	Fruit juices, oranges, old potatoes, new potatoes, tomatoes, fresh green vegetables, frozen peas.
Vitamin D	Margarine, fatty fish, eggs, fortified breakfast cereals, liver, butter.
Dietary fibre	Dried beans, All-bran, wholemeal bread, baked beans, white bread, potatoes, whole-grain breakfast cereals and pasta.

Possible problems

Some elderly people may have medical or social problems which prevent them from achieving a healthy diet.

Social problems   Many elderly people live on low incomes and may need advice about low-cost meals. Cookery classes for retired people can help. Many elderly people live alone and may lose interest in food and lack the motivation to cook for only one.

Medical problems   Some elderly people may have difficulty eating and digesting food. They need to eat foods which are easy to digest, such as fish, chicken and eggs, and may need to drink pure fruit juice if they are not able to eat fruit.

If elderly people have physical disabilities such as arthritis, they may have difficulty shopping and cooking. Friends and relatives can help with the shopping and the Meals on Wheels service can provide hot meals for elderly people who are unable to cook. A good store of easy-to-cook convenience foods is essential for emergencies such as bad weather.

Workshop

1   Mrs Jones has just retired. She is fit and well but is on a low income. Plan a day's meals for her. Cook a selection of low-cost dishes from the day's meals. Cost one dish. Evaluate this assignment.
2   Mr Williams is 75 and suffers from arthritis. He enjoys his food and likes to eat well but has difficulty with shopping, especially in winter. Suggest some convenience foods which he could keep in his store cupboard for emergencies. Plan a day's meals using these foods. In the practical session cook a selection of these dishes. Evaluate this assignment.
3   Mrs Brown is 80, and since her husband died has had little enthusiasm for cooking. Suggest some healthy and economical snacks and simple meals which she could prepare. Cook some of these in the practical session. Evaluate this assignment.
4   Prepare a talk about healthy eating to be given at an over 60s club. List any foods or visual aids you would take to illustrate your talk.

Extra research

What is hypothermia? Research the causes and prevention. What part does food play in the prevention of hypothermia?
Find out about schemes in your area for insulating homes for the elderly.
Investigate housing provision for the elderly in your area.
Find out about Meals on Wheels and Age Concern.

Vegetarian meals

What is a vegetarian?

As a general rule, vegetarians avoid all meat, fish and poultry. Beyond this, vegetarianism covers a range of diets.

Ovo-lacto-vegetarians include milk, milk products (like cheeses, yoghurt and butter) and eggs in their diet.

Lacto-vegetarians eat milk and milk products but not eggs.

Vegans exclude all foods of animal origin including milk and its products, eggs, honey and processed foods that use any animal products. Their diet consists of food from plant sources only.

Why vegetarianism?

There are many reasons why people change to a vegetarian diet. These are some of the main ones:

Moral reasons   Most people become vegetarian because they object to the slaughter of animals for food.

Ecological reasons   Some vegetarians think the consumption of meat is much more costly in terms of land and crop resources.

Vast quantities of cereal crops, which could be used for human consumption, are currently used to feed farm animals. Many see this as a very inefficient way to feed people.

10 acres of land (that's about 5 football pitches) will support
61 people on a diet of soya beans
24 people on a diet of wheat
10 people on a diet of maize
2 people on a diet of cattle meat

Health reasons   Many people are turning to vegetarianism because they feel it is a healthier and more wholesome way of eating.

Religious reasons   A number of religions advocate vegetarian diets, for example Buddhism.

Taste   Some people do not like the taste of meat.

Did you know?
1 3% of British adults are vegetarians.
2 5.5% of adults avoid red meat.
3 9.3% (1.2 million) children are said by their parents to be vegetarian or beginning to avoid red meat.
4 Women and girls are far more likely to be non-meat-eating than men.
5 Famous vegetarians include Madonna, Michael Jackson, Chrissie Hynde, Gaz Top and Morrissey.

Animal foods	Vegetarian alternatives
Meat, fish, poultry	Lentils, beans (wide variety), nuts, cereals, textured vegetable protein made from soya beans, quorn mycoprotein.
Milk, yoghurt	Soya milk made from soya beans, soya milk yoghurt.
Cheese	Vegetarian cheese is made without rennet which is obtained from calves' stomachs.
Eggs	Most vegetarians prefer free-range eggs because they object to the battery system of egg production.
Animal fats, lard, suet	Pure vegetable fats and margarines which do not contain any animal fats, vegetable suet.
Meat stock cubes	Vegetable stock cubes and vegetable concentrates such as Marmite.

Changing to a vegetarian diet

Changing to a vegetarian diet should be a carefully thought out and well planned step. Here are some suggestions for anyone considering a vegetarian diet:

- Do it gradually – start by trying a few non-meat meals in a week.
- Visit health-food shops and look at vegetarian products.
- Visit large supermarkets and look at their vegetarian meals.
- Have a meal in a vegetarian restaurant and study the menu.
- Borrow some vegetarian cookery books from the library.
- Write to the Vegetarian Society for information and advice. Their address is: Parkdale, Dunham Road, Altrincham, Cheshire WA14 4QG.

The Vegetarian Society's symbol, found on foods suitable for vegetarians

Vegetarian nutrition

A well-balanced vegetarian diet can be very healthy. Vegetarians eat less fat and more fibre than most meat eaters. Ovo-lacto vegetarians generally have no problem achieving a healthy diet, but they may have to limit the amount of butter, cream and cheese they eat otherwise their diet may contain too much fat.

Vegans, who eat no animal products, have to plan their diets with care to make sure that they obtain enough high-quality protein, but this can easily be done by combining two or more low-quality proteins.

Vegetarian nutrition

Vegans need to eat a good mixture of pulses (dried peas, beans and lentils), nuts, cereals and vegetables. A vegan diet may be deficient in Vitamin B_{12} because this vitamin is not generally found in vegetable foods, so vegans may need to take a regular supplement of Vitamin B_{12}.

How to improve protein quality

Bread + Peanut butter → Sandwich

Vegetables + Lentils → Vegetable soup

Wholemeal breadcrumbs + Nuts and vegetables → Nut loaf

Spaghetti + Lentils and vegetables → Spaghetti with tomato and lentil sauce

"A veggy week"

The following meals for one week for an ovo-lacto vegetarian have been suggested by The Vegetarian Society.

Monday

breakfast
wholewheat cereal
(e.g. Bran Flakes, All-bran)
wholewheat toast
fruit juice

lunch
French onion soup
wholewheat roll
fruit

dinner
pasta with lentil & red pepper sauce
green salad
sliced tomatoes
apricots with yoghurt

Tuesday

breakfast
mushrooms on wholewheat toast
fruit juice

lunch
cottage cheese and salad in wholewheat rolls
fruit

dinner
cheese & sweetcorn flan
green peas
baked potatoes
oaty apple crumble & custard

Wednesday

breakfast
whole-grain muesli with milk
wholewheat toast
fruit juice

lunch
tomato soup
salad sandwich
fruit

dinner
spinach & cream cheese pancakes
mashed potatoes
grilled tomatoes
natural yoghurt & maple syrup

Thursday

breakfast
chopped fresh fruit, yoghurt & raisins
wholewheat toast
fruit juice

lunch
veggyburger & onion in wholewheat bap
fruit

dinner
brown rice risotto
home-made coleslaw and green salad
slice banana loaf

Friday

breakfast
poached egg on toast
fruit juice

lunch
watercress soup
wholewheat bread
small packet cashew nuts

dinner
mushroom & cheese macaroni
green beans
apple cake

Saturday

breakfast
baked beans on toast
fruit juice

lunch
wholewheat pitta bread
grated cheese & salad stuffing
fruit yoghurt

dinner
black-eyed bean pie
roast parsnips
raspberry whip

Sunday

breakfast
boiled egg and toast
fruit juice

lunch
avocado, mushroom & beansprout salad
French dressing
wholewheat bread and peanut butter
potato crisps

dinner
chunky nut & vegetable roast
roast potatoes
cabbage
peas
veggy gravy
fruit pie and nut cream

Workshop

1 Draw the following chart into your book and complete it.

Type of vegetarian	Foods eaten
Ovo-lacto vegetarian	
Lacto-vegetarian	
Vegan	

2 Explain the meaning of protein quality. Give examples of how protein quality can be improved by combining foods.

3 Plan a day's meals for an ovo-lacto vegetarian. Give reasons for your choice.

4 Plan a day's meals for a vegan. Give reasons for your choice.

5 You have a friend who is considering becoming vegetarian. Write her a letter in which you advise her where to get information about vegetarianism. Suggest some simple non-meat meals she could try.

6 Investigate the use of textured vegetable protein as a substitute to minced beef. Make two versions of *either* shepherd's pie *or* spaghetti bolognaise, one with TVP and one with minced beef. Assess each for appearance, taste and texture. Write an evaluation of your findings.

7 Many favourite meat-based recipes can be adapted to make them suitable for vegetarians. Adapt a lasagne recipe by using either a vegetable or pulse mixture in place of the meat sauce. Cook the recipe you have adapted and evaluate your results.

The staple diet

Tracy lives in Liverpool and has Quiche Lorraine for lunch.

Guiseppe lives in Naples and has Spaghetti Marinara for his evening meal.

Sonia lives in New York and had a pizza yesterday evening.

Rajesh lives in Bombay and has chapatti with his main meal.

Imad lives in Baghdad and always has bread at mealtimes.

All the above dishes have one thing in common: they contain flour made from **wheat**. Tracy, Giuseppe, Sonia, Rajesh and Imad will eat food made with wheat flour on most days of their lives. Tracy and Sonia will also eat baked potatoes and chips, and Rajesh and Manal will eat rice on most days too.

These foods – wheat, potatoes and rice – are the most important foods in the diets of the people who eat them.

They are **cheap**
They are **readily available**
They have **little taste** but they **easily absorb flavours and liquids such as sauces**
They are **mainly starch** so they are **filling**
They are called **staple foods**

Wheat

Before it can be baked, the wheat grain must be broken down into very fine particles. This is called *milling*, and the original process involved rubbing the wheat between two round, flat stones to open it and extract the starch. This can still be seen in some flour mills, but almost all commercial flour today is milled by passing the wheat between metal rollers to separate the starch from the bran and the germ. The more starch that is extracted, the lower the *extraction rate*: wholemeal flour has an extraction rate of 95% and white flour of 75%.

Wheat is an important ingredient for many foods e.g. bread, cakes and biscuits.

Rice

Rice is the staple food for over half the population of the world but it is grown on less than half the area needed to grow wheat. *Brown rice* includes the bran but *white rice* has had the bran removed by polishing. This process removes most of the B vitamins too.

Most savoury dishes need dry, separate grains so a long-grain rice such as Basmati is best for this. Risotto needs a rice which will absorb flavours so a short-grain Italian rice is used.

As well as the usual rice dishes (plain rice, fried rice, risotto, pilau, paella) try using gluten-free rice flour in biscuits and for thickening sauces, and rice flakes in muesli. Wild rice is often added to plain rice as an interesting variation in appearance and taste. However, it is not really a rice but a type of grass seed and it is also very expensive.

Potato

Unlike wheat and rice, the potato is a root vegetable. It is a very important staple, though, because it is a good source of vitamin C as well as providing energy and protein.

As potatoes are vegetables they are difficult to store for long periods, unlike cereals. The vitamin C content deteriorates during storage and potatoes can be infected by fungi. They also begin to sprout before the following year's crop is ready.

Despite all these disadvantages, potatoes are very popular in various forms: boiled, mashed, baked, roasted, sautéed and as chips. Processed potatoes are expensive but convenient: canned new potatoes, dried mashed potatoes and many varieties of frozen potatoes, e.g. chips, croquettes, waffles and hash browns. Crisps are extremely popular and the number of varieties increases yearly.

The Fact Cards for the three staples most widely available in Britain show the composition of the foods, and give some recipe ideas.

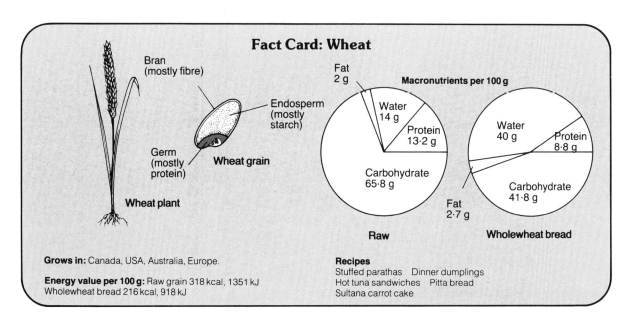

Fact Card: Wheat

Bran (mostly fibre)

Endosperm (mostly starch)

Germ (mostly protein) **Wheat grain**

Wheat plant

Macronutrients per 100 g

Raw:
Fat 2 g
Water 14 g
Protein 13·2 g
Carbohydrate 65·8 g

Raw

Wholewheat bread:
Water 40 g
Protein 8·8 g
Carbohydrate 41·8 g
Fat 2·7 g

Wholewheat bread

Grows in: Canada, USA, Australia, Europe.

Energy value per 100 g: Raw grain 318 kcal, 1351 kJ
Wholewheat bread 216 kcal, 918 kJ

Recipes
Stuffed parathas   Dinner dumplings
Hot tuna sandwiches   Pitta bread
Sultana carrot cake

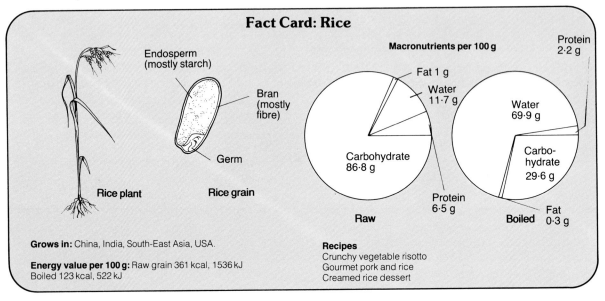

Fact Card: Rice

Endosperm (mostly starch)

Bran (mostly fibre)

Germ

Rice plant

Rice grain

Macronutrients per 100 g

Fat 1 g
Water 11·7 g
Carbohydrate 86·8 g
Protein 6·5 g

Raw

Protein 2·2 g
Water 69·9 g
Carbohydrate 29·6 g
Fat 0·3 g

Boiled

Grows in: China, India, South-East Asia, USA.

Energy value per 100 g: Raw grain 361 kcal, 1536 kJ
Boiled 123 kcal, 522 kJ

Recipes
Crunchy vegetable risotto
Gourmet pork and rice
Creamed rice dessert

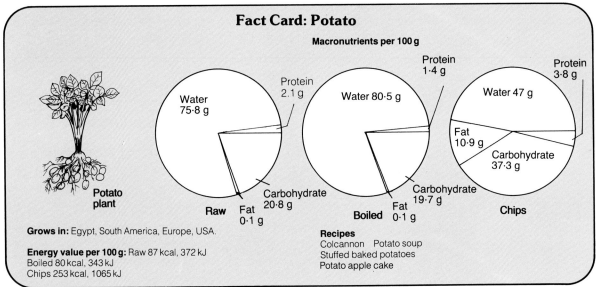

Fact Card: Potato

Macronutrients per 100 g

Water 75·8 g
Protein 2.1 g
Carbohydrate 20·8 g
Fat 0·1 g

Raw

Protein 1·4 g
Water 80·5 g
Carbohydrate 19·7 g
Fat 0·1 g

Boiled

Water 47 g
Protein 3·8 g
Fat 10·9 g
Carbohydrate 37·3 g

Chips

Potato plant

Grows in: Egypt, South America, Europe, USA.

Energy value per 100 g: Raw 87 kcal, 372 kJ
Boiled 80 kcal, 343 kJ
Chips 253 kcal, 1065 kJ

Recipes
Colcannon   Potato soup
Stuffed baked potatoes
Potato apple cake

Workshop

1 Apart from the three staples mentioned, there are also oats, rye, millet, sorghum, cassava, yam, plantain and sweet potato. As a class, write fact cards for each of these on large sheets of paper and make a wall display. Include information and pictures to show what these staples look like, where they are grown, nutritional value, processing, cooking. Also include one or two (tried and tested!) recipes, together with the cost and nutritional value of each dish.

2 Look at the Fact Cards. If you got all the energy you need for the day (see page 188) from *only* potatoes or *only* rice or *only* wheat, how much would you need to eat? (Remember to look at the cooked values!) If the need for energy is satisfied, is there enough protein present?

3 Work out the percentage of energy from fat in boiled potatoes and chips (see page 12 for how to do this).

From contented cows . . .

1

Milk and milk products in this country come mainly from cows, although you can buy goats' milk, and some cheeses are made from sheep's milk.

Milk is a source of protein (casein and whey proteins), fat and carbohydrates. The fat is mostly saturated fat. The carbohydrate in milk is a sugar called **lactose**.
This table shows what 100 ml of milk (or 100 g of dried milk) contains:

	Pasteurized Whole*	Channel Island	Skim	Semi-skimmed	Evaporated	Condensed	Dried skim
Water (g)	87.3	86.3	90.9	89.7	68.6	25.8	4.1
Protein (g)	3.3	3.6	3.4	3.3	8.6	8.3	36.4
Fat (g)	3.8	4.8	0.1	1.6	9.0	9.0	1.3
Carbohydrate (g)	4.7	4.7	5.0	4.8	11.3	55.5	52.8
Energy							
kcal	65	76	33	46.4	158	322	355
kJ	272	316	142	194	660	1362	1512
%Energy from							
fat	53	57	3	31	51	25	3
Calcium (mg)	120	120	130	125	280	280	1190

* and untreated, homogenized, UHT, sterilized.

2

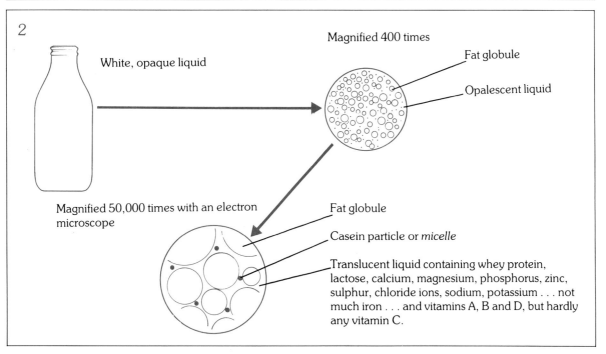

White, opaque liquid

Magnified 400 times

Fat globule

Opalescent liquid

Magnified 50,000 times with an electron microscope

Fat globule

Casein particle or *micelle*

Translucent liquid containing whey protein, lactose, calcium, magnesium, phosphorus, zinc, sulphur, chloride ions, sodium, potassium . . . not much iron . . . and vitamins A, B and D, but hardly any vitamin C.

3

Many people in the world cannot drink milk without getting stomach pains – they can't digest the sugar and are said to be *lactose intolerant*.

However, in northern Europe the majority of people are able to drink milk, and the vitamin D we get from milk helps us to remain healthy in the winter when we do not get much vitamin D from the sunlight.

For people who can tolerate milk, it is a very nutritious food . . . but it's also nutritious for **bacteria**.

$$\text{LACTOSE} \xrightarrow{\text{BACTERIA}} \text{LACTIC ACID}$$

The lactic acid makes casein curdle. Other bacteria then attack the sour milk. This makes the milk smell.

4

1860, PARIS

Louis Pasteur invents a way of stopping wine going off: it is heated gently, just enough to kill bacteria.

This was found to be ideal for milk, which is now **pasteurized** by heating to 72°C for 15 seconds.

5

Pasteurization kills many of the bacteria which cause souring, but does not spoil the taste and the 'cream line'.

Some people think that milk looks and tastes better if the cream is evenly spread throughout, so it is **homogenized**.

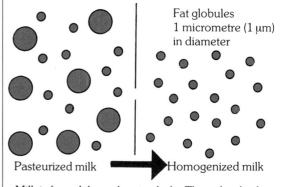

Fat globules 1 micrometre (1 μm) in diameter

Pasteurized milk   Homogenized milk

Milk is forced through a tiny hole. This splits the fat globules to make them all the same minute size. They no longer rise to the top of the milk.

Before trekking across the outback, Alligator Alistair needs milk for his cornflakes . . . but there are no fridges for miles. So he takes **sterilized milk** on his expedition. He can choose in-bottle sterilized milk (heated in the bottle at 112°C for 15 minutes) or UHT sterilized (heated at 132°C for one second, then packaged). Both will keep for months.

For your delectation . . .

. . . there is also **dried milk**, which is spray or roller dried. A bit of water is added so it will 'wet' when you put it in your coffee.

. . . and **evaporated milk**, which has had half the water removed and then been canned and sterilized so that some of the lactose caramelises.

. . . and **condensed milk**, which is only ¼ water but is *over 50% sugar* . . . try (if you dare) condensed milk on a slice of bread . . . in Liverpool these sandwiches are called *connie onnies*.

Workshop

1 Milk contains most nutrients but it is not a 'complete' food. What is missing from it?

2 a Milk is often thought of as a 'protein food'. How much milk would you have to drink to get your recommended daily amount of protein (see page 188) just from whole milk?

 b This wouldn't necessarily be a healthy thing to do – why not?

3 What is lactose intolerance?

4 What makes milk go sour? How is it prevented?

5 Why does homogenized milk not have cream on top?

6 Why does evaporated milk have such a distinctive colour and taste?

7 "Skim milk might be healthier, but it doesn't taste as good." This comment is often made when suggestions are made about improving diets. Try a triangle taste test (see page 11) to prove whether people really can tell the difference between skim and full-fat milk. Next, try a triangle test using banana milkshakes made from the two types of milk. (Whisk together 1 ripe banana, 1 tbsp ice-cream, 1 tsp honey and a glass of milk.) Finally, do a triangle test using the two types of milk in Quiche Lorraine. Work out the energy value and the percentage energy from fat for the different types of milkshake and quiche.

8 Write a magazine article explaining the advantages and disadvantages of pasteurized, sterilized, dried, evaporated and condensed milk for children, expectant mothers and the elderly.

Milk products

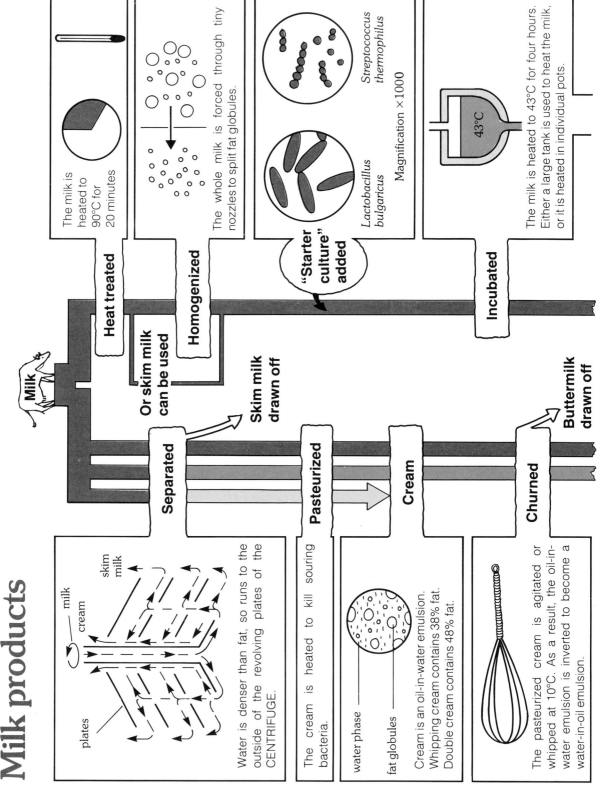

Heat treated

The milk is heated to 90°C for 20 minutes

Or skim milk can be used

Homogenized

The whole milk is forced through tiny nozzles to split fat globules.

"Starter culture" added

Streptococcus thermophilus

Lactobacillus bulgaricus

Magnification ×1000

Incubated

The milk is heated to 43°C for four hours. Either a large tank is used to heat the milk, or it is heated in individual pots.

43°C

Milk

Separated

Skim milk drawn off

milk
cream
skim milk
plates

Water is denser than fat, so runs to the outside of the revolving plates of the CENTRIFUGE.

Pasteurized

The cream is heated to kill souring bacteria.

Cream

water phase
fat globules

Cream is an oil-in-water emulsion. Whipping cream contains 38% fat. Double cream contains 48% fat.

Churned

Buttermilk drawn off

The pasteurized cream is agitated or whipped at 10°C. As a result, the oil-in-water emulsion is inverted to become a water-in-oil emulsion.

Fermentation takes place:

lactose → starter culture → lactic acid
(milk sugar) (pH 4.5)

The acidity makes the protein COAGULATE so that the yoghurt sets.

Cooled

This stops the bacteria working.

Fruit added

Put into pots

The bacteria are still in the yoghurt, so it must be kept cool.

Yoghurt

Yoghurt contains all the nutrients of milk (or skim milk) plus sugar.

MINIMUM 0.7% BUTTERFAT
Added ingredients:
Cherries, Sugar

150 g

AVERAGE CONTENTS
PER 150 g POT
Fat 1·5 g
Energy value 135 kcals
Protein 9 g
Carbohydrate 24 g

Butter

water droplets

fat phase

Butter is a water-in-oil emulsion made up of 85% fat and 15% water.

Salt added

This adds flavour, and helps to prevent bacteria, yeasts and moulds from growing. However, unsalted butter is becoming more popular.

Packaged

Butter is sold in foil, greaseproof paper, tubs and cans.

FARM BUTTER

BUTTER

Energy value per 100 g: 740 kcal, 3041 kJ. The butter on a typical slice of toast contains 60 kcal/250 kJ.

Melted

Centrifuged

Ghee

Ghee consists of butter fat only. It contains no water and no soluble proteins, so keeps much longer – especially in hot climates.

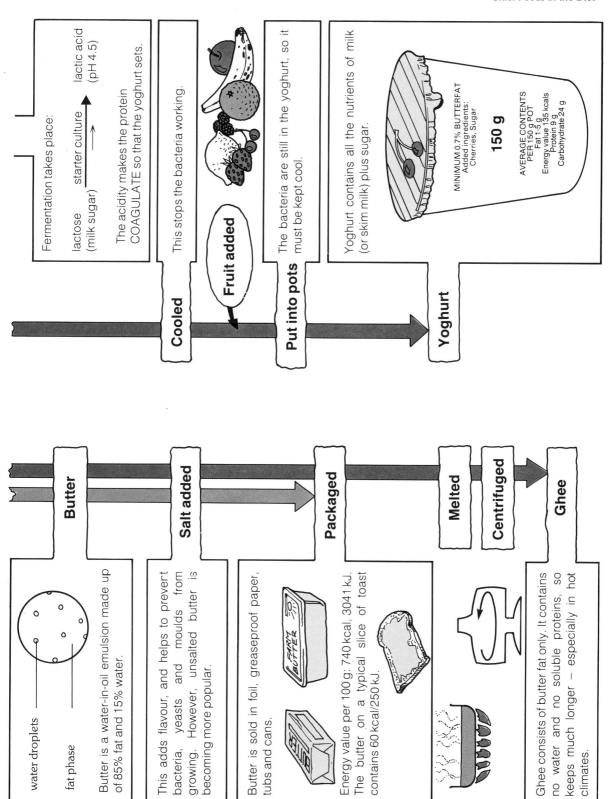

Workshop

1 Put a very small amount of butter on a slide, squash with a cover slip and look at it under the microscope at magnification × 100 and × 400. Repeat with cream. You should see the water droplets in butter and the fat globules in cream.

2 Whisk the contents of a small carton of cream until it forms peaks, then carry on whisking until you see small yellow specks of butter. What has happened to the emulsion?

3 Look in a delicatessen or health-food shop for a carton of buttermilk. It will probably be cultured buttermilk – bacteria have been added and it has been incubated so that it becomes more acidic and thickens slightly. Drink some and describe the taste, then use it to make some scones. This is the traditional way of making scones in Ireland.

4 Look for low-fat butter in the supermarket and compare nutritional values with ordinary butter. Carry out a triangle test (see page 11) to see if your friends can tell the difference when it is spread on thin white bread.

5 Try making some low-fat butter. You will need some lecithin capsules, available in health-food shops. Mix 200 g butter with 200 g water in a liquidizer. Add the contents of a lecithin capsule and liquidize for a few seconds more. Note what happens before and after adding the lecithin. Taste the spread and compare it with a low-fat butter and with ordinary butter.

6 Make some ghee by melting 100 g butter in a small saucepan and simmering gently over a very low heat for five minutes. Remove from the heat and skim off the foam. Allow the clear oil to cool slightly, then strain it through a metal sieve or a double layer of muslin into a container for storage. The ghee will keep for about four months. Fry an egg in ordinary butter and in the ghee. What difference do you notice?

7 Try an Enterprise Project:
Collect empty yoghurt pots. Sterilize them with baby-bottle sterilizing solution, then rinse *very* thoroughly with boiled water. Almost fill the pots with sterilized skim milk and add a teaspoon of dried milk and a teaspoon of sugar to each pot. Then put a teaspoon of commercial natural yoghurt in each pot and stir. Cover with circles of aluminium foil. Put all the pots on a tray in a warm place such as an airing cupboard or a drying cabinet at 30–35°C overnight. The yoghurt should be set by morning. If you like, you could stir in chopped orange, apple, raspberries or strawberries.

   If the yoghurt is good enough to sell, your Enterprise Group should:
a Work out the cost of the ingredients, the other materials, and the electricity, and decide how much to charge for the yoghurt.
b Design labels and stick them on to the pots.
   (You could work out the nutritional value per 100 g and per pot and put this on a label too.)
c Advertise the product.
d Sell the yoghurt and then work out the profit.

To make a hard cheese, such as Cheddar

a A starter culture of souring bacteria is added to pasteurized milk so that the lactose becomes lactic acid and the pH falls from 6.5 to 4.5.

b Rennet, an enzyme from the stomach of calves, is added. This makes the protein coagulate so that the mixture sets into a gel.

c The gel is cut into small pieces so that the whey drains off. The pieces left are the curds.

d The curds are 'scalded' at about 39°C for about 45 minutes, and are stirred so that more whey is released. The starter culture is not killed and the rennet carries on working. The curd is allowed to 'pitch' – it settles on the bottom of the tank it is in.

e The pieces of curd are piled on top of each other to squeeze out even more whey. This is called cheddaring.

f The curds are 'milled' – they are cut into small granules.

g Salt is mixed in to draw more whey out of the curd and to slow down the work of the starter bacteria.

h The curd is pressed into moulds and loses the last of the whey. It is left at a low temperature to mature. The texture and flavour change slowly because:
  - the starter culture carries on working
  - ripening organisms are put in some cheeses, e.g. blue cheese
  - some cheeses have ripening organisms on the outside, e.g. Brie

i The cheese is coated with a cloth, wax or plastic to stop physical damage and any more loss of moisture.

The food value of a hard cheese such as Cheddar

Cheese is ten times as concentrated as milk. It contains all the casein from milk, all the fat, most of the calcium and all the vitamin A – but none of the lactose, no vitamin C and very little iron. Because of the fat, hard cheeses such as Cheddar are high-fat foods, but they are also high in good quality protein.

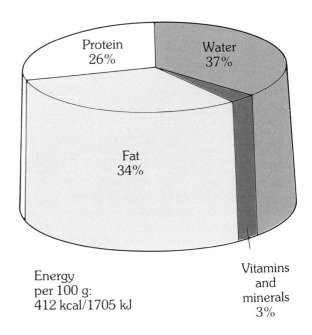

Protein 26%

Water 37%

Fat 34%

Energy per 100 g: 412 kcal/1705 kJ

Vitamins and minerals 3%

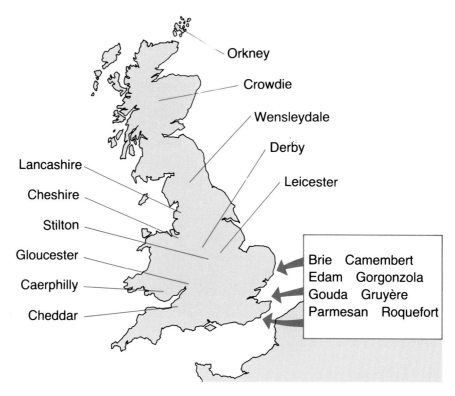

Orkney
Crowdie
Wensleydale
Derby
Leicester

Lancashire
Cheshire
Stilton
Gloucester
Caerphilly
Cheddar

Brie   Camembert
Edam   Gorgonzola
Gouda   Gruyère
Parmesan   Roquefort

Workshop

1 Soft cheeses such as cottage cheese, Brie,
Lymeswold and feta are made in a similar way
to hard cheese, but they are not matured or
pressed.
State three differences between soft and hard
cheese that result from the difference in
manufacture.

2 Try making a soft 'cheese'.
Bring $250 \, \text{cm}^3$ milk to boiling point, and then
add a large pinch of salt and 1 tsp lemon juice.
Simmer for 15 minutes, stirring occasionally.
Place a double layer of muslin or a scrupulously
clean tea-towel over a pudding basin and pour
the milk mixture through it. Allow to drain.
When almost all the liquid has passed through,
squeeze the cloth gently. Pack the 'cheese' in a
clean carton and refrigerate. Try as a sandwich
with cucumber and tomato, or peanut butter
and honey, or granary bread.

(a) What is the main difference between this
and the industrial method of making soft
cheese?

(b) What are the names of the 'cheese' that
stays in the muslin and the liquid that drains
away? (Remember Miss Muffet!)

3 Carry out a cheese tasting. Take six different
cheeses and choose a symbol for each one. For
example:

○ Cheddar   *   White Cheshire
□ Red Leicester   +   Edam
△ Danish Blue $ Brie

Cut the cheeses into 1·5 cm cubes, as far as
possible (some will crumble), put them on
separate plates and label the plates with the
appropriate symbol. Ask your tasters (you
should have at least four) to try each cheese and
to write down THREE words to describe it such
as * is PALE, CRUMBLY, MILD. They must
keep their words secret at this stage. When all
the cheeses have been tasted, make a list of the
words that have been used to describe each
cheese. How many were identical? Could you
have identified any of the cheeses just by the
description?

Fruits and vegetables

All food, however complicated, comes from plants because plants are the start of the food chain. Unlike animals, plants can make complicated molecules like amino acids, protein, sugars, starches and even fats from minerals, gases from the air, water and sunlight.

The building blocks

Plant foods are made up of CELLS: a cell wall and cell membrane enclose the cytoplasm.

Nucleus

Regulates the cell – it contains the genetic material DNA.

Cytoplasm

A watery solution containing everything needed for the plant to grow: sugars, enzymes, vitamins and minerals. It may also contain water-soluble pigments (e.g. the red/blue colouring of beetroot, red cabbage). If the cell is pierced by slicing, bruising or freezing, cytoplasm contents can mix and come into contact with air, or an enzyme can cause destruction of vitamin C, or browning can occur.

Plastids

Special structures within the cytoplasm. They contain water–insoluble substances such as chlorophyll, carotenoids and starch.

Cell wall

Made of rigid cellulose molecules embedded in pectins (like steel reinforcing rods in concrete). These are the source of dietary fibre in the diet. When plant foods are cooked, the pectins become soluble so they no longer support the 'reinforcing rods', and the cell loses its shape.

Cell membrane

Surrounds the contents of the cell. Lets nutrients pass in and waste materials pass out.

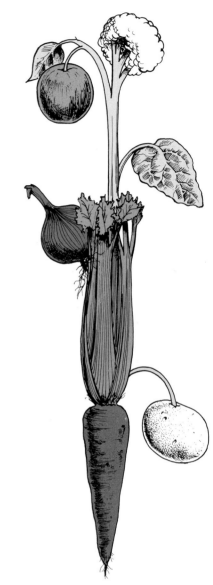

Have you ever seen a plant like this? It would be useful to cooks because all the parts of this plant can be eaten:

The ROOT holds the plant in the ground and takes in water and nutrients to be passed to the rest of the plant. Examples of roots we eat are carrot, radish and yam.

The STEM supports the plant and carries nutrients between the root and other parts of the plant. Celery and rhubarb are two stems we eat.

Some stems turn into storage organs or TUBERS, to hold nutrients for the plant. Potatoes and water chestnuts are tubers.

LEAVES make sugar from carbon dioxide and water by photosynthesis, as long as sunlight is available. The leaves are flat so that they can have the greatest surface area exposed to the light, and they are full of plastids containing chlorophyll. Examples of leaves we eat are cabbage, Brussels sprouts, lettuce, spinach. Strictly speaking, onions and garlic are leaf bases.

FLOWERS are the reproductive organs of the plant. No flowers are eaten alone – broccoli and cauliflower are mainly stem with small, unusual flowers.

The FRUIT is a tissue that surrounds the ovary and seed of a plant. The tissue is usually sweet, brightly coloured and pleasant-smelling, and is at its sweetest when the seeds are ready to be sown. Animals eat the inviting fruit, and this means that the seed will be dropped on the ground away from the parent plant, so that it has more of a chance of growing. Examples of fruits that we eat are apples, pears, cherries . . . and cucumbers, tomatoes, peppers.

Why eat fruits and vegetables?

Fruits and vegetables provide half the vitamin A in the diet, virtually all the vitamin C, and about a fifth of the B vitamins. It is best to eat them raw or lightly cooked to preserve the vitamins. Vitamin C and thiamin are destroyed if food is alkaline – but all fruits and vegetables are naturally acid. Fruits and vegetables are good sources of dietary fibre.

Most fruits and vegetables are mainly water – lettuce is 96% water – so they provide very little energy . . . as long as they are not covered in gravy, butter or custard!

Fruits and vegetables LOOK good because pigments give them bright colours: chlorophyll makes them green (e.g. cabbage, Brussels sprouts), carotenoids make them orange, red or yellow (e.g. carrots, tomatoes, sweet potato) and anthocyanins make them dark red (e.g. beetroot, aubergine).

They have a good TEXTURE because of the cell walls and water. If the cell walls are thick, the plant will have a crisp texture, like celery and Iceberg lettuce. The cells are full of water, blown up like a balloon (but kept in shape by the cell wall) so the plant is firm . . . unless it is stored in a dry place where it loses water and wilts.

They TASTE good because fruits increase in sugar content when they are ripe, and they usually contain acids to give a refreshing 'bite'. Vegetables have hundreds of different types of flavour molecules, giving each a distinctive taste. Some vegetables contain starch which gelatinises when it is cooked, making the food soft and able to absorb other flavours.

Workshop

1 How many fruits and vegetables do we eat? There are the common ones like carrots and peas, apples and pears. Then there are more unusual ones like aubergine and kiwi fruit. Visit your local greengrocers and supermarket, then make a class list of as many as possible – try to reach 100. Write beside each a dish that the fruit or vegetable can be used in. Choose one of the dishes that you have not tried before, follow the recipe for it and record your opinion.

2 "What is the best way to cook fruit and vegetables for the best taste, texture and colour?"

PLAN and INVESTIGATE this brief, taking care to use controls and to record your results (see on 'Your guide to investigation assignments' page 6). Some hints:
- Use only one vegetable or fruit, e.g. cabbage, Brussels sprouts or rhubarb.
- Compare no more than three methods of cooking, e.g. boiling, microwaving, pressure cooking, and decide on cooking times beforehand.
- EVALUATE the results by using a hedonic scale for the taste test. In other words, ask the tasters (there should be at least ten) to look at and taste a sample, then to grade for taste, texture and colour on this scale:
  5 like very much
  4 like slightly
  3 neither like nor dislike
  2 dislike slightly
  1 dislike very much

3 In the past, baking soda (sodium hydrogen carbonate) was added to green vegetables to keep them green. This is not now advised. Why?

4 "Which fruits and vegetables are best for vitamin C?"

You can investigate this with a practical test, and by looking up vitamin C content in the *Manual of Nutrition* (HMSO).

For the practical test, you will need a solution of blue dye (2,6-dichlorophenolindophenol – DCPIP), and a piece of filter paper for each fruit or vegetable to be tested. Dip the filter papers in the dye until they are soaked, then hang them up to dry. They are now ready to use, but if you need to keep them for more than a few days they must be stored in a polythene bag in the fridge.

Cut the fruits and vegetables and press the cut surface on the DCPIP paper. If vitamin C is present, the blue dye turns colourless. If the DCPIP goes pink it shows that acid is present – this will tend to preserve vitamin C, but does not mean that the vitamin is present.

Record your results, and also record the amount of vitamin C per 100 g from the *Manual of Nutrition*. List the foods in descending order of vitamin C content. How does this list compare with the experimental results?

5 When is a fruit a fruit? Many years ago in the USA, a court had to make a decision about this because fruits did not have to pay import duties but vegetables did. Imagine that the British government is proposing to introduce such a tax, and that you work for a fruit and vegetable importer so you want to pay as little tax as possible. Your partner works for the government which wants as much tax as possible. What definition of 'fruit' and 'vegetable' would you each use, and why? Can you arrive at an agreement?

Meat

Meat is probably the most expensive item in the family food budget. Is it worth the expense of buying it and the effort of cooking it? Sara and Joe are doing an assignment to find out more about meat. After a planning session, they are ready to begin.

"So what exactly *is* meat?"

"What we usually call meat is the muscle tissue of cattle, pigs and sheep."

"Isn't liver meat then?"

"Er . . . yes, but liver, heart and kidney are called OFFAL. They aren't the same kind of muscle."

"What's the muscle tissue made of?"

"Well, there's the red MUSCLE, made up of muscle fibres. Then there are two types of CONNECTIVE TISSUE, one type that looks like a veil, and gristle. Lastly, there's FAT. Fat can be round the muscle, like this lamb chop, or it can be inside the muscle, like this topside – then we call it MARBLING."

"How do the muscles turn into meat?"

"The animals are taken to an abattoir and killed humanely. The muscles contract – that's called rigor mortis. The weight of the carcase breaks the muscle fibres, so the muscle goes soft again in a few hours, but the carcase is hung for longer so that flavour develops."

"Why is meat red?"

"It contains a red pigment that's a protein called MYOGLOBIN – it stores oxygen in the tissues. It's similar to the haemoglobin in blood, *except* that haemoglobin carries oxygen *to* the muscle."

The next person Sara and Joe have arranged to see is a dietitian . . .

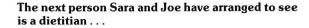

"We know that meat is made of muscle, connective tissue and fat, but is it good for us?"

"It depends on the kind of meat, but on average, meat is made up of about two-thirds water, one-sixth protein and one-sixth fat. The protein is very good quality – the amino acids are in just the right proportions."

"What about vitamins and minerals?"

"Yes, they are in meat of course, especially B vitamins, but meat isn't the best source of vitamins. It's very important for one particular mineral though – IRON. That's in the myoglobin molecule."

"Does cooking have any effect on nutritional value?"

"Not really, though some minerals and vitamins might be lost in the juices if they aren't used in a sauce or gravy."

"I love pork crackling. What about the nutritional value of that?"

"I'm afraid it's mostly saturated fat. You should remove fat when possible, for example you can cut off the fat round chops. The 'marbling' fat in joints is harder to avoid."

A chef is able to provide a bit more information . . .

"What's the best way to cook meat?"

"It all depends on the cut. Fat in meat just melts when it's cooked, and even though it might not be so good for you it does help to make the meat moist and tender. But the other two components of meat behave in different ways."

"You mean the muscle and the connective tissue?"

"Yes. Inside the muscle fibres are molecules that give meat flavour. These are dissolved in water. The water makes it nice and juicy too. But when meat is cooked the fibres shrink and the juices are squeezed out, so the meat goes hard and dry. If the joint is then fibrous and chewy, all you can do is make the fibres shorter by slicing them across the grain."

"What about the connective tissue? Aren't there two types – the sort-of veil-type and the gristle type?"

"Yes – the veil-type is mostly COLLAGEN and this is all round the muscle fibres too, though you can't see it. It acts as a kind of cement. When collagen is cooked it becomes soluble – then it's called GELATIN, and it makes meat more moist. The other type of connective tissue is ELASTIN. This is greatest in muscle that has had to work hard, or in older animals. And no matter how much you cook it, it won't go tender."

"What can you do then? Just throw it away?"

"Not necessarily. You can cut the meat up small, or mince it so that you don't notice the elastin when you're chewing it."

89

"How can you tell when meat is cooked?"

"Well, steak tartare is on the menu tonight and it won't be cooked at all, but it'll be delicious . . . and people who ask for rare steaks will get steak that's so red in the centre that some people think it's *not* cooked. But it will be tender and juicy. Usually, though, meat is 'cooked' when it's brown in the middle. This means the myoglobin has been denatured by the heat, so the centre of the meat has reached 72°C. Another way of testing whether meat is done is to pierce it with a fork to make sure no more juices come out."

"Why doesn't bacon go brown?"

"It's cured with nitrites, and they react with the myoglobin so that it goes pink."

At this stage Sara and Joe go back to their Home Economics class to tackle the next stage in their assignment: Joe is going to develop some recipes, and Sara has some scientific investigations to do . . .

"These muscle fibres look about the same size as a hair."

"What are you making, Joe?"

"I'm adapting four recipes so that they can be put in a booklet called *Meat on a budget*. They're meals for one person, and the recipes will include the cost and the energy value."

"I'm investigating the effects of cooking on meat. I've cut a piece of braising steak into quarters and I'm frying one quarter, grilling one, microwaving one and simmering one. Then I'll ask people to try them and to give a score out of 4 for tenderness and taste."

Workshop

1 Carry out the tasks that Sara and Joe started when they were back in the Home Economics room.

2 Sara and Joe could have seen other people during their investigation; for example someone from The Vegetarian Society, and a farmer.

What questions would you ask them? Have a class discussion based on the questions.

3 Imagine you are Sara and Joe. Using the information from the interviews, and the results of the practical tasks in (1), write a report of the meat assignment under the headings: Analysis, Investigation, Implementation and Evaluation.

Pulses and nuts

Pulses are a type of edible seed – usually peas, beans and lentils. Another name for them is 'legumes'. They are good sources of protein, and have plenty of fibre. Look at the table below. Now compare the nutritional value of boiled beans with the nutritional value of stewed minced beef. 100 g of stewed minced beef contain 23 g protein, 15 g fat, no carbohydrate and no fibre. There are 220 kcal (955 kJ) in 100 g.

What about the quality of the protein?

The protein quality is not quite as good as the protein quality of milk, eggs and meat, but can be improved by complementing the pulses with small amounts of other foods (see page 71).

Nutritional value per 100 g of boiled beans

	Energy kcal	kJ	Protein g	Fat g	Carbohydrate g	Fibre g
Butter bean	95	405	7.1	0.3	17.1	5.1
Haricot bean	93	396	6.6	0.5	16.6	7.4
Kidney bean	94	393	7.6	0.6	15.6	8.6
Lentils	99	420	7.6	0.5	17.0	1.2

The most common pulses available

Butter beans	Large, white, with soft texture and a bland creamy flavour.
Chick peas	Pale brown, round, nutty in both texture and flavour.
Haricot beans	White, smaller and plumper than butter beans but also with a bland flavour.
Red kidney beans	An attractive, dark red colour and a satisfying, strong taste and firm texture. These beans contain a naturally-occurring toxin so they *must* be boiled for ten minutes at the start of cooking.
Black-eye beans	Small, oval-shaped with a black 'eye' on one side.
Soya beans	These are best known for their products, such as soy sauce and tofu.
Lentils	Very small, usually orange. They cook very easily to become a tasty purée.

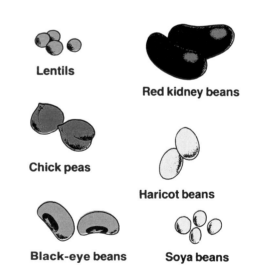

Lentils

Red kidney beans

Chick peas

Haricot beans

Black-eye beans   Soya beans

If you look in a supermarket or health-food shop, you will find many more varieties of pulses – experiment with aduki, borlotti, cannelini and pinto beans.

Cooking the beans

Apart from lentils, all dried beans need soaking and long cooking in plenty of boiling water, though cooking can be speeded up in a pressure cooker.

Cooking times for beans in minutes

	Soaking	Cooking	Pressure cooking (15 lb pressure)
Butter beans	Overnight	50	17
Chick peas	Overnight	50	20
Haricot beans	Overnight	60	18
Kidney beans	Overnight	50*	17
Black-eye beans	Overnight	30	12
Soya beans	Overnight	90	25
Lentils	None	20	–

* Kidney beans should be fast boiled first for 10 minutes.

Here are some ways beans can be used in cooking:

- Make stews with beans instead of meat, or use beans to replace some of the meat.

- Make your own baked beans with 250 g *cooked* (from 100 g dried) haricot beans. Put these beans in a saucepan with 1 finely chopped onion, 2 tsps mustard pickle, a small can of tomatoes, a vegetable stock cube and 1 tsp black treacle. Bring to the boil and simmer for 30 minutes. Serves two, but you decide whether to serve on toast!

- Cook butter beans (save the liquid), and make a dip by puréeing in a blender with lemon juice, salt, pepper, a small amount of vegetable oil and enough cooking liquid to give a creamy consistency. Add a crushed garlic clove if you like the taste.

Nuts

Nuts are also edible seeds, with a hard shell. Unlike pulses, nuts are usually eaten fresh. They are also high in protein and fibre; most of them are oily too.

Nutritional value per 100 g of selected nuts

	Energy kcal kJ	Protein g	Fat g	Carbohydrate g	Fibre g
Almond	565 2336	16.9	53.5	4.3	14.3
Brazil nut	619 2545	12.0	61.5	4.1	9.0
Chestnut	170 720	2.0	2.7	36.6	6.8
Peanut	570 2364	24.3	49.0	8.6	8.1

Nuts are eaten with drinks and at Christmas, but how can they be more important in the diet? They can be made into interesting dishes, for example:

Almonds   Sprinkle flaked almonds on to vegetables just before serving. For extra taste, toast the almonds first.

Cashew nuts   Make a flan base by mixing together 100 g fresh wholemeal breadcrumbs, 100 g crushed cornflakes, 75 g chopped cashew nuts, 100 g grated cheese, 2 eggs, a large pinch dried mixed herbs, salt and pepper. Grease a 20 cm diameter flan tin and press the mixture on to the base and up the sides. Bake 'blind' in an oven at 200°C (400°F) for 25 minutes, then use as for a baked shortcrust pastry flan base.

Peanuts   (strictly speaking, not a nut at all but a legume). Toast 50 g peanuts under the grill, turning frequently, until brown (but not burnt). Cool and chop coarsely. Mix with similar amounts of vegetables such as chopped cucumber, celery, onion, pepper. Just before serving the salad, mix with a vinaigrette dressing made with 60 ml oil and 30 ml lemon juice, plus a pinch each of dried herbs, salt, pepper and brown sugar.

Workshop

1 Explain why the energy value of nuts is much higher than that of pulses.

2 After Christmas you have about 500 g of mixed nuts left. Suggest some quick-to-cook recipes in which these could be used. Try the dishes in class.

3 When supermarkets start selling an unusual food they often promote it by producing a free informative leaflet. You have been asked by your local supermarket to write one of these leaflets to promote pulses, especially the less familiar ones. The manager would like sections on where the pulses are grown, cost, storage, cooking, nutritional values, and some recipes. The leaflet must be illustrated. Organize your class to produce the leaflet. You will need to do some research, as well as recipe development (see page 33). If you have desk-top publishing in your school the leaflet could look very professional – your local supermarket might be very interested in the finished product, and so might the health promotion unit.

Don't be waste fuel!

Energy is measured in many different units. What unit of measurement is used to measure energy in food?

Joules can be used as a unit of measurement for any form of energy (e.g. heat produced by burning gas or using electricity).

Look at the gas and electricity bills opposite. What units are used on these bills? Electricity is sold by the unit. One unit of electricity equals 1 kilowatt hour (1 kWh), that is the amount of electricity used to run a 1000-watt appliance, such as a one-bar electric fire, for an hour. (For more information about how to calculate the amount of power used by appliances, see page 105.) The gas bill shows how many therms have been used. One therm equals 100,000 British Thermal Units (BTU).

Because energy is expensive, it is important to think of ways in which it can be saved. Below are some ways to save energy in the home in general, and when cooking in particular. Can you think of any more?

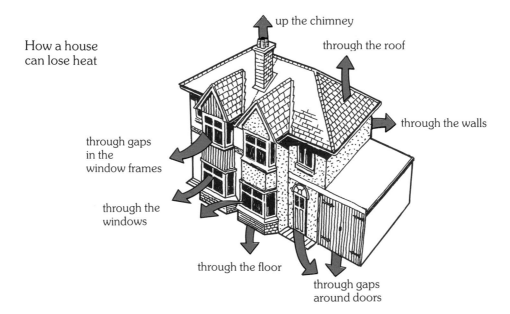

How a house can lose heat

up the chimney

through the roof

through the walls

through gaps in the window frames

through the windows

through the floor

through gaps around doors

A Heating and lighting

- Choose the most comfortable temperature for each room, e.g. living room 19°–21°C, bedroom 14°–15°C.
- If you have central heating, decide what the most appropriate type of fuel is. It could be electricity, gas, oil or solid fuel.
- Regulate the water temperature and the times at which heating is switched on and off. Use room thermostats or radiator thermostats.
- Insulate the house to prevent heat loss.
- Position lights for maximum efficiency.
- Fluorescent lights of the same wattage use less energy than tungsten bulbs.

A gas bill

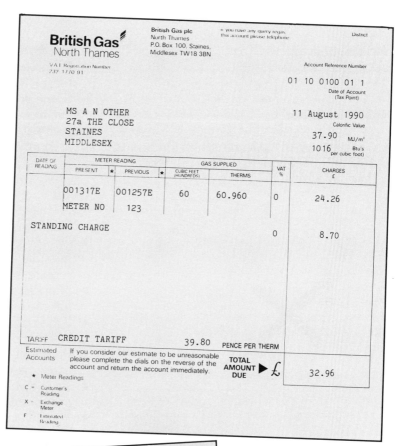

An electricity bill

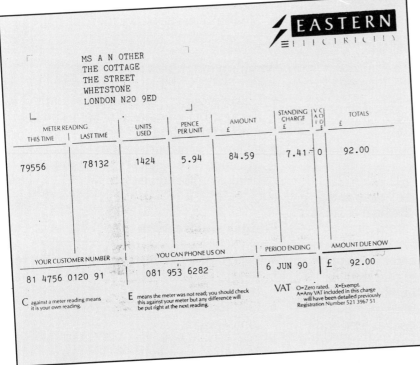

B Using appliances

Use economically and do not leave running longer than necessary.

Hob or hotplate

- Use a saucepan the same size as the heated area or burner and do not use more heat than necessary.

- Use the minimum amount of water in the saucepan and turn down the heat as soon as the water boils.
- Cover the saucepan.
- Two or more vegetables can be cooked in the same saucepan – wrap one in foil to keep separate, or one vegetable could be boiled and the other steamed on top of it.
- Use a pressure cooker – it saves time and therefore fuel.

Grill

- Use from cold, except for making toast.
- If possible use a toaster, not the grill for toast – it is more economical.
- Some grills on electric cookers have a dual circuit so that either the whole or part of the grill may be used, depending on the amount of food to be cooked.

Oven

- Use the timer if there is one on the cooker.
- Do not preheat the oven whenever possible; there are very few dishes which require a preheated oven.
- Manage the oven economically, making full use of the heat zones.
- If the cooker has a small oven use it if the amount of food to be cooked is small.
- Frequent opening of the oven door will cause heat to be lost.
- Take care not to overcook foods – food and energy may be wasted.
- Microwave cookers use much less fuel than the oven of a gas or electric cooker (see page 106).
- Slow cookers also save fuel (see page 110).

Washing machines and driers

- Select programmes carefully according to the type of detergent and fabric and the amount of soiling.
- When possible, dry washing outside or overnight in a suitable room rather than using a tumble dryer.

Fridges and freezers

- Do not position the refrigerator or freezer next to the cooker or the central heating boiler.
- Use the thermostat to control the temperature.
- Defrost regularly.

Workshop

1 Plan a meal that could be cooked using the hob only. Cook the meal in a practical session, taking careful note of how long you use each ring or burner and the grill. Copy out and fill in the tables below.

2 Plan a meal that could be cooked using the oven only. Cook the meal in a practical session, taking careful note of how long the oven was used. Draw up a table similar to that in question 1. Calculate the cost of cooking the meal using either gas or electricity. The loading of an electric cooker is 2·5 kW. A gas oven uses 9900 BTU/hour. Assume full power was used.

3 Investigate the length of time bread takes to toast when you vary the distance the bread is placed from a preheated grill. Display your results on a graph. (Remember that the same grill setting should be used, the bread should be of the same thickness and toasted to the same degree of brownness each time.)

4 Suggest two ways in which energy could be saved when
a using the grill
b using the hob or hotplate
c using the oven.

5 How could you prevent heat loss from a house?

Electricity

Part of cooker	Loading (kW)	Time used (mins)	Fuel used (kW)	Cost of electricity (p per unit)	Cost of electricity used (p)
Small ring	1.1			6.2	
Small ring	1.1			6.2	
Large ring	1.8			6.2	
Large ring	1.8			6.2	
Grill	2.5			6.2	
					Total

Assume that full power was used.

Gas

Part of cooker	Loading (BTU/h)	Time used (mins)	Fuel used (BTU)	Cost of gas (p per therm)	Cost of gas used (p)
Medium burner	6500			38.5	
Medium burner	6500			38.5	
Large burner	11000			38.5	
Large burner	11000			38.5	
Grill	11500			38.5	
					Total

Assume that full power was used. 100,000 BTU = 1 therm.

How heat travels

Heat is a form of energy. Gas, electricity, oil and solid fuel are the main sources of energy for heating the home and for cooking in this country.

Heat is applied to food in order for the physical and chemical changes in cooking to occur. These changes make food more appetising, palatable and digestible.

Sometimes only one method of heat transfer is involved in the cooking, but usually more than one is used, depending on the method of cooking.

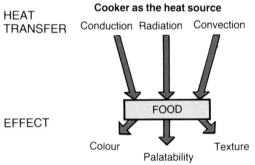

Cooker as the heat source

HEAT TRANSFER — Conduction Radiation Convection

FOOD

EFFECT — Colour Palatability Texture

Conduction

This type of heat transfer occurs in frying, boiling, roasting, baking and microwave cooking. The molecules nearest to the heat absorb energy and vibrate. The vibrations pass from molecule to molecule. In solid substances and good conductors such as metals the molecules are closely packed and allow the heat to pass through quickly. In liquids and poor conductors or *insulators* such as wood, glass and plastic the molecules are further apart and the heat does not pass through so easily. It is for this reason that a metal pan will get hot while the handle remains cool.

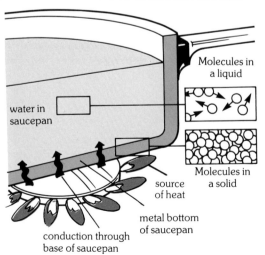

water in saucepan

Molecules in a liquid

Molecules in a solid

source of heat

metal bottom of saucepan

conduction through base of saucepan

Convection

Heat is transferred by convection in boiling, frying, oven roasting and baking. When gases and liquids are heated the molecules expand, become less dense and therefore lighter, and consequently rise. Cooler, denser molecules further from the heat fall to take their place and so currents are set up and the heat is circulated.

warm water rising

cold water sinking

Convection currents in a saucepan

In a conventional oven, convection currents circulate so the top of the oven is the hottest part and the bottom the coolest. In a fan-assisted oven a circular element and a small fan at the back of the oven circulate the hot air very quickly. Consequently, all parts of the oven are the same temperature.

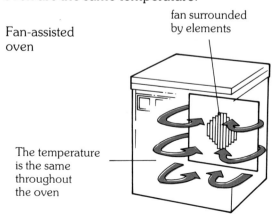

Fan-assisted oven

fan surrounded by elements

The temperature is the same throughout the oven

Radiation

This occurs in grilling and microwave cooking. The heat is transferred in waves which travel in straight lines from the source. The energy is reflected by smooth, shiny surfaces such as metals. Other substances, such as glass, allow the waves to pass through them. Matt substances, such as food, absorb the waves and get hot.

radiant waves

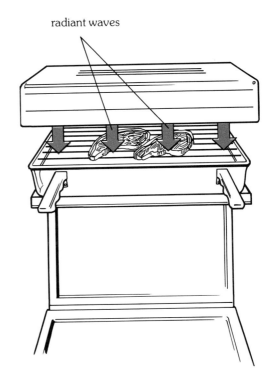

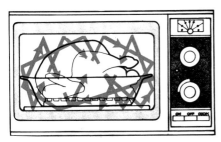

Microwave energy being absorbed by food

Workshop

1 Investigate how well the different materials used for the manufacture of cooking basins conduct heat. Make an "all in one" pudding mixture, place a third of it into a plastic basin, a third into a foil basin and a third into a china basin. Cover all three basins with foil, place in a steamer and compare cooking times. Check to see if the pudding is cooked by putting a skewer into the centre. If the skewer comes out clean, the pudding is ready. Display your results on a bar chart.

   In future, which type of basin would you choose for cooking your pudding if you wanted it to cook as quickly as possible?

2 Investigate whether the cooking of jacket potatoes is speeded up if greater use is made of good conductors of heat (e.g. skewers, foil, potato bakers). Try to choose even-sized potatoes.

3 Explain why a thermos flask will keep hot liquids hot and cold liquids cold.

Cooking methods (1)

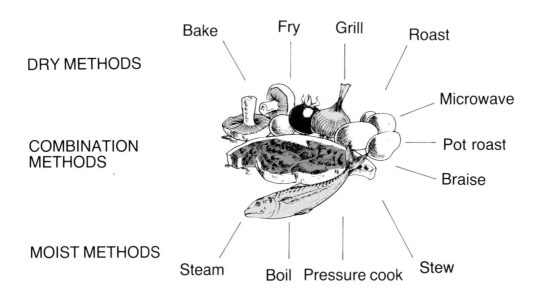

DRY METHODS — Bake, Fry, Grill, Roast, Microwave

COMBINATION METHODS — Pot roast, Braise

MOIST METHODS — Steam, Boil, Pressure cook, Stew

Why cook food?

- To make it more digestible and in some cases less bulky.
- To make it attractive so that people want to eat it.
- To make it safer to eat – the heat kills many of the micro-organisms present.
- To improve the flavour.
- To change the texture.
- To improve the colour (e.g. a pale cream cake mixture becomes a golden brown cake).

How food cooks

The dry methods of cooking, the moist methods and the combination methods are all ways of transferring heat to food during cooking. In some cases (such as grilling) the heat is transferred directly. In other cases the heat is carried by another material or medium such as air, water or fat, which is heated and in turn heats the food.

In dry methods of cooking the heat is either transferred directly, or the medium of air is used, or the medium of fat. In moist methods of cooking water is the cooking medium and the heat turns the water to steam. Some methods of cooking combine both dry and moist heat, e.g. braising.

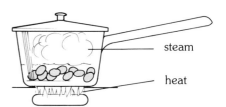

steam

heat

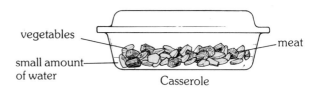

vegetables

small amount of water

meat

Casserole

Dry methods

Usually dry methods use a large amount of energy for a short time. You should use tender food because of the high temperature.

Dry methods of cooking

Method	Suitable for	How heat is transferred	Further information
Baking/oven roasting	Meat, fish, poultry, vegetables, cakes, pastry	Air in the oven is heated, setting up convection currents which heat the surface of the food. Heat is then conducted to the centre.	Produces a crisp, brown surface. To keep food moist, use oven bags or foil. (Remove foil before the end of cooking for a crisp outside.)
Roasting on a barbeque or rotisserie	Good quality meat, poultry, fish, potatoes	Radiant heat produced from a glowing fire heats the surface of food. Heat is conducted to the centre.	Fat drips away during cooking. A rotisserie can be used for roasting in front of a grill.
Grilling	Small, tender pieces of meat, fish, poultry, some vegetables, bread	Radiant heat cooks the surface of the food, and heat is conducted to the centre.	Fat drips away. With infra-red or contact grills the food is in direct contact with the grill (see p. 108)
Microwaving	Foods of even texture and thickness with high moisture content	The energy of radiated microwaves is absorbed by the food and causes the water molecules to vibrate and produce heat, which is conducted to the centre of thick products. Microwaves have longer wave lengths than heat from radiant grills.	Microwaves only penetrate up to 5 cm deep (see p. 106).
Frying	Small, tender pieces of meat, fish, eggs, some vegetables	Convection currents in hot fat heat the surface of the food. Heat is conducted to the centre.	*Dry frying* will remove some fat from foods like sausages and bacon. *Shallow and deep-fat frying* add fat to food. *Stir-frying* is a very quick method of cooking food cut into small pieces. Very hot fat is used in a wok or frying pan.

Workshop

1 Why should foods be tender if dry methods of cooking are used?

2 State three reasons why food is cooked.

3 Explain the differences between the following methods of frying, and suggest a suitable food for each method.
   a Stir-frying
   b Shallow-fat frying
   c Deep-fat frying
   d Dry frying

4 Investigate the following methods of cooking a chicken joint: microwaving, grilling, baking in an oven.
   - Try to use even-sized chicken joints.
   - Time each method of cooking carefully.
   - The chicken is cooked if the juices run clear after a sharp knife has been placed into the thickest part of the joint.

Evaluate your results for length of cooking time, colour, flavour and tenderness. Present these results as a chart. What conclusions can you draw from your investigations?

Cooking methods (2)

Combination methods

Method	Suitable for	How heat is transferred	Further information
Pot-roasting	Small joints of meat such as topside or middle neck (the less tender cuts)	Conduction through the container, convection currents in the liquid, conduction from the outside of food to the centre.	The meat is browned and then cooked in the oven, in a container with tightly fitting lid. The meat cooks in its own juices and added vegetables provide additional moisture.
Braising	Topside, middle neck, some vegetables, e.g. onions, celery	As for pot-roasting.	The meat is browned, then placed on a bed of vegetables and stock or water. The container is covered. The hob or the oven may be used.

Moist methods

Moist methods of cooking use lower temperatures and take longer. The moisture present helps to tenderise tougher foods.

Moist methods

Method	Suitable for	How heat is transferred	Further information
Boiling	Vegetables, eggs, pasta, rice, larger and tougher cuts of meat	Conduction through the base of the saucepan, convection currents through the medium of water, conduction to the centre of the food.	Water boils at 100°C. Large bubbles rise to the surface, the water moves vigorously. Water simmers at about 90°C. Small bubbles rise to the surface and the movement is less vigorous.
Steaming	Sponge puddings, some vegetables, small pieces of fish	Conduction through base of saucepan converts water into steam which rises. Convection currents heat the outside of food. Heat conducted to the centre.	

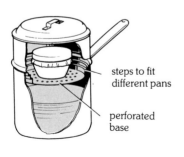

steps to fit different pans

perforated base

A steamer

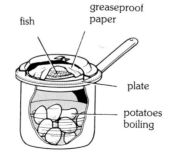

greaseproof paper

fish

plate

potatoes boiling

Steaming fish on a plate

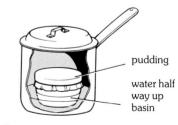

pudding

water half way up basin

Steaming in a saucepan

Method	Suitable for	How heat is transferred	Further information
Stewing	Tougher cuts of meat, fresh and dried fruit	As for boiling.	Small amount of liquid used. Food is simmered either in a saucepan on the hob or a casserole in the oven. The liquid is part of the dish.
Pressure cooking	Wide variety of foods including soups, stews, vegetables, puddings	As for steaming, but because the steam is under pressure it reaches higher temperatures (up to 121°C).	Cooking time cut considerably – a stew cooks in about 2 hours in a saucepan, but 20 minutes in a pressure cooker.
Slow cooker	Tougher cuts of meat, soups, offal, steamed puddings	As for boiling.	Food is brought to boiling point in an ordinary saucepan and then transferred to the slow cooker. A low heat cooks food for 8–12 hours. Saves energy.

Workshop

1 List the methods of cooking which are:
   a energy saving
   b time saving
   c energy and time saving.
2 Complete the following table.

Food	Suitable methods of cooking	Reason
Potatoes		
Tough piece of steak		
Chicken joint		
Rice		
Green vegetables		
Fillet of fish		

3 Explain the difference between simmering and boiling.
4 Cook an "all in one" sponge-pudding mixture by the following methods: (a) pressure cooking; (b) steaming; (c) microwaving.
Make one sponge-pudding mixture and divide into three *equal* portions and place in three *equal-sized* basins made of the *same* material. (Remember that you should not use a metal basin in a microwave cooker.) Cover each basin with a piece of cling film. Check recommended cooking times in a recipe book and the manufacturer's handbook. Time the cooking of the three puddings accurately. Evaluate your results for length of cooking time, colour, flavour and texture. Prepare a chart showing the results. Which method of cooking did you find the most successful?
5 Assuming that a slow cooker, a microwave oven, a pressure cooker and a gas cooker are available, which method(s) of cooking would you recommend to the following people, and why?
   a A working mother who has bought some tough steak, a mixture of root vegetables and potatoes.
   b A student living in a bedsitter who has bought a frozen pizza.
   c A young man who has invited his girlfriend for an evening meal and has bought pork chops and a selection of vegetables including mushrooms and tomatoes.

Testing, testing

There is a wide variety of cooking appliances on the market. If you want to buy a cooking appliance you must ask yourself some questions to make sure you make the right choice. The most important of these is:

Do I Need it?

Your answer will depend on the:
- size of your household
- amount of money available
- type of meals to be prepared
- size of your kitchen

If you decide you do need the appliance, you must think about these points:

Performance

Using and cleaning

Flexibility

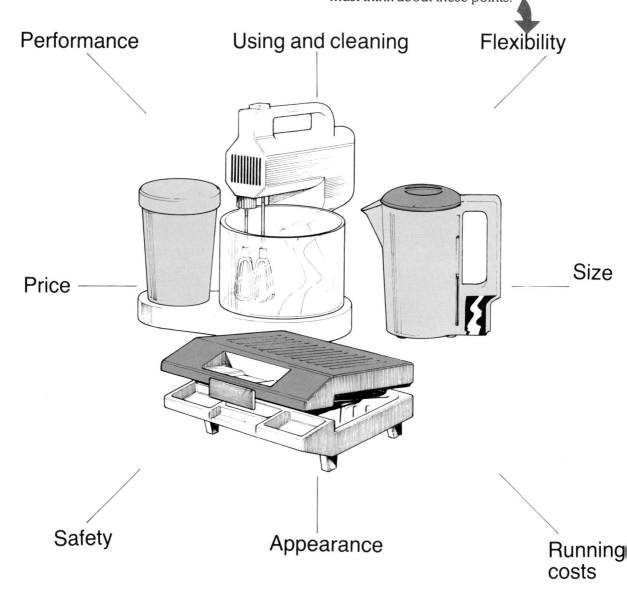

Price

Size

Safety

Appearance

Running costs

Performance   Will it carry out the job for which it was designed efficiently? A demonstration or reports in magazines such as *Which?* or *Good Housekeeping* will help you answer this question.

Flexibility   Will it perform one task only, or can it do several jobs? Accessories may be useful, but check whether you have to pay extra for these.

Using and cleaning   Is it easy to assemble and easy to clean, or are there nooks and crannies in which food will lodge? Are the dials and switches in a convenient place and easy to use? If hand held, is it comfortable?

Price   Check the prices in several stores before buying and find out if each store will carry out repairs.

Running costs   As most appliances are electrical, the manufacturer's rating plate on the base or rear will give a power rating in watts. This states how much electricity is used if the appliance is used continuously for one hour.

Safety   Has the appliance got BEAB approval or a BSI kite mark? Both indicate the appliance has reached a safety standard (see page 161). Is the appliance stable when in use? Is it built of strong material, with no sharp edges that could cut fingers?

Appearance   Does it look attractive? Does it match the colour scheme in the kitchen?

Size   Will it fit in the kitchen, and can it be easily stored? Is it light enough to lift if it cannot be kept permanently on a kitchen bench? Is the height, when in position, comfortable for the task to be carried out?

How to calculate running costs

This rating plate from a hand mixer shows the rating to be 150 watts (W), so if it was used continuously for one hour, 150 W or 0·15 kW of electricity would be used. Electricity costs 6·17p per unit and one unit of electricity is the amount used to run a 1000-watt appliance for one hour, so 1 unit = 1 kilowatt hour (1 kWh). Therefore, using the mixer for one hour would cost $6·17 \times 0·15 = 0·93$p, almost 1p. But it is more likely that the mixer would only be used for about ten minutes continuously, in which case the cost would be

$$\frac{6·17 \times 0·15 \times 10}{60} = 0·15\text{p}$$

By carrying out similar calculations you can compare the running costs of different appliances. Remember, the higher the rating and the longer you use an appliance, the greater the cost will be.

Workshop

1 Give, in order of priority, the points you would consider when deciding whether you needed to buy a microwave cooker.

2 You decided to buy a microwave cooker. List six points which would help you to decide whether to buy microwave A or microwave B. Explain why you think these points are important.

3 Select one cooking appliance, either in school or at home, and investigate whether it was a good buy. Write a report on it using the headings around the drawing on page 104.

4 The loadings on the rating plates of some cooking appliances are:
Toaster   850 watts
Food Processor   500 watts
Coffee Maker   700 watts
Kettle   2400 watts
Blender   350 watts
Deep-fat Fryer   1000 watts
Calculate the running cost if each appliance is used continuously for 20 minutes.

Save it! (1)

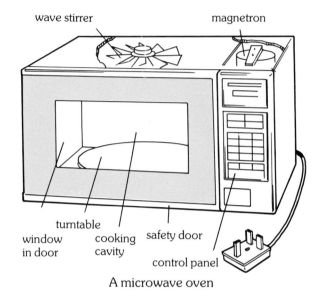

A microwave oven

A microwave oven

Energy can be saved by using equipment such as microwave ovens, pressure cookers, infra-red grills and slow cookers. Microwave ovens, pressure cookers and infra-red grills save fuel by cooking food more quickly. Slow cookers save fuel because the amount of electricity used is very small, although cooking takes a long time.

Microwave ovens

How they work
Electricity is changed into energy with a short wave length but a high frequency by the magnetron at the top of the cooker. These *microwaves* are spread evenly by the wave stirrer. The energy is absorbed by the water molecules in the food, causing them to vibrate rapidly and so produce heat, which cooks the food. Microwaves penetrate the food up to a depth of 5 cm, whereas in a conventional oven only the outside of the food is heated and the heat is then conducted to the centre.

Materials such as glass, china, paper and plastic used for making cooking containers allow microwaves to be *transmitted* – the microwaves pass through them.

Types of microwave ovens

The majority of microwave cookers are table-top models, but they can be built into kitchen units.

Basic or Compact microwave ovens generally have a small cooking cavity, an on/off switch, a defrost control, and they may have a turntable. The output is 400–500 W.

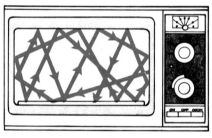

Microwave energy being reflected off cooking-cavity walls

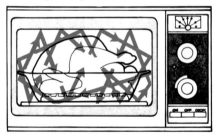

Microwave energy being absorbed by food

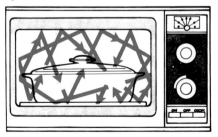

Microwave energy passing through cooking container

Standard microwave ovens have a larger cooking cavity, a higher output (650–700 W) and usually a variety of power levels and a defrost facility. A temperature probe to measure the internal temperature of foods such as meat may be fitted.

Sophisticated microwave ovens have all the features of the standard cooker as well as automatic timers, touch controls, longer timing and memory facilities. Some also have a grill so that two-level cooking is available. The food can be browned at the beginning or end of the cooking time.

Controls

Timing   The microwave oven either has dials or more often digital touch buttons, which give greater accuracy.

A **temperature probe** is useful when cooking large joints of meat.

Variable power controls regulate the energy output so that power levels suitable for different foods can be selected. A variety of different markings may be used on either a dial or digital touch buttons. The level of energy can be marked in words, numerals, watts or percentage of total wattage (see diagram on the right).

Sensor cooking is available on some cookers. It switches the cooker off when the moisture given off in the cooker reaches a certain point.

A **turntable** enables foods to be automatically turned, ensuring more even cooking.

Cooking containers

Glass, china, paper and plastic are all suitable materials.
As metal reflects microwaves, metal containers should not be used. They may also damage the magnetron – check in the handbook about the use of foil. Thin plastic may become misshapen, especially if the recipe contains high amounts of sugar or fat. To get the best results, use a round container.

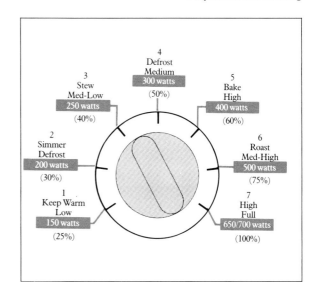

A variable power control panel

Advantages and disadvantages

- Food is cooked quickly, saving time and energy, but it is easy to overcook foods because of the short cooking time.
- A variety of foods can be cooked but not all foods give good results, for example Yorkshire puddings do not cook well.
- It is a clean method of cooking.
- Food keeps its colour, flavour and nutritive value, but foods do not brown nor will they have a crisp coating on the outside.
- Only food which is even in shape and texture will give the best results.
- It is very useful for thawing and cooking frozen foods.

Care and maintenance

Special cooking film is available to cover foods to prevent splashing, but if splashes do occur they are easily removed from the inside using a damp cloth. The outside also just needs wiping with a damp cloth. The microwave oven should be checked by a safety expert every three to five years to ensure that the microwaves are not leaking.

Infra-red grills

These are sometimes called contact grills. They are portable.

How they work
Two heavy aluminium plates, which are usually coated with Teflon or some other non-stick material, are heated by electricity. The plates are in contact with the food, which is heated by conduction and infra-red heat. The top plate is hinged so that foods of different thicknesses can be cooked, or a baking tin may be fitted in. Other plates may be fitted in some grills, for example a waffle-making plate. The output of infra-red grills is 1–2 kW.

A contact grill

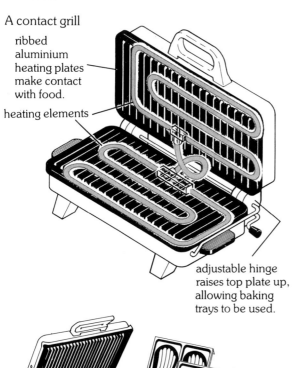

ribbed aluminium heating plates make contact with food.

heating elements

adjustable hinge raises top plate up, allowing baking trays to be used.

'Lift and lock' adjustable hinge in operation.

Detachable plates are available for making waffles and toasted sandwiches.

Controls

There are a small number of settings, which are thermostatically controlled. A small neon light shows when the grill is switched on and when the pre-set heat is reached it goes out.

Use and maintenance

Cooking time depends on the food to be cooked, varying between 1–2 minutes for rare steak to 6–10 minutes for sausages in the tray. As cooking time is short, careful timing is needed. The food is put on the bottom plate, which may need brushing with oil for some foods. You should select foods of the same thickness for cooking together.

After use, switch off the grill and allow to cool slightly before wiping with kitchen paper to remove the fat. Use a nylon scourer or brush dipped in hot soapy water to remove food particles which have stuck. Some grills have detachable plates which, when cold, can be removed and washed in hot soapy water. The outside only needs wiping with a damp cloth.

Sandwich toasters are very similar to infra-red grills.

Workshop

1 How can fuel be saved by using
   a a microwave cooker
   b an infra-red grill?
2 Explain how a microwave cooker works.
3 What materials will
   a absorb
   b reflect
   c transmit microwaves?
4 What features would you expect to find on a sophisticated microwave cooker?
5 Give three advantages and three disadvantages of microwave cooking.
6 Why are infra-red grills sometimes called contact grills?
7 Does an infra-red grill use more or less electricity than a standard microwave cooker, if used for the same number of minutes?

Save it! (2)

Pressure cookers

Food is cooked by steam in pressure cookers. The steam, produced when the water boils, is not allowed to escape, and so pressure builds up. As the pressure increases, so does the temperature at which water boils. The higher temperature reduces cooking time.

Pressure	Boiling point of water
Normal atmospheric pressure at sea level	100°C
Low 5 p.s.i. (0.35 kg sq cm)	108°C
Medium 10 p.s.i. (0.7 kg sq cm)	115°C
High 15 p.s.i. (1.05 kg sq cm)	121°C

p.s.i. pounds per square inch

The "Hi dome" pressure cooker

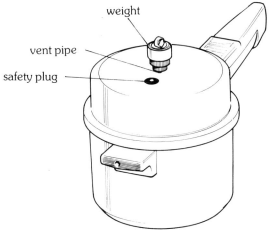

weight

vent pipe

safety plug

This is the standard pressure cooker. Three weights are available: 5 lb, 10 lb and 15 lb, so the pressure can be altered.

When steam rises in the pressure cooker, air is expelled through the vent pipe. Then the weight is fitted over this pipe so that the temperature will rise.

The "Ultra" pressure cooker

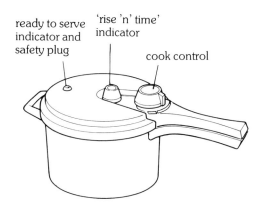

ready to serve indicator and safety plug

'rise 'n' time' indicator

cook control

The weight has been replaced by a cook control, which forms part of the lid. This means only 15 lb pressure is available. The Ultra has a ready-to-serve indicator/safety plug through which air is expelled before the indicator rises to seal the pressure cooker. This makes the pressure increase and the temperature rise.

A "Rise 'n' time" indicator shows that the correct temperature has been reached and is being maintained during cooking.

The automatic pressure cooker

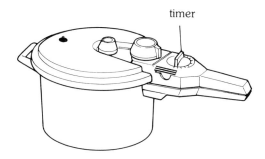

timer

A timer, which is built into the lid, can be set for the required length of cooking time.

Advantages and disadvantages

- Saves cooking time, but accurate timing is necessary to prevent overcooking.
- Reduces loss of nutrients because of the short cooking time and the use of a small amount of liquid.
- Saves fuel because of reduced cooking time.
- Tough cuts of meat can be made tender in a short time.

Care and maintenance

Always make sure the vent is kept clear. If steam escapes from the pressure cooker, either round the lid or from the safety plug, it may be necessary to replace the gasket or the safety plug.

After use, wash in hot soapy water and if necessary use a nylon scourer or a steel wool pad to remove particles of food.

Safety

There are three built-in safety features:

- The cooker body is extra thick to withstand the pressure.
- A locking lid ensures that the pressure cooker cannot be opened until the pressure is reduced.
- A safety plug is fitted. This will either melt or be pushed out if the pressure is too great. It allows the steam to escape and the pressure to be reduced.

You should, of course, always follow the manufacturer's instructions.

Slow cookers

Slow cookers are pottery casseroles which are electrically heated. They are used mainly for the cooking of stews and dishes which require long, slow, moist heat. The output is between 80 and 170 W. Because of the low output, there is no thermostat.

Slow cookers

Some slow cookers are removable from the plastic or metal case which contains the heating element.

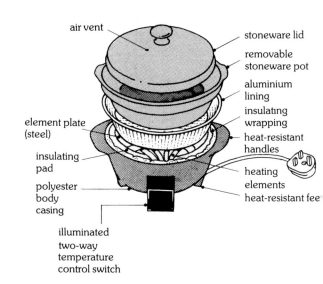

air vent

stoneware lid

removable stoneware pot

aluminium lining

insulating wrapping

heat-resistant handles

element plate (steel)

insulating pad

polyester body casing

heating elements

heat-resistant fee

illuminated two-way temperature control switch

Removable-pot slow cooker

In others, the heating elements are wound round the sides and base.

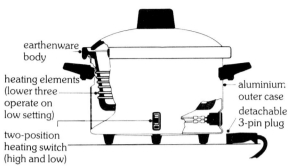

earthenware body

heating elements (lower three operate on low setting)

aluminium outer case

detachable 3-pin plug

two-position heating switch (high and low)

Fixed-pot slow cooker

In some models there are two heat settings, and on large models the switch from high to low setting may be automatic.

Use and maintenance

- The manufacturer's instructions must be followed to ensure that the slow cooker reaches the temperature required for the destruction of harmful micro-organisms present on the food.
- Pulse vegetables do not always get cooked thoroughly in slow cookers. Red kidney beans should be boiled for ten minutes before they are put in a slow cooker, as they contain a toxin which can only be destroyed by boiling for a short time.
- As food will not brown during cooking, any necessary browning should be done in a separate pan before cooking.
- There is less evaporation so you should reduce the amount of liquid in a recipe.
- No attention is necessary once cooking has started.
- The pots are easily cleaned because at the temperature used for cooking, food does not stick firmly to the sides.
- If the slow cooker is of the fixed pot type do not put into water. The casing of the removable type should not be put into water either. Soapy water can be put into the pot.
- The outside should be wiped with a damp, soapy cloth.

Workshop

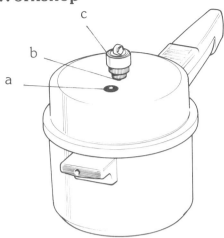

c

b

a

1 How should parts a, b and c be labelled?
2 Explain in your own words how a pressure cooker works.
3 Describe three *new* features which are now present on pressure cookers.
4 Give numbered instructions for the making of a beef stew using a pressure cooker, and explain the reasons for each stage.
5 List three advantages of a pressure cooker.
6 Explain the difference between a pressure cooker and a slow cooker.
7 What should you avoid when cooking red kidney beans in a slow cooker?
8 Give three disadvantages of using a slow cooker.

Mixer or processor?

Both food mixers and food processors help with food preparation, but each type of machine is designed to carry out some jobs more efficiently than others. There may be some overlap in what the appliances can do, but the two machines are not completely interchangeable.

What they do

Food mixer

- Creams fat and sugar
- Makes pastry
- Kneads dough (free-standing mixers only)
- Beats, whisks

Mixers do several types of food preparation prior to cooking and they aerate food as they mix it. It is an advantage to be able to regulate the mixing speed when food is being aerated.

A free-standing food mixer

Food processor

- Chops, slices, shreds, grates and blends raw ingredients which do not require cooking.

Some food processors will mix ingredients prior to cooking, but less air is added to the mixture because of the speed and design of the blade, so the mixture will not rise so well.

A food processor

Attachments

Optional attachments that can be purchased are shown on the next page.

These attachments are supplied with the processor:

S-shaped stainless steel blade
S-shaped plastic blade
Discs – slicing, grating
Additional discs can be bought, as can an egg-whisking attachment.

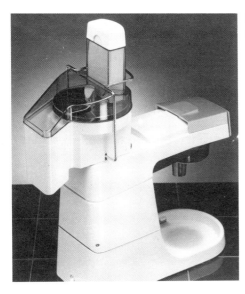

Slicer and
shredder

Mincer

Liquidizer

Optional attachments
for a food mixer

Food mixer *continued* | **Food processor** *continued*

How they work

This depends on the type of mixer. There are two main types:

a *Large free-standing mixer*, e.g. Kenwood Chef
   The motor is housed in the case and it has a rating of about 375–1000 W. The beater is

The motor is housed in the stand or base and it has a rating of between 200 and 700 W. It drives the belt turning the central spindle on which are placed the attachments. A bowl or mixing container is positioned over the central spindle.

113

Food mixer *continued*

driven by the motor. It rotates rapidly, and moves round the bowl so that all the ingredients are mixed thoroughly.

b *Small food mixer*
The mixer is much smaller and the motor less powerful (100–300 W). It can be hand held as well as used with a bowl and stand. Small mixers will carry out most tasks performed by large mixers, but smaller quantities should be used.

Both free-standing and smaller mixers require mains electricity to power the motor but there are now some cordless mixers available. These are automatically recharged after use from the mains power supply, when placed in position on the wall bracket.

Food processor *continued*

Belt-driven food processor

The lid is locked into position. If the shredding/slicing discs are to be used, the food is put into the feed tube and held in place by the food pusher. Liquids are also added via the feed tube.

Controls

These vary according to the size of the mixer. Large free-standing mixers usually have a dial which operates as an on/off switch as well as controlling the speed at a variety of levels. Small mixers usually have a 3-speed control on the handle, but some only have one or two speeds.

Controls for food processors vary considerably. Some processors have only one speed and the processor starts as soon as the lid is locked into position if the power is switched on. Others have a "pulse" control which gives short bursts of power and therefore greater control. Some models have a choice of speed.

Use and maintenance

- The manufacturer's handbook will help you choose the type of beater, the quantity of food and the speed to select for the task to be carried out. Take care not to exceed the quantities recommended, or the motor may be damaged.
- The sides of the bowl may need scraping with a plastic spatula from time to time during use. Switch off the mixer first!
- Before cleaning after use, switch off and unplug. Take care not to get any water on the motor. Just wipe the plastic case with a damp cloth. The bowl and beaters can be washed in warm soapy water.

- Check the manufacturer's handbook for the choice of attachment, quantities, timing and speed.
- Do not operate continuously for long periods, or the motor will become overheated.
- The bowl may need scraping with a plastic spatula from time to time during the mixing.
- After use, switch off, unplug and ensure the blades have stopped moving before removing the lid.
- The bowl and attachments can be washed in warm soapy water and a damp cloth used to wipe the rest of the machine.

Food mixer *continued*   Safety   **Food processor** *continued*

Check the mixer has a BEAB approval label before buying (see page 161).

Keep fingers and kitchen utensils well away from the beaters when the machine is operating.

Do not touch switches with wet hands.

A BEAB label will ensure the food processor meets electrical safety standards.

As the processor does not work unless the lid is locked, this helps prevent kitchen utensils and fingers coming into contact with the blades while the machine is working. The feed tube is too small for a hand to fit into it and its height is designed to prevent fingers coming into contact with the discs. Cutlery and spatulas should not be placed down the feed tube.

Some models have a brake to stop the blades quickly when the machine is switched off.

Care is needed when washing the metal discs and blade as the edges are very sharp.

Do not touch switches with wet hands.

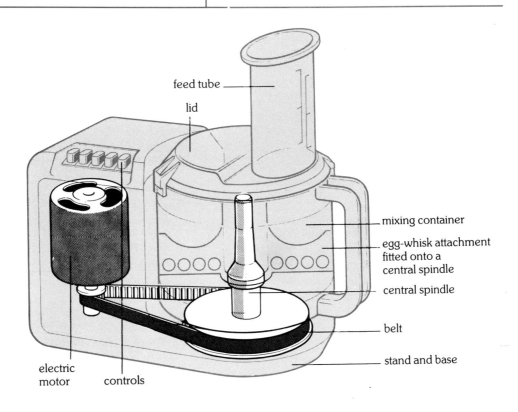

feed tube

lid

mixing container

egg-whisk attachment fitted onto a central spindle

central spindle

belt

stand and base

electric motor

controls

How a belt-driven food processor works

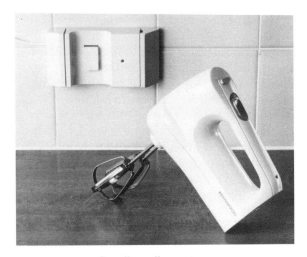

Small cordless mixer

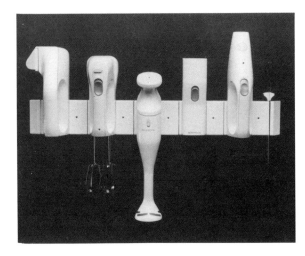

Wall storage-bracket for a small
cordless mixer and its attachments

Workshop

1 Name two tasks which are most successfully
carried out by:
a a food processor
b a food mixer

2 Give three safety factors which are built into a
food processor and explain how they work.

3 Investigate the making of a Victoria sandwich
cake using a food processor and an electric
mixer (either free-standing or hand held).
- Use the "all in one" method with 100 g of the
margarine, sugar and flour mixture in each
sandwich tin.
- Check in the handbooks for machine speed
and processing time.
- Remember to divide the mixture evenly, to
bake it in two identical 15 cm (6″) sandwich
tins, at the same temperature, in the same
oven and for the same length of time.
- Evaluate your results for the time, colour,
texture and appearance, paying particular
attention to texture.
- How would the result help you to decide
which machine to use for cake making in the
future?

4 Investigate the making of shortcrust pastry using
a food processor and a food mixer.
- Use 100 g flour and 50 g fat to make the
pastry for a small fruit plate tart.
- Check in the handbooks for speed and
processing time.
- Remember to time the pastry-making
carefully, use the same amount of water for
each tart, use identical plates for each tart,
bake at the same temperature, in the same
oven and for the same length of time.
- Evaluate the results for the time, colour,
texture and appearance.
- In future, which machine would you choose
for making your pastry? Why?

Keep it cool

Refrigerators and freezers help to keep perishable food in good condition.

How they work

When a liquid evaporates or changes into a gas it uses heat. In a refrigerator heat is drawn from the foods in the cabinet as the liquid or *refrigerant* evaporates in the evaporator. The gas is pumped under pressure to a condenser where it is changed back into a liquid. The liquid passes back to the evaporator and the cycle starts again. Insulation in the walls of the cabinet helps keep the temperature inside

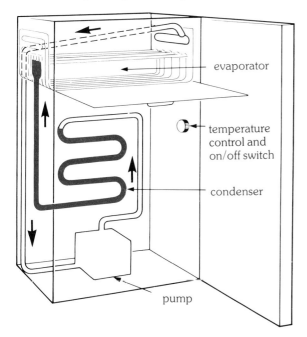

low. A freezer works in the same way, but the temperature in the cabinet is much lower. In both fridges and freezers the refrigerant is sealed into the system and is harmless to the environment until the seal is broken. This happens when the refrigerator is discarded and broken up. New refrigerators contain 50% less of the refrigerant which damages the environment and are better insulated, so last longer.

Controls

A dial, usually inside a refrigerator but on the outside of a freezer, operates a thermostat which keeps the temperature constant. The temperature in a refrigerator should be between 2°C and 5°C and in a freezer −18°C. (See page 124 about the importance of low temperatures when storing food.) A freezer usually has a "fast freeze" or "super freeze" control which can be switched on to reduce the temperature further when a batch of food is to be frozen.

Frozen food compartments have star markings to indicate temperature and therefore how long frozen foods can be stored.

Types of freezers

A **chest freezer** opens at the top. Food is usually stored in wire baskets. The chest freezer takes up a lot of space.

An **upright freezer** opens from the front, which makes it easier to load, unload and check stocks. Food can be placed directly on shelves or packed first in baskets. Some shelves have coils containing refrigerant passing under them, and food to be frozen should be packed on these shelves.

A **fridge/freezer** or **freezer/fridge** is a combined refrigerator and freezer in one unit, but with separate doors. The name depends on which is the larger unit. The advantage of this appliance is that it only takes up the floor space of a refrigerator, although in some larger models the units are placed side by side.

Types of refrigerators

A **standard refrigerator** has a frozen food compartment and an evaporator at the top.

A **larder refrigerator** does not have an evaporator box. Instead, near the back or top of the cabinet, is a thin vertical or horizontal cooling plate.

Marking	Approximate temperature	Maximum time for frozen foods
*	− 6°C	1 week
**	−12°C	1 month
***	−18°C	3 months
****	−18°C	3 months

The four star marking indicates that the freezer can be used for freezing fresh foods.

Care and maintenance

- Avoid putting hot food in refrigerators and freezers as it raises the temperature in the cabinet.
- All foods should be covered; otherwise they will dry out.
- Food to be stored in a freezer should be suitably packaged to keep it in good condition.
- The coolest part of the refrigerator is below the frozen food compartment, and meat and fresh fish should be stored here. The other shelves and the door are less cool.

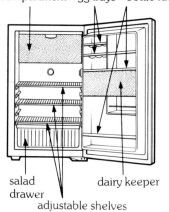

frozen-food compartment egg trays bottle rack

salad drawer dairy keeper adjustable shelves

- Refrigerators and freezers should be defrosted regularly to remove the ice, which acts as an insulator. When a lot of ice collects, food will not cool as well and more electricity is used to keep the temperature low.
- Some refrigerators and freezers have automatic defrost so that no ice builds up.
- Push-button defrosting in a refrigerator works by stopping the pump when the button is pressed. When defrosting is finished the pump starts again and the refrigerator cycle begins. The water from the melted ice collects in the evaporator tray and should be emptied away.
- Manual defrost is necessary if there is no automatic or push-button system. The control should be set to off or defrost, the food removed (wrap frozen food in newspaper) and stored in a cool place. A bowl of hot water placed inside the cabinet will melt the ice more quickly. Wipe down the inside of the cabinet and reset controls.
- Occasionally it is necessary to wash the inside of the cabinet with warm water plus a little bicarbonate of soda. The outside can be washed with warm soapy water.

Workshop

1. Carry out a class survey on the types of refrigerators and freezers you have at home. Present the results as a bar chart showing numbers owning refrigerators, larder refrigerators, chest freezers, upright freezers, fridge/freezers and freezer/fridges. What percentage of pupils have a refrigerator at home and what percentage have a freezer?
2. Name the parts of a refrigerator and explain how a refrigerator works.
3. What is the recommended temperature for (a) a refrigerator and (b) a freezer? Why is it important to keep food cool?
4. Explain why food should be covered before putting it in a refrigerator.
5. Give three advantages of owning (a) a refrigerator and (b) a freezer.

Which cooker?

A cooker is the most important piece of equipment for the preparation of food in the kitchen. It is made up of three parts: the hob or hotplate, the grill and the oven. In the standard cooker, which is free standing, all three parts are in one unit. In split-level cookers the parts are separated and built into kitchen units. Either the grill and oven are separate from the hotplate/hob or the hotplate/hob is placed over the grill and oven

The two main fuels used for cooking in Britain are gas (either natural or bottled) and electricity.

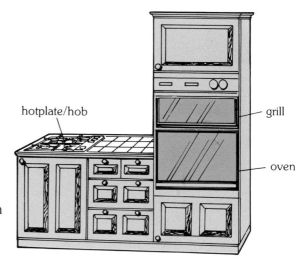

hotplate/hob — grill

— oven

A free-standing cooker

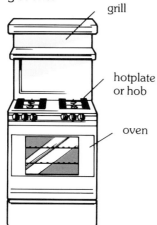

grill

hotplate or hob

oven

hotplate/hob

grill and oven

Split-level cookers

Gas

Hotplate

With their compact flames, modern hotplates provide better heat transfer between the flames and the saucepan. The heat is easily controlled from full heat to a low setting for simmering. All the burners may be of the same power rating or there may be two higher-rated and two lower-rated burners.

Ceramic hobs and individual **ceramic discs** have now been introduced on some cookers. These tend to slow down heat transfer but the cooker looks attractive and cleaning is easier.

Electric

Hob

There are several types of boiling rings available. *Radiant rings* are the most common. The element is enclosed in a tube which glows red when full heat is used. *Disc rings* have a flat top with a shallow sunken part in the centre. The disc, which covers the heating element, does not glow red on heating. A *ceramic hob* is a smooth sheet of ceramic glass on which the heated areas are marked. Underneath these areas are the elements. When high heat is used the glowing elements can be seen through the ceramic surface.

119

Gas *continued*

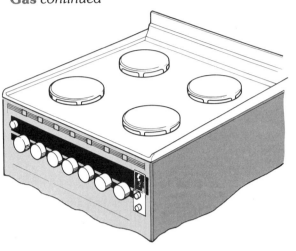

A ceramic gas hob

Electric *continued*

Halogen ceramic hobs

The elements on some of the newer ceramic hobs now contain tungsten halogen filaments which heat up more quickly and are much easier to control. The heat glows under the ceramic hob at all heat settings.

Magnetic induction hob

Magnetic wire coils replace the heating elements. Control is very easy, with almost immediate response to changes of setting.

Use perfectly flat pans the same size as the boiling rings for economy and efficiency.

Some rings have a dual circuit so that either the central portion or the whole ring can be used. The rings can also vary in size and rating.

Radiant rings

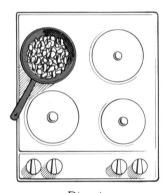

Disc rings

Ceramic electric hob

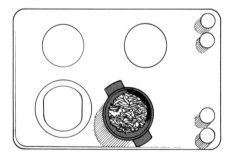

Halogen ceramic hob

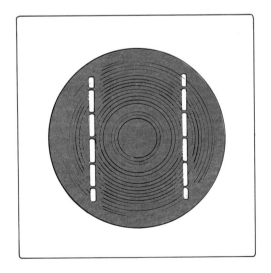

Magnetic induction hob

Gas *continued*

Grill

The size and position varies. Grills are either at eye level or at waist height. The conventional grill has a long burner. Flames from the burner heat a metal fret which glows red. Newer **surface-combustion grills** mix the air and gas before burning on the surface of the metal gauze. This spreads the heat more evenly, and even when the heat is reduced there is still a large grilling surface.

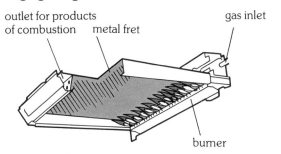

outlet for products of combustion — metal fret — gas inlet — burner

Conventional grill

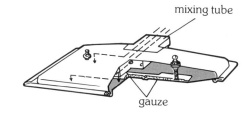

mixing tube — gauze

Surface combustion grill

Electric *continued*

Grill

There is variation in size and positioning. Some grills in larger cookers serve as a second oven.

The electric element is contained in a metal tube built into the roof of the grill. It is usually the full width of the cooker. Some grills have a **dual circuit** so that either the whole grill or only half can be heated.

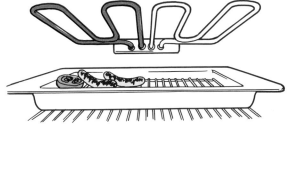

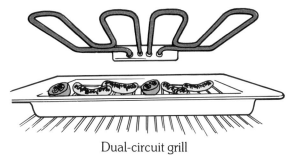

Dual-circuit grill

A **rotisserie** (spit) is available on some cookers. The food is placed on a metal rod which fits under the grill. An electric motor turns the rod, so for gas cookers a nearby electric socket is needed.

Gas oven

- Usually the burner is in the oven itself so it is heated directly.
- Most ovens have "easy clean" linings.
- Glass panels are built into many oven doors.
- A valve is fitted as a safety device. This controls the gas supply to the main burner. If the burner flame goes out, the valve closes and stops the flow of unburnt gas.

Electric oven

- The main heating elements are on both sides of the oven behind removable "easy clean" panels. In some ovens there is also a low-rated element underneath the oven floor.
- Two ovens are present on some cookers – the main one and a smaller secondary one.
- The door may have a glass panel or there may be an inner glass door.

Convection currents are set up so that there are zones of heat. A variety of dishes requiring different temperatures can be cooked in the oven at the same time.

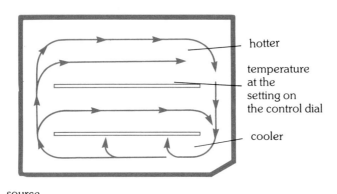

Shelf 1:	
Shelf 2:	Roast Lamb Jacket Potatoes
Shelf 3:	
Shelf 4:	Carrots with Orange Braised Vegetables
Shelf 5:	
Base:	Baked Apples

hotter

temperature at the setting on the control dial

cooler

source of heat

Use of heat zones with an oven set at 190°C, gas mark 5.

Fan-assisted ovens

The fan is fitted at the back of the oven and distributes the heat more evenly so that foods will cook just as quickly and evenly on any shelf. If a fan is fitted in a gas cooker, a nearby electric socket is required as the motor is driven by electricity.

Combination ovens

A fan-assisted oven is combined with a microwave oven. It can be used in a variety of ways:
- as a conventional oven with heat zones
- as a fan oven
- as a microwave oven
- as a combination oven with microwaves plus heat from gas or electricity.

Fan-assisted oven

Microwave combination oven

Gas *continued*

Gas oven controls

Gas ovens have a temperature range between 93°C and 260°C. This can be accurately regulated. Some ovens have a slow-cooking setting with a temperature between 80°C and 110°C. This is useful for casseroles and for keeping food hot, without it drying out, at the end of normal cooking time.

Automatic timers and interval timers or reminders are available, but a nearby electric socket is required.

Electric *continued*

Electric oven controls

The temperature range is 100–270°C, and the temperature is easy to control. When the oven is switched on an indicator light shows. This switches off when the set temperature is reached.

Most cookers have an electric clock and automatic oven timer which can be set to switch on the oven automatically for a set period and then switch it off at the end of that period. In addition to this, 60-minute interval timers are usually fitted. These ring or buzz at the end of the set time. Some electric cookers have digital automatic timers with touch control.

Cleaning

The outside of cookers is finished in vitreous enamel in a variety of colours. A wipe with a damp cloth will keep the surface clean.

Spillage trays on hobs or hotplates can usually be removed for cleaning. Ceramic discs or hobs should be regularly cleaned with a special cleaner.

In ovens with "easy clean" liners grease splashes burn off, so it is only doors and shelves which need regular cleaning.

Workshop

1 Compare the features of one gas cooker and one electric cooker using the following headings:
   a Hotplate/hob
   b Grill
   c Oven
   d Controls
   Which cooker did you prefer and why?

2 a Make a scone mixture using 200 g of flour. Divide the mixture in half – weigh to be accurate. Make two sets of scones and bake one set in an electric cooker and the other in a gas cooker. If an oven thermometer is available, check the temperature in the two ovens is the same on the same shelf before baking the scones. Remember that the scones should be of the same size, thickness and number. They should be baked for the same length of time on baking trays of the same size and material.
   b Explain why each step in 2a is important.
   c Evaluate your results for colour, flavour and texture. Which batch of scones did you prefer and why?

3 Describe three types of boiling ring which may be found on a modern electric cooker.

4 a You are planning to buy a new cooker and have £500 to spend. Visit your local gas and electricity showrooms and decide which cooker you would buy.
   b Write a report about this cooker, describing the hob/hotplate, grill, oven and any other important features which made you choose the cooker. Include a picture or a drawing of the cooker.

Your meat . . . or your poison?

Steve and Emma are thinking about starting a small business, making sandwiches for local office workers. Before they start work, they visit Mr Williams, the local Environmental Health Officer.

> From what I've said, can you think of a good slogan for all food preparation?

> Well, bacteria multiply if food gets warm . . . they are put on to food by dirty hands, or even by putting them on a dirty worktop . . .

> and flies might land on them . . . so how about "KEEP FOOD COOL, CLEAN AND COVERED!"

Is your fridge cool enough?

To be sure that food is safe we should know the temperature of our fridges – but how many people do? Carry out a SURVEY of your friends and neighbours:

ASK – "Do you know the temperature of your fridge?"
Most people will say "I've no idea!" so:

ASK – "Have a guess at what you think the temperature is."

ASK – "Do you keep a thermometer in the fridge?"
If the answer is "YES", read the temperature. It's much more likely that the answer will be "NO", but in any case,

ASK – if you can take the temperature of the fridge.

Use a portable thermometer such as an ESMI from British Gas, and put the temperature probe on the middle shelf. Leave it for five minutes and write down the temperature.

An ESMI thermometer

Put all the class results on to a table and answer these questions:

- What percentage of people knew the temperature of their fridges?
- What percentage of fridges had thermometers in them?
- Were they accurate?

Now plot "guessed" temperature against actual temperature, using a graph like the one below.

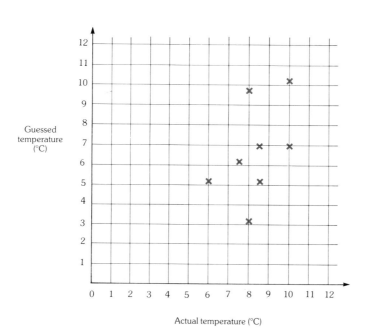

Correlation of Actual and Guessed Temperature in a Recent Survey

Guessed temperature (°C)

Actual temperature (°C)

What conclusions can you draw about the general public's knowledge of fridge temperatures and about how safe food is in their refrigerators?

Workshop

1 What are the four most important ways of preventing food poisoning?
2 Can you suggest three reasons for the increase in food poisoning cases over the past few years?
3 When Steve and Emma take Mr Williams' advice and "check their suppliers", what questions should they ask?
4 Design a poster about food hygiene, to be displayed in small food-producing firms like Steve's and Emma's.

Bacti-fax

Food poisoning can be caused by metals or by chemicals such as bleach and even arsenic. It can also be caused by viruses and by toxins produced by certain moulds. However, most food poisoning is caused by bacteria, which are very small single-celled organisms. If you know how and why the bacteria grow you will be able to prevent them from growing in food, so the food you cook will be safe. Some facts about the most important food poisoning bacteria are shown here.

Salmonella

- Does *not* form spores.
- Does *not* form a toxin. The illness is caused by eating large numbers of bacteria which have grown in the food.
- Grows best between 10°C and 40°C.
- Does not grow below 5°C.
- Is killed by heating to 70°C.
- Is found mainly in chicken, red meat and sometimes in raw egg.

Staphylococcus

- Does *not* form spores.
- *Does* form a toxin. It is difficult to destroy with heat as it withstands boiling for 30 minutes. The illness is caused by eating food that contains the toxin, even if the bacteria themselves have been destroyed by heat.
- Grows best between 10°C and 40°C.
- Does not grow below 5°C.
- Is killed by heating to 70°C but the toxin is *not* destroyed at this temperature.
- The bacteria are spread by people – they are in most people's noses, and on hair, skin and hands. They are especially dangerous if you have a cut, spots or a boil. So you must always wash your hands before preparing food; hair should be covered completely; and cuts or skin blemishes must be covered.

Salmonella food poisoning makes you vomit, you have diarrhoea, abdominal pain and a fever. You will probably feel so ill that you have to go to the doctor, and the illness will last a week or more. It is a serious illness and can be fatal to children and the elderly. After the illness you will excrete the bacteria in faeces for a while – some people excrete them for the rest of their lives. So it is *vitally* important that you wash your hands well after visiting the lavatory or you will spread the bacteria to the food you are preparing.

To prevent: wash hands after visiting the lavatory and before preparing food; thaw frozen food thoroughly; cook all food thoroughly.

Staphylococcus food poisoning occurs very soon after eating the food. It is fairly mild though unpleasant – just (!) vomiting – and it usually only lasts about 24 hours. So you might not visit the doctor even though the illness is inconvenient. If it occurs in *your* restaurant it will be bad for business.

To prevent: cover all cuts, sores, spots and boils; cover hair; wash hands; refrigerate properly; avoid cross-contamination from raw to cooked food.

Clostridium perfringens

- *Does* form spores.
- Does *not* form a toxin in the food itself. The illness is caused by eating large numbers of bacteria which have grown in the food.
- Grows best between 10°C and 50°C.
- Does not grow below 5°C.
- The spores are heat-resistant, so ordinary cooking is unlikely to kill this bacterium completely. After cooking, it is *most* important that the food is chilled quickly and completely if it is not eaten immediately. Any reheating must be rapid, and must be done just before the food is served.

Clostridium perfringens is found in meat and meat products because it lives in animal intestines. It is also found in the gut of some people, so washing hands after visiting the lavatory is very important.

The illness is most often a result of meals for large groups of people, such as wedding receptions or celebration dinners. The people affected will have diarrhoea and abdominal pain, and it can be serious for the very young and the elderly.

To prevent: avoid cross-contamination from raw to cooked meat; cook thoroughly, cool quickly, store properly, reheat quickly, eat immediately.

Campylobacter

- Does *not* form spores.
- Does *not* form a toxin.
- Does not usually grow in food but it is carried by food, and very few cells are needed to cause the illness.

Campylobacter can be found in raw chicken and unpasteurized milk, but since it does not form spores it is easily destroyed by normal cooking.

The illness is very common – since 1984 there have been more cases per year of illness caused by *Campylobacter* than *Salmonella* food poisoning. It usually lasts about three weeks, and it can be serious.

To prevent: cook food thoroughly; avoid cross-contamination between raw chicken and other foods, work surfaces and plates.

Listeria

- Does *not* form spores.
- Does *not* form a toxin.
- Is killed by heating to 70°C.
- Very commonly found on vegetables; also found in pâté and many common ready-made foods.
- Can grow at temperatures below 5°C, especially when refrigerated for a long period of time, e.g. over two weeks.

Listeria can be extremely serious – it can cause abortion in pregnant women and serious illness in the elderly and in people with underlying illness.

To prevent: cook food thoroughly; buy chilled food within the 'sell-by' date and eat promptly; store food at 3°C; rotate refrigerated food carefully.

Workshop

1 You have been asked to prepare food for a party to be held in seven days' time. You have one small, domestic refrigerator. The menu is to be: broccoli quiche, chicken and rice salad, coleslaw, baked potatoes, strawberry cheesecake, trifle. Everything will be made from fresh ingredients. Prepare a time-plan from the shopping to the serving, showing very carefully the steps you will take to make sure the food is safe to eat.

On the shelf

A family of four will eat their way through 28 kg of food in an average week. All of that food has to be transported to their home. Years ago most of it would have been bought on the daily trip to the local shop. Now most food is bought in supermarkets in a 'one-stop-shop' that may take place once a week or even only once a month.

When the food arrives in the house it has to be stored correctly or else . . .

. . . cans will go rusty
. . . eggs will go bad
. . . meat will make us ill
. . . cheese will dry out
. . . frozen fish fingers will thaw
. . . biscuits will go soft
. . . cake will go mouldy
. . . bread will go stale
. . . lettuce will wilt
. . . carrots will rot
. . . flour will be eaten by mice
. . . sugar will attract ants

It is highly unlikely that all these things would happen to one load of shopping, and in any case some of these things only occur after a long time. But food is expensive and it is hard work to carry it home, so it should not be wasted because it has not been stored properly.

Why do these changes happen, and how can they be prevented?

A can will rust if it has a tiny pinhole in the tinplate that covers the steel, and is in a damp atmosphere. Water can get through the hole and cause the iron in the steel to form *iron oxide* – rust. It is possible for the rust to pass completely through the can so that the contents leak out and bacteria get into the food.

Prevent it by storing cans in a cool, dry cupboard and making sure that when new canned food is bought, the old stock is brought to the front of the cupboard. Do not store canned food in the fridge unless the label tells you to.

Eggs will go bad if bacteria from the outside shell manage to get through a crack in the shell and then through the white (difficult because the white is alkaline) to the yolk.

Even if eggs *don't* contain bacteria, the quality deteriorates as the eggs age because the amount of thin white increases and the amount of thick white decreases.

Prevent by buying only clean, uncracked eggs from a reputable supplier and using them quickly. It is not necessarily a good idea to store eggs in the fridge because water might condense on them and carry bacteria inside.

Meat can make us ill if it contains certain bacteria that cause food poisoning, especially *Salmonella* and *Clostridium perfringens*. These bacteria are in the intestines of most farm animals, including chickens, and they can get on to the surface of meat when the animals are killed and sliced by the butcher.

Prevent by storing meat below 4°C in a fridge, by thawing frozen meat completely before cooking, by cooking meat thoroughly, and by refrigerating leftovers immediately.

Cake will dry out, biscuits will go soft. If biscuits, which are dry, are left out they will go soft because they take up water from the air. On the other hand, if cake, which is moist, is left out then water will be lost to the air and the cake will taste dry.

Prevent by enclosing dry food in an airtight box or tin, but moist food should be loosely wrapped in a polythene bag or placed in a container with a few ventilation holes, because . . .

Cheese will go mouldy, and so might cake and bread, if it is *too* moist and if mould spores land on it. Moulds are a type of fungus which multiplies by producing millions of **spores**. A common mould is *Penicillium* – its spores are often in the air, even inside the house. If one lands on a piece of cheese which has a moist surface it will grow to form a hairy mat called a **mycelium**.

Prevent by storing away from the air, but in a container which is ventilated. Cheese should be kept cool in a fridge where mould will grow more slowly.

Bread will go stale. This might be confused with drying out, but while drying is simply loss of water from the bread to the atmosphere, staling is an alteration of the molecular structure. When bread is cooked, the starch granules swell as they absorb water, and the starch molecules separate from each other. You cannot see this, even with the most powerful microscope, but this is what happens:

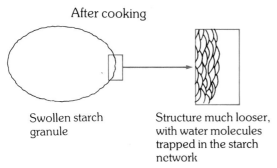

Before cooking

Wheat-starch granule

Starch molecules very tightly packed together, lying alongside each other.

After cooking

Swollen starch granule

Structure much looser, with water molecules trapped in the starch network

If the bread is kept for a few days, even if it is stored perfectly so that it neither dries out nor goes mouldy, you might notice when you chew it that it feels slightly gritty and grainy. This is because the water molecules have moved from the swollen starch granules outwards towards the crust (which is why a crusty loaf becomes less crusty as time goes on), leaving the starch granules with less water even though the loaf as a whole has the same amount. So the starch molecules have begun to go back to the position they had before they were cooked – tightly packed and lying alongside each other.

Prevent by adding a very small amount of fat to bread dough, using bread quickly, not storing it in the fridge (staling is more rapid at low temperatures). Reverse the effects by putting the loaf in a hot oven for a few minutes or a microwave for a few seconds.

Lettuce will wilt if water is lost from the cells so that they no longer keep their shape. This will happen if lettuce and other green vegetables are kept in warm, dry air.
Prevent by storing green vegetables at low temperatures, preferably in the fridge, and in a closed container such as a polythene bag or a crisper.

Carrots will rot if the skin is bruised or cut so that bacteria or mould can get into the cells. They use the nutrients in the carrot to multiply, and they pierce the cell walls so that cell contents mix and often react to form brown compounds.
Prevent by treating fruit and vegetables gently and storing in a cool, dry cupboard.

Frozen fish fingers will thaw if the temperature rises above 0°C. This will damage the cells, and if the temperature rises even higher, bacteria will be able to grow. If the fish fingers are frozen again the bacteria will not be killed and you might not be able to tell that the bacteria are there.
Prevent by wrapping frozen food when carrying it home to keep it at 18°C, and by putting it in the freezer as soon as you get home. To find out more about frozen food see page 139.

Flour will be eaten by mice, sugar will attract ants. It is estimated that, worldwide, about a fifth of all food which is harvested is eaten by pests. Rats, mice and insects find our food as delicious as we do!
Prevent by storing flour, sugar, cornflour, muesli etc. in tins or polythene boxes so that insects cannot get to the food. Also make sure that there are no holes in the walls and that cupboards are clean.

Workshop

1 Leave bread on a plate in a warm place, moisten a little each day and observe mould growth. Look at the mould with a hand lens or a low-power binocular microscope. Draw what you see.

2 A friend runs a small grocery shop. She would like to produce a leaflet to advise customers about storing food they buy from her, and she has asked you to write it.

3 Develop a new fruity snack-bar product that can be advertised as a 'healthy break-time biscuit'. Try different packages to find the best one. The packaging can be tested by an 'accelerated storage test', i.e. storing the product at a high temperature (about 40°C) and in a humid atmosphere (in a large polythene box containing a cup of water).

4 Use an ESME thermometer and a stopwatch to monitor frozen fish fingers. Asking a shopkeeper for permission first, insert the thermometer probe into a small hole at one end of a packet of fish fingers. Record the temperature while it is in the freezer, and start the stopwatch. Put the packet in your trolley, buy other goods if possible, take them through the checkout, carry the shopping home, unpack it and put it in your freezer. Watch the time very carefully and record the temperature every five minutes. Draw a graph of the 'cold chain'.

Food processing for beginners

Have you ever . . . washed lettuce . . . peeled potatoes . . . made a cake . . . grilled a pork chop . . . frozen bread?

If you have, then you have processed food yourself. But why did you carry out each of these activities? If you make a list of the reasons, it will probably look something like this:

- to make food edible
- to make food attractive
- to make food more digestible
- to make food last longer.

Food is processed industrially for very similar reasons.

1 To prevent spoilage

All plants and animals contain biological catalysts called **enzymes**. When plants are growing and animals are living, the enzymes catalyse reactions that, for example, turn starch into sugar, produce growth, digest food, etc. When the plants are harvested and the animals are killed the enzymes carry on working, often with undesirable effects:

- light-coloured plants may turn brown
- fruit and vegetables become over-ripe and soft
- the fat in meat may become rancid
- vitamin C (ascorbic acid) may be destroyed by the enzyme ascorbic acid oxidase.

Food can also spoil because of **microorganisms**, especially yeasts, moulds and bacteria. These are naturally present on growing plants and living animals, but they are far more likely to increase and spoil the food after harvesting the plants or killing the animals because there is no longer any natural resistance to them. The effects can be seen on damaged and rotting fruit. They can be seen – and smelled – on minced beef that has been stored in a refrigerator for three or more days: bacteria grow and act on the protein to produce nasty-smelling small molecules.

Plums affected by brown rot

How can the actions of enzymes and microorganisms be prevented?

- Low temperatures slow down or stop their effects. Very few bacteria will grow, or enzymes act, between 0°C and 7°C. At freezer temperatures bacteria are not killed and enzymes are not destroyed but they cannot act on the food.

- High temperatures can destroy both enzymes and microorganisms. Enzymes are destroyed at 65°C and microorganisms are destroyed at 100°C unless they contain heat-resistant spores.

- Acidity prevents enzymic and microbial action. Most foods are neutral and few bacteria can grow at a low pH. Pickling therefore prevents spoilage. Yoghurt and cheese (which are actually made with the help of some bacteria that can produce acid from lactose) will keep much longer than milk.

- Irradiation kills bacteria and stops enzymic action. Irradiation can kill bacteria, and it can stop enzymic action. It is an expensive method which is likely to be made legal in the UK shortly. Gamma rays from a radio-active isotope, cobalt-60, are used to sterilize food or, at a lower level of radiation, to pasteurize it. Irradiation will also prevent sprouting in potatoes and spoilage in strawberries. The food itself does not become radioactive but some nutrients can be destroyed and taste can be affected. It is legal in other countries for certain foods, e.g. in Holland for chicken and spices.

- Removal of water prevents the action of bacteria and enzymes, but does not destroy them.

2 To make food safe to eat

As well as spoilage bacteria, all foods can contain bacteria that are harmful to humans. It is important to remember that most spoilage bacteria are *not* harmful. The bacteria that are harmful, most of which do *not* make food look or small bad, can be destroyed in the ways listed in (1) above. (See also page 128.)

3 For convenience

A lot of processed food is partly or fully prepared, for example: canned baked beans, canned potatoes and canned peaches are ready to eat straight from the can. A lot of canned food does not even need heating.

Frozen peas, cauliflower and courgettes need no preparation, though they do need cooking for a few minutes in boiling water or a microwave oven. Frozen meat and fish, however, are usually uncooked so need just as much preparation and cooking as fresh meat – except that it is vitally important that extra time is allowed for thawing.

Chilled ready meals are completely prepared and only need reheating. Instructions on the packet should be followed *exactly* so that the food is thoroughly heated.

Foods such as bread, cakes and breakfast cereals are ready to eat.

Dried soup, packet cake mixes and 'instant' puddings all need added liquid to rehydrate the ingredients.

Workshop

1 Write headings as follows: FRESH; DRIED; FROZEN; CANNED; CHILLED; PASTEURIZED, then subheadings for each: ADVANTAGES; DISADVANTAGES. Make a list of the advantages and disadvantages of each method. From the lists, which do you think is best for:
a Brussels sprouts
b soup
c milk
d beefburgers
e haddock
f lasagne?

2 Look at the food at home in the fridge, freezer and in cupboards. For TEN foods, list the reasons for the particular method of preservation that was used.

3 Prepare two meals. One should be made from fresh ingredients and served immediately and the other should contain the same ingredients which have all been processed. The meal could be beefburgers, peas and new potatoes, followed by apple pie and custard. The 'processed' meal would have frozen beefburgers, dried peas, canned new potatoes, ready-made packaged apple pie and canned custard. Compare the cost, the time spent on cooking and preparation, any special storage conditions for the raw and the processed food, the taste and the appearance of the meals. If the processed food has nutritional information on the packets you could compare the nutritional values as well, by using food tables or a computer program for the 'fresh' meal. From all this information prepare and give a talk to the class. You could call it 'Fast food, real food'.

Steam heat

Why use high temperatures in food processing?

- Because enzymes are inactivated above 65°C.
- Because bacteria are killed above 65°C.
- Because bacterial spores are destroyed above 100°C.

What temperatures are used?

100°C for a few seconds will **blanch** fruit and vegetables so that they
- do not discolour
- do not lose vitamin C
- soften and reduce in size in order to fit into a carton or can

72°C for 15 seconds will **pasteurize** milk so that
- harmful bacteria are killed
- the number of spoilage bacteria is reduced so that the milk stays fresh while it is delivered, while it stands on your doorstep for an hour or so, and in your fridge for 24 hours.

But pasteurization also destroys the small amount of vitamin C that is in fresh milk.

100°C for about 10 minutes **sterilizes** cans of fruit. This is a fairly low temperature and a short time because
- the food is acid (it has a pH below 4.5), so bacterial spores cannot germinate and grow
- heat is only needed, therefore, to kill yeasts and moulds, and boiling for a few minutes will be enough
- if stronger heat were used, the fruit would be overcooked and spoiled.

121°C for up to 15 minutes **sterilizes** canned vegetables, meat and fish. This higher temperature is required because
- these foods have a pH of 4.5–7.6, so bacterial spores can germinate and the bacteria can grow
- the foods need cooking for longer periods than fruit.

The most dangerous bacterium in the canning industry is *Clostridium botulinum*. It produces a deadly poison or *toxin* when it is able to grow in a can, so it is vitally important that every can of vegetables, meat and fish is treated as though *Clostridium botulinum* is in it. It has to be heated by steam under pressure (just like a pressure cooker) at 121°C for up to 15 minutes. This kills the *Clostridium botulinum* spores and any others that might be present.

How is the food processed?

Let's look at two examples:

1 Pasteurized milk

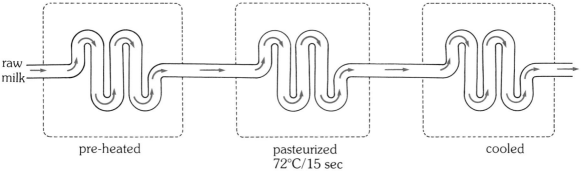

raw milk

pre-heated

pasteurized
72°C/15 sec

cooled

2 Canned peas

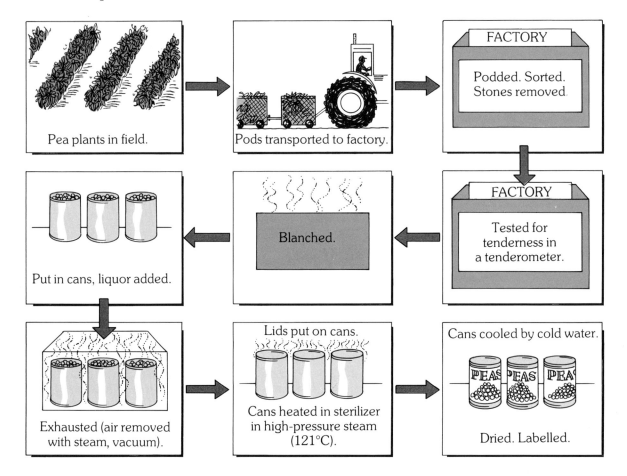

Pea plants in field.

Pods transported to factory.

FACTORY
Podded. Sorted. Stones removed.

FACTORY
Tested for tenderness in a tenderometer.

Blanched.

Put in cans, liquor added.

Exhausted (air removed with steam, vacuum).

Lids put on cans.
Cans heated in sterilizer in high-pressure steam (121°C).

Cans cooled by cold water.
Dried. Labelled.

Pasteurization is not only for milk. Fruit juices are pasteurized, but not to destroy bacteria. (Can you work out why this is not necessary?) It is done to destroy **yeasts** which might grow and ferment the fruit juice. Liquid egg, used in catering, is also pasteurized at 63°C for one minute.

Sterilization is not only done inside cans. The food can be sterilized by heating it first, then putting it into a sterile can and sealing it. The food is heated at a higher temperature for a much shorter time, so it tastes less 'cooked' (for example, canned custard). This process is called **aseptic canning**.

Food can also be sterilized in plastic containers (for example, plastic trays with a sealed foil lid). When the lid is removed the dish and its contents can be heated in a microwave oven.

Retort pouches have been in existence for a long time, but are still not widely used. They are laminated plastic or aluminium foil bags into which food is placed. Air is removed from the bags and they are sealed. The food must be heated to the same temperature as in conventional canning, but because the pack is much flatter it takes less time to reach the required temperature. This means the food is 'cooked' less strongly, and should have a better flavour. Delicate sauces such as a wine sauce can be packaged in this way. This, plus the fact that the process is more expensive than canning, means that retort pouches tend to be used for 'gourmet' food.

Where should heat-processed food be stored?

While pasteurized milk contains no harmful bacteria, it does contain bacteria which can multiply and make the milk sour, called spoilage organisms. So pasteurized milk, and other pasteurized food, must be stored in the fridge below 5°C and consumed by the eat-by date.

The great advantage of heat-sterilized food is that it costs nothing to store, unlike frozen, chilled or pasteurized food. But the cans, trays or pouches should be kept in a dry and fairly cool place. While the food is sterile, it does not keep for ever. Chemical reactions between food constituents can take place, and sometimes the food reacts with the metal in cans.

Workshop

1 List the advantages and disadvantages of:
   a pasteurizing milk
   b conventional canning
   c aseptic canning
   d retort pouches
   e food in sterilizable trays

2 One of the reactions that blanching is intended to prevent is enzymic browning (the browning that happens when light-coloured fruits and vegetables are cut). Devise an experiment to find an alternative treatment for sliced apples. Have a brainstorming session to decide on possible treatments. In your experiment have a control (an untreated apple slice), and treat each slice in exactly the same way, with just one variable. Record the amount of browning every 10 minutes for an hour. Which is the best treatment? What are the advantages and disadvantages of each?

3 Using the flow diagram for canned peas as a guide, draw a flow diagram for (a) canned potatoes and (b) canned baked beans. Take care to include *every* process, and explain the reason for each process.

Ice and cold

Alex's Menu

Moules marinière

—

Four Seasons Pizza
Rice and carrot salad
Coleslaw

—

Cheesecake

To celebrate the start of his new job, Alex is inviting his friend Suriya to a meal. As he is very busy, he has decided on ready-prepared, 'convenience' foods that have been preserved using low temperatures.

Alex's foods have been **chilled**. The dishes have been prepared at a factory under very strict hygienic conditions, then put in a container and rapidly chilled in a blast of cold air to below 3°C. The foods are transported in lorries to the shops, and are displayed for sale in a chilled cabinet until their 'sell-by' date. The label on the package may say, for example, 'eat within two days of purchase', or it may give an 'eat by' date. In either case, the instructions must be carefully obeyed, for three reasons:

(a) If the foods are stored correctly, at or very near 3°C, most food poisoning bacteria will not grow. But one, called *Listeria*, can grow at this temperature. It only grows slowly, but if the food is refrigerated first in the factory, then in a lorry, then a shop, then in the home, the storage time can be so long that there are enough bacteria to make people ill. The illness is rare, but it can be very serious.

(b) While the low temperature stops most dangerous bacteria from growing, the bacteria, moulds and yeasts that make foods look, smell and taste bad can still grow – though the growth will be very slow. So food can go bad, even when it is chilled, and then it will be wasted.

(c) Enzymes in food will also continue to act. Again, the action will be slower than at room temperature. The enzymes will make the food decay.

As long as the temperature is low – though not so low that the food freezes – commercially-produced chilled food should be just as good as food you make at home.

Packaging is very important with chilled foods: water must not be allowed to evaporate from the food, nor must drops of water condense on it. Foods must be carefully stored, below 4°C, in the fridge. Raw foods must never touch, or drip onto, any other foods. It is especially important to keep raw food away from cooked or ready-to-eat food.

Chilled food should be gently but thoroughly reheated on the hob, in a conventional oven or in a microwave oven. The centre of the food should reach at least 70°C.

Since Alex took care to store his food for only one day at 4°C, and he reheated the food in his microwave oven following instructions exactly, the food looks and tastes almost as good as it would if he had made it himself. Also, the nutritional value has not been reduced by processing.

Anant is having a quick meal with his friend Kitty before they go to their evening class. Anant's meal is entirely from the freezer. The manufacturers will have chosen one of the following methods to freeze the food:

A **blast freezer** is used for irregularly-shaped food. The food is on perforated shelves, and air at about −30°C is blown over the food.

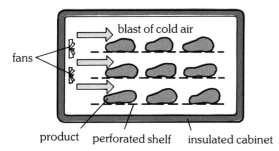

A **fluidized bed freezer** also blows a blast of cold air over the food, but this time vertically, from *below* the food. Foods like chips and peas float in the stream of air, so freezing is rapid.

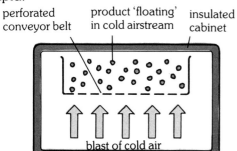

A **plate freezer** works best with food that fits into a regular package. Flat, hollow plates through which a very cold liquid is passing are pressed above and below the packages.

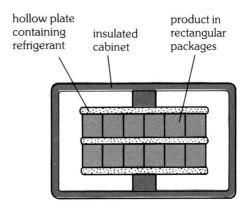

A **cryogenic freezer** sprays harmless liquid gas on to the food. The gas can be carbon dioxide, at −78°C, or nitrogen at −196°C.

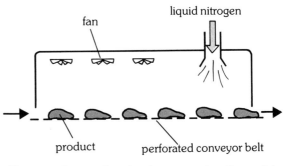

You can freeze food at home, using the cold, still air in your **chest or upright freezer**.

Ice-crystal formation during freezing

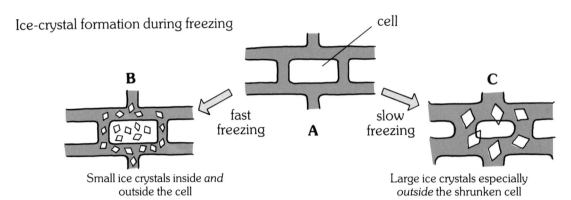

B — Small ice crystals inside *and* outside the cell

fast freezing **A** slow freezing

C — Large ice crystals especially *outside* the shrunken cell

The faster the freezing, the better the quality of the food. As the food cools down, the water in the cells freezes at about −2°C. But the ice crystals do not all form at once: it can take anything from a minute to 48 hours for all the water to freeze, depending on the method used and the size of the food. While the ice crystals are forming, the temperature of the food does not fall but stays at around −2°C. This period is called the *latent heat period*.

If the latent heat period is very short (freezing is very fast), then ice crystals in the food are small both inside and outside the cells. But if for the same size of food the latent heat period is long, then large ice crystals form outside the cell. The cell shrinks and the crystals might pierce the cell wall.

When the food thaws and the ice crystals melt, the shrunken cell in C can never return to what it was like before freezing, and the sharp ice crystals will have pierced the cell walls so that the contents of the cell come into contact with air. The texture, taste and nutritional quality are all affected by slow freezing.

After the latent heat period, the temperature continues to fall, and the food should be stored below −18°C.

The fastest freezing is cryogenic, followed by plate, then blast, then chest. But it depends very much on the size of the food, so the fluidized bed freezing can also be very rapid because the pieces of food are so small.

Workshop

1 Freezing does not kill bacteria in food, though it reduces the numbers a little. When the food is thawed it is even more nutritious for bacteria because of the pierced cells. Draw a poster, with an appropriate slogan, to discourage people from refreezing frozen food.

2 Look carefully at Anant's and Alex's meals. How would you rate their nutritional value? What changes would you suggest to make sure they conform to NACNE guidelines?

3 a Write a five-point plan that must be followed when cooking, chilling/freezing and thawing, to ensure good hygiene.

 b Using your five-point plan, develop a main-course dish and a sweet that Alex could prepare on Friday, chill in his refrigerator overnight and serve on Saturday. Then develop a different main course dish and a sweet that Anant could prepare, freeze, and serve the following week.

4 To observe the effects of freezing on the cellular structure of food, cut a cube of potato, about 2 cm × 2 cm × 2 cm. Freeze it overnight, then put it on a plate and allow to thaw at room temperature. Observe what happens (the colour, texture and appearance) and explain what you see.

5 Test cooking instructions by buying two samples of chilled, ready-to-eat lasagne. Record the temperature of each sample, then cook one in a conventional oven and one in a microwave oven (make sure the dish is not metal), following instructions exactly. Then measure the temperature of the lasagne in the middle. It should be at least 70°C in both cases. (Note: you should not use a mercury thermometer to take the temperature of food. Use, for example, an ESMI thermometer from British Gas.)

Not a drop . . .

1 Drying is one of the oldest methods of food preservation. Bacteria and *enzymes* can spoil food but they need plenty of water in order to be active. Removing the water does not destroy them, but as long as the food is dry they cannot harm it. In hot countries fish, meat, fruit and vegetables are **sun dried**. But it is a slow method, the food shrinks, and it can be difficult to reconstitute. Insects can attack the food during drying too.

2 Most drying involves a stream of warm air passing over the food, carrying away molecules of water.

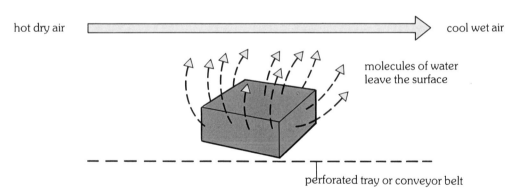

hot dry air ⟶ cool wet air

molecules of water leave the surface

perforated tray or conveyor belt

The food dries quickly as long as the water molecules can leave the surface easily, but after a while the outside layers will be dry (and may have shrunk) but the centre is still wet.

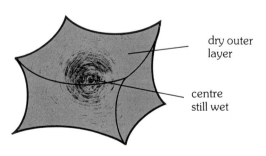

dry outer layer

centre still wet

There is a danger that the outside will now get *too* dry and that no more water will be able to evaporate. This means that the drying must be carefully controlled or the quality of the food will be very poor.

3 Food dries more quickly if it is in small pieces.

Food is heated during drying, so nutrients might be lost.

Blanching is needed before drying to destroy enzymes.

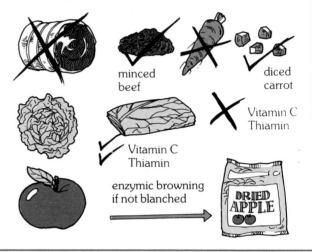

minced beef

diced carrot

Vitamin C Thiamin

Vitamin C Thiamin

enzymic browning if not blanched

DRIED APPLE

4 The simplest method of artificial drying is to use a **kiln**. This is traditionally used for hops and seasonal vegetables.

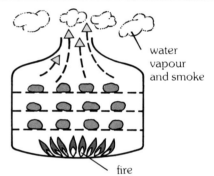

water vapour and smoke

product on perforated shelves

fire

5 Another fairly simple method is to use a **tunnel drier**. The food is on a conveyor belt or on trolleys and hot dry air is blown over it.

TUNNEL

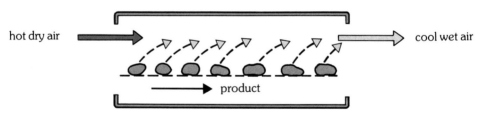

hot dry air

cool wet air

product

Or, using the same principle, a **fluidized bed drier**.

Hot dry air is blown *through* the product, which 'floats' in the air stream. The food should be in small pieces so that it dries quickly to give a good quality product.

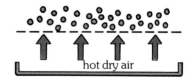

hot dry air

6 For liquids, a **spray drier** is used.

The liquid is sprayed into a very large cone into which hot air is blown. The droplets dry very quickly and the dry product falls to the bottom of the cone. Sometimes, e.g. with milk, the product is *too* dry and has to be re-wetted a little so that it will mix easily with water.

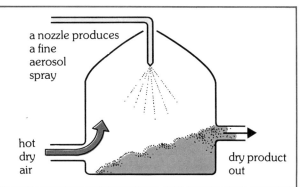

a nozzle produces a fine aerosol spray

hot dry air

dry product out

7 A method of producing dried food of much better quality is **accelerated freeze drying.**

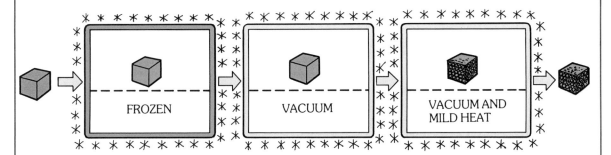

FROZEN

VACUUM

VACUUM AND MILD HEAT

The food is first frozen, by any of the usual methods, then it is put in a chamber from which air is removed so that the food is under very low pressure. It is heated slightly, while still in the vacuum chamber, and the ice *sublimes* – it goes straight from ice to vapour without becoming water. Then air is let into the chamber and the food is packaged. A very dry product is obtained, with no shrinkage. It has a 'honeycomb' structure and is very easy to rehydrate. But it can be fragile.

Workshop

1 Choose a meal that can be bought both dried and frozen, such as chilli-con-carne or beef curry with rice. Find a recipe for the same dish. Prepare the fresh, frozen and dried versions and compare them for:
a price per portion   e taste
b portion size   f appearance
c time to prepare   g overall acceptability
d convenience
Draw a poster to communicate your results to the rest of the class.

2 How convenient *is* dried food? Look in the store cupboard at home and list all the dried foods you can find. Write a comment next to each item on the list, for example on advantages and disadvantages, and state its uses. Is the food available in any other form? If so, why has the dried one been bought?

3 Write a few lines about each of the following, in relation to dried food:
(a) enzymes (b) blanching (c) vitamins
(d) reconstitution (e) packaging (f) storage
(g) wetability.

4 Work in a team of four. You have been asked to make suggestions for a new dried food product. The brief is that it should be unusual (nothing quite like it already in the shops), convenient, savoury, and should appeal particularly to young people. Present your ideas, showing evidence for likely success, and include a mock-up of a possible label.

Be a careful consumer

Legislation for consumers

The main piece of legislation which protects consumers is the Sale of Goods Act 1979. This act lays down three main rules:

1 Goods must be **as described**. If a jumper is labelled "all wool" it must not contain any other fibre.
2 Goods must be **of merchantable quality**. This means that they must work properly and must not be damaged. A dress is not of merchantable quality if the hem is falling down.
3 Goods must be **fit for their normal purpose**. Dressmaking scissors are not fit for their normal purpose if they are not sharp enough to cut fabric.

  Goods covered include those bought in sales, street markets, by mail order and from door-to-door salesmen.

How the law works

If you buy any article which is faulty (not of merchantable quality), does not work or does not do the job adequately (not fit for its normal purpose), or is not as described, then you have rights as a consumer. If you act correctly and promptly you may:

- Reject the goods and get your money back.
- Get a cash payment to make up the difference between what you paid and the reduced value of the faulty item.
- Receive a replacement or free repair.

Knowing your rights as a consumer and knowing how to complain correctly can make problems easy to rectify. Remember that most shopkeepers are honest and helpful and want to retain the goodwill of their customers – but you have a duty to be fair and honest.

How to complain

1 Stop using or wearing goods.
2 Complain quickly.
3 Return to the shop with the article and receipt.
4 Ask to see the manager or the person in charge.
5 Be polite, firm and calm.
6 Be sure of the facts and stick to them.
7 Be clear about what you want: your money back, replacement or repair.
8 If you complain in writing keep a copy of the letter. If you telephone keep details of date, time, person with whom you spoke and what was said.
9 Goods returned by post should be sent by recorded delivery and the record of delivery kept.
10 If the goods are heavy or bulky (a wardrobe or washing machine), write to or telephone the firm asking them to collect the goods or to inspect them in your home.

Extra help

If you have a consumer problem which you need help with, look in the telephone directory for the local Consumer Advice Centre, the Citizen's Advice Bureau or the Trading Standards Department.

Mark decides to spend his birthday money on a personal stereo, so he goes into town on Saturday and buys one from a large electrical store. When Mark gets home he finds that the stereo is faulty. It will not rewind. He immediately puts it back in the box with the receipt. On Monday after school, Mark returns to the shop.

Mark was a careful consumer. He knew the law and his rights and was able to obtain a replacement personal stereo without any difficulty. It might not have been as easy if Mark had lost the receipt and thrown the box away or had tried to remove the back of the stereo to repair it himself.

Role play

Act out some complaints procedures in class. Choose whether you want to play the customer or the shop assistant. The products returned are:

a Pair of shoes with broken heel, bought the previous week, receipt kept.

b Dress worn to a party, washed, customer decides she doesn't like it and returns to the shop with the receipt.

c School bag with broken strap, bought six months ago, no receipt.

What would you expect the outcomes to be?

Customers: Describe your reactions to helpful and unhelpful shop assistants.

Assistants: Describe your reactions to polite customers and unpleasant customers.

Remember

Keep the receipt and the packaging until you are sure that the goods are satisfactory.

Be polite and make sure that you know your facts.

Be fair. You are not entitled to anything if you change your mind about wanting the item or if you damaged it yourself or if you got it as a present (the buyer must claim).

Workshop

1 Name the main law which protects consumers, and explain how this law works.

2 Design a flow chart to show the correct procedure to use when making a complaint.

3 Invite someone from the local Trading Standards Office to talk to your class about consumer law.

4 Do you think that consumers are well protected and get a good deal? If possible, illustrate your answer by giving examples of consumer problems your family has had to deal with.

5 Visit your local Citizen's Advice Bureau or Consumer Centre and pick up some leaflets designed to help consumers, especially leaflets produced by the Office of Fair Trading.

145

Safe food: The law

There are strict laws which apply to the manufacture and sale of food. The main laws are the Food Safety Act 1990 (England and Wales) and the Food and Drugs Act 1956 (Scotland). Selling or stocking food which is unfit for human consumption is a criminal offence.

Preparing food

It is an offence to prepare food for sale in any place where there is a risk of its being contaminated.

- The room where food is prepared must be clean, well ventilated and in good repair.
- There must be hand-washing facilities.
- First-aid materials must be available.
- Rules about the cleanliness and siting of lavatories must be obeyed.

Handling and selling food

Those who handle or sell food must be clean and wear clean clothing. Food must not be placed anywhere where it might become contaminated, such as above the load line of a freezer. A catering business must keep perishable food (meat, fish, milk and eggs) at below 5°C or above 63°C – in other words *cold* food must be kept *cold* and *hot* food must be kept *hot* (read about the growth of bacteria and temperature on page 124). Perishable foods which are sold loose (not wrapped or in containers) must be kept covered or screened when displayed for sale. Think about the glass delicatessen counters at supermarkets.

Anyone intending to prepare food for sale must tell the local Environmental Health Department. The regulations even apply if you are preparing and selling food for charity, so if you make and sell cakes in school to raise money for a school fund you must follow the hygiene rules.

If you have a complaint about food bought in a shop or about a dirty cafe or restaurant, contact the local Environmental Health Department (look in the telephone directory).

Workshop

1 Visit your local supermarket and make a report about the handling and storage of food for sale. You may like to use headings: General Cleanliness; Cleanliness and Appearance of Assistants; Storage and Handling of Food at delicatessen counter; Loading of Food in freezers.

2 You buy a meat pie from a baker's. When you get home you discover that the pie is mouldy. Explain what action you would take.

3 You are buying a cream cake from a supermarket. The assistant licks her fingers before putting the cake into a bag. What should you do?

Is real money going out of fashion?

How much real money do we spend? When we buy goods we can pay by cash ("real money"), by cheque, by credit card or by EFTPOS card. There is an increasing number of credit cards available ("plastic money"). Most people now have their wages paid directly into their bank or building society accounts, and see only a fraction of it in real money. Is real money going out of fashion? Will notes and coins disappear?

There are two main ways of buying goods:
1 Buying Outright — Buy now, pay now.
2 Borrow Money — Buy now, pay later.

Buying outright

Buying outright and paying immediately may be the easiest and cheapest way of paying for goods. You may pay by cash, cheque or EFTPOS.

Cash If you pay by cash it is quick and easy – but be careful when carrying large sums of money around. You can sometimes get a discount for paying by cash.

Cheque You can have a cheque account at a bank, building society or post office. If you have one of these accounts you can pay for goods by writing a cheque, as long as you have a cheque guarantee card. This guarantees that cheques up to £50 will be paid by the bank. Cheques must be filled in correctly. Always write in ink. Write the amount in words and figures as close to the left as possible. Draw a horizontal line through any remaining spaces (so that nothing can be added to your cheque later). If you make any alterations add your initials above them (to prove it was altered by yourself). Some shops now have tills which print your cheques for you. All you have to do is sign the cheque, once you have read it to make sure the information printed on it is correct.

EFTPOS A newer way of paying immediately is by EFTPOS, which is Electronic Funds Transfer at Point Of Sale. If you pay by EFTPOS you have a card which looks like a credit card and is called a 'switch' card. On the back of the card is a magnetic strip which stores details of your bank account. When the card is placed in a machine in a shop your account is instantly debited. This type of payment is likely to be very popular at supermarkets and petrol stations where it will save a lot of time.

A switch card

Front

Reverse

Buying on credit

Buying on credit is when you buy something and pay for it over a period of time. In other words, you are borrowing money, which can be an expensive way to buy goods. Buying on

147

credit or borrowing money is now an acceptable way of obtaining goods, but this was not always so.

Neither a borrower, nor a lender be;
For loan oft loses both itself and a friend.
And borrowing dulls the edge of husbandry.

Shakespeare, *Hamlet*

The Consumer Credit Act 1974

This protects you when you buy on credit. It controls who can offer credit, the way they can advertise, the information they must give before you sign, the procedure for ending a credit agreement, the steps a trader can take if you default, and almost every aspect of almost every kind of credit transaction up to £15,000. The act covers most forms of credit including cash loans, credit sales and hire purchase.

APR

All traders who give credit must work out the total charge for credit in terms of an Annual Percentage Rate of charge (APR). APR is a measurement of the total cost for credit. It includes the interest on the loan itself and any other charges you may have to pay. Credit traders must calculate APR according to a standard formula laid down in regulations under the Consumer Credit Act. This means that you can use APR to compare different forms of credit. The lower the APR, the cheaper the credit will be.

Examples of APR

The examples on the right show how a television , cash price £375, might be bought from the same store, using different types of credit.

Interest-free credit

Shops often advertise interest-free credit. By law, the total repayments must not exceed the cash price, but check the cash price – you may be able to buy the item more cheaply elsewhere.

Use credit wisely

Buying on credit can be very useful, but you must be careful. It is easy to take out too many loans and then not be able to keep up the repayments. Think before you borrow.
Never borrow for goods you do not want.
Never over-commit yourself.
Always check the APR to find the best deal.
Always borrow from reputable companies.
Always read the agreement carefully and check the figures for yourself.

Different forms of credit

Hire purchase or conditional sale   This is a loan arranged to tie in with a particular purchase. You pay a deposit, take the goods and repay the rest by instalments. A hire purchase (HP) agreement must show clearly the cash price, the total hire purchase price and the amount of each instalment. You do not own the goods until the last instalment is paid, so you must not sell or dispose of them. However, once you have paid one third of the total amount payable, the seller cannot take the goods back without a court order.

Credit sales   You have to pay by instalments, but you usually own the goods immediately you have paid the deposit. This means that goods cannot be taken back, but you can be sued if you fail to pay.

Hire purchase arranged through the store
Cash price £375 to be repaid by
24 equal monthly instalments of   £20.93
                Total amount payable = £502.32
                             APR = 34.2%

Personal loan from a bank
Loan £375 to be repaid by 24
equal monthly instalments of   £18.61
                Total amount payable = £446.64
                             APR = 18.8%

The store's own budget account
Customer chooses to pay £20 a month
(which gives a credit limit of £480)
                      APR = 29.8% as stated
To clear the account will require 24 payments of £20
plus £8.88 taken from the 25th payment.
                Total amount payable = £488.88

Bank or building society loans If you have a bank or building society account you may be able to borrow money from them to buy goods. Check the APR to see if you are getting a good deal.

Plastic money There are three main types of credit cards:

Bank credit cards: such as the Access and Visa cards. You can use these cards to pay for goods up to your credit limit. You get a statement each month which shows how much you owe and what the minimum payment is. If you choose to pay off only some of what you owe, then you have to pay interest on what is left. If you pay your account in full each month you do not have to pay any interest and you have the advantage of six weeks' free credit and the convenience of shopping with a credit card. Some banks charge an annual fee.

A bank credit card

Charge cards: For example American Express and Diner's Club cards. These cards give the advantage of paying by credit card, but you have to pay the account in full each month. There is no interest but you have to pay an annual fee.

A charge card

Shop cards: Most large retail chains now have their own form of credit card. The advantage to the shop is that it encourages people to shop there. The advantage to the customer is that you do not have to write cheques and you can spread the payments. Some shop cards work like credit cards, some work like charge cards and some are budget accounts. For budget accounts you have to make a regular payment each month and are then allowed to buy goods worth up to twelve times this amount (or some other multiple of the amount). If you are in credit on this account (there is money saved up) you do not get any interest.

A shop card

Where to get help

If you have a credit problem or need advice about credit, there are several places where you can get help. Look in the telephone directory for your local Citizen's Advice Bureau, Trading Standards Department, Consumer Advice Centre, Money Advice Centre, or Neighbourhood Law Centre. The advice is free.

How old do you have to be to take out credit?

Generally you have to be over 18 to apply for credit like HP, credit cards and bank loans. Sometimes you have to be over 21. At any age under 25 you may be asked for a guarantor. A survey in 1989 for the Office of Fair Trading and Radio 1 revealed that 71% of 18–20 year olds now use one or more types of credit.

What does it mean?

Guarantor:
Someone who will take over the payments on a credit arrangement if you are unable to pay.

Interest:
An additional amount of money you have to pay in most types of credit agreements in order to borrow the cash or buy the goods. Interest rates can vary.

Security:
Security is what you have to be prepared to lose if you can't keep up the repayments. If a loan is secured on property and you fail to keep up the repayments you could lose your home.

Creditors:
People you owe money to.

Debtors:
People who owe money.

Workshop

1 Make a summary chart for buying goods outright. Copy the chart below into your book, and fill it in. Each space needs to be large enough for 3–4 sentences.

BUYING OUTRIGHT		
Advantages		**Disadvantages**
Cash		
Cheque		
EFTPOS		

2 What is plastic money? Write a paragraph to explain how each of the following types of credit cards work.
   a Bank credit cards like Barclaycard
   b Charge cards such as American Express
   c Shop cards like the Boots card.

3 Your parents are intending to buy a new freezer on credit.
   a Explain how each of these forms of credit could be used to buy the freezer: Hire purchase, Credit sale and Bank or Building Society loan.
   b When examining credit agreements with your parents you see APR quoted. What does APR mean, and why is it important to compare the APR of different credit deals?

4 Study the examples of APR on page 148 and answer these questions.
   a Which is the cheapest credit deal?
   b Which is the most expensive credit deal?
   c What is the difference in price between the cheapest credit deal and the most expensive credit deal?
   d What is the difference between the cash price and the most expensive credit deal?

5 Explain the problems which could arise if too many goods are bought on credit, and say where people can get advice on credit matters.

The lure of the supermarket

- A supermarket is a large self-service store which stocks between 3000 and 5000 separate items of grocery.
- The first supermarket to open in Britain was a Co-op store which opened in London in 1942. But supermarkets were rare before the 1950s.
- American surveys suggest that more than two-thirds of supermarket purchases are unplanned or "impulse" buys.
- There are six major supermarket chains: Co-op, Sainsburys, Presto, Tesco, Asda and Safeway. These six chains sell approximately half of all the grocery bought in this country.

How supermarkets persuade us to buy

It is not by accident that more than two-thirds of supermarket purchases are impulse buys – the supermarkets plan it that way. There are many ways in which supermarket customers can be influenced to buy goods. These ways of influencing customers can be grouped under two headings:

1 Design of the supermarket

The supermarket is designed to be bright, colourful and attractive, a place that we enjoy spending some time in. It may have a coffee bar to encourage us to make shopping a leisurely outing.

Aisles of shelves run longitudinally down the supermarket to encourage us to walk past as many shelves as possible.

Ventilation makes sure that bread smells are wafted into the supermarket but fish smells are wafted out.

Trolleys are large, and a few purchases in the bottom of them look lost so we feel we have to fill the trolley.

2 Positioning of goods

"Eye level is buy level". Foods with the highest profit are placed at eye level.

Basic items may be placed at the back or far end of the store so that we have to walk past lots of other tempting goods to reach them.

Fruit and vegetables are often placed near the entrance because they are colourful and attractive, and also because they are commonly-purchased items, so we get into a buying frame of mind early on.

Foods may be placed in groups with other foods. Salad cream may be placed above a freezer unit which contains food often eaten with salads, such as quiches and pizzas.

Sweets and magazines are placed near the checkout to tempt us as we are waiting in the queue. Sweets may be placed at low level where children will see them and want them.

Powerful giants

Supermarkets may have many ways to persuade us to buy more, but sometimes they act in our interest by responding to our demand for healthier foods and supplying us with healthy eating information. The major supermarket chains are now so powerful that they are able to dictate to the food manufacturers. A recent example of this is that most of the major supermarket chains have asked food manufacturers to use less artificial additives in foods. The large supermarket chains are also able to insist on standards of quality, and to negotiate special prices from the food manufacturers. They are able to do this because of the huge quantities they order. If they took their custom elsewhere it could put the food manufacturer out of business.

Supermarkets can influence the way we eat

We can influence supermarkets

How to Get the Best From Your Supermarket

1 Take a shopping list with you and try to stick to it, especially if funds are limited.

2 Buy large quantities if possible. Larger packs are usually better value for money.

3 Compare prices of different brands. Some supermarkets display unit prices to help you to compare prices, for example the cost of soap powder per kilogram.

4 Look for special offers. Some supermarkets reduce items when they are close to the sell-by date, but remember that they need using quickly.

5 Buy fruits and vegetables when they are in season. They will be cheaper and better quality.

6 Read nutrition information labels and look for nutrition information leaflets and recipe leaflets.

New technology in the supermarket

Supermarkets have been quick to make use of new technology in order to become more efficient. Here are some examples of how supermarkets have used new technology.

Automatic Checking Out   Laser scanning of bar codes gives the customer a detailed print-out of purchases, speeds up the queues at the check-outs and also helps the supermarket with stock control. The computers linked to the check-outs give the store a record of foods sold. This makes re-ordering of stock easier and it can also be used to analyse the effectiveness of advertising or special offers. A supermarket can use the information stored in the computer to see if yoghurt sales went up when it was on special offer or to compare the types of food bought on different days of the week.

Automated Payment   It is now possible to pay by EFTPOS at supermarkets. This speeds up the check-out process and is more convenient (see page 147 for more about EFTPOS).

The Future   Supermarkets may offer a phone-in service in which goods are ordered by phone and delivered the same day. We already have the technology to go one better than this and provide computer shopping. Details of goods available are displayed on a screen and a linked home computer transmits the orders to the supermarket.

Workshop

1 Make a list of the ways in which supermarkets influence us into making impulse buys.

2 Complete this paragraph about the advantages of supermarket shopping, using the words given below the paragraph.
Supermarket prices are usually _____ and a _____ range of goods is available. There is a rapid turnover of stock and so food is _____. Most people like to _____ their own goods. Supermarkets are very _____ conscious.
FRESH, SELECT, WIDE, HYGIENE, COMPETITIVE

3 Collect a selection of supermarket healthy eating leaflets. How useful are they? How much advertising do they contain?

4 Write a short essay (one side of A4 paper) with the title The Power of the Giant Supermarket Chains.

5 Some large supermarket chains will give conducted tours to school groups. Arrange to visit a large supermarket to find out about the new technology used in that store and also about the positioning of goods on the shelves.

Open all hours

As we saw in the last unit, the six major supermarket chains sell approximately half of all grocery sold in this country. The other half of all food sold is sold by a variety of retailers such as small supermarket chains, independent grocers, specialist shops, butchers, greengrocers, fishmongers and market stalls. Let's look at these shops.

The small supermarket

Mr Wilson is the manager of a Supavalu store. There are twelve others in the area, most of which are in small local shopping precincts. Opening hours are 9 a.m. to 5.30 p.m. Monday to Saturday, with late opening until 7 p.m. on Thursdays and Fridays. There is a total staff of eight, including some who work part time. Mr Wilson thinks that his prices are competitive, but because his store is small he is not able to stock a wide range of goods. Most customers live near the store. There is no delivery service.

Key points   Good prices • Convenient for local houses • Normal opening hours • Limited range of stock • No deliveries

The independent grocer

Mr and Mrs Singh own and run a small grocery shop. They live on the premises. They belong to a group of independent retailers who band together to get better prices from the wholesalers, but in spite of this their prices are still higher than supermarket prices. Because their shop is small they are not able to keep a large stock, so they concentrate on stocking basic items. Opening hours are long – usually 8 a.m. to 8 p.m. Monday to Saturday and 9 a.m. to 1 p.m. on Sunday. Most of their customers live locally and are regular customers. Mr and Mrs Singh like to chat to their customers, especially the elderly ones who like to take their time over the shopping. Customers can serve themselves or be served. There is a delivery service.

Key points   Prices generally higher than supermarkets • Limited range of stock • Long opening hours • Convenient for local houses • Friendly personal service • Self-service • Delivery service

The specialist shop

Bill Brown and Son is a family-run butcher's shop in the high street of a small town. Most customers are regulars. The Browns pride themselves on offering good service to their customers, and will bone joints and prepare cuts of meat to the customers' requirements. They also advise customers on the cooking of meat and best buys available. They keep a fairly large stock of fresh meat and a large stock of frozen meat, so are able to provide most cuts of meat. They make their own sausages. Their prices are competitive. They will take orders by phone and will deliver.

Specialist shops offering a similar service   Greengrocers, fishmongers, bakers.

Key points   Offer expert service and advice
- Personal service   ● Competitive prices
- Delivery service   ● No self-service

BROWN & SON BUTCHERS

Workshop

1 Make a chart of the advantages and disadvantages of each type of retail outlet described on this page.
2 Bearing in mind the information on supermarkets on p. 151, write down where you would shop and why in each of the following circumstances
   a You need to stock up on basic items.
   b You need some meat for a barbeque, advice about the best type of steak to buy and some spare ribs cut.
   c You need some fresh vegetables but are short of money. You also need advice about what is in season and what is good value for money.

The market stall

Mr and Mrs Murphy rent a stall in a city market on Tuesdays, Fridays and Saturdays. Because they have low overheads (no heating, lighting etc.), they are able to offer cheap prices. They have a rapid turnover of goods and have to buy fresh stock each day. The Fruit Basket sells mainly basic fruits, but other traders in the market sell unusual fruits and vegetables. Murphy's fruit is always good quality but some stalls display the best goods and sell inferior ones.

Key points   Cheap prices   ●   Fresh foods, but quality may vary   ●   No self-service
● Hygiene may not be good on stalls selling perishable foods

d It is 7.30 p.m. on Saturday evening and you have run out of sugar and teabags.
   e You need plantains and sweet potatoes for a Caribbean dish.
3 How good are your local food shopping facilities? Make an evaluation of them using the following headings: Prices, Variety of shops available, Opening hours, Range of goods available, Service offered.

Further Research
Conduct a shopping-basket survey in your area. Compile a list of basic food items and compare the cost of these items at different shops and supermarkets in your area. This could be done as a class exercise. Present your results on a large chart to be displayed on the notice board.

Food labels

The 1984 Food Labelling Regulations require pre-packed foods to be labelled with:

1 The name

The product name must describe the food. If a manufacturer gives food a fancy name the label must describe what it is, for example Chocolate Delight must also be described as chocolate and cream dessert. Strawberry yoghurt must contain strawberries, but strawberry flavour yoghurt does not need to contain strawberries – it may just contain flavouring.

2 The ingredients

The ingredients must be listed in descending order of inclusion by weight, so the ingredient present in the largest quantity will be first on the list. If added water accounts for more than 5% of the contents it counts as an ingredient and must be shown on the list. Additives must be shown by name or by E number, which is an officially accepted code which applies throughout Europe.

3 A datemark

Most foods are now datemarked. The main exceptions are long-life foods (foods lasting longer than 18 months). The datemark is the date up to and including which food will remain at its best if it is stored correctly. Look for the words "Best Before" or "Sell By".

4 Storage instructions

The label must give instructions for the storage of the food.

5 Name and address

The name and address of the manufacturer, packager or seller within the EEC must be on the label.

6 Place of origin

If a food is imported and then packed by a British manufacturer it may be misleading if the country of origin is not mentioned.

Weight — 225g e

BEST BEFORE END SEPT. 91 — Datemark

Name — Auntie Betty's
Homebake Luxury Sponge Mix
Just add one egg & filling!

Required

Ingredients — Ingredients

Nutrition Information

Preparation — To Prepare

To Mix

Picture of product — To Bake

Store in a cool place — Storage instructions

Auntie Betty's Quick Foods Ltd.
Mill Lane
Westhampton
ENGLAND — Name and address

7 Preparation

There should be instructions for preparation if this is necessary, for example in the case of a cake mix.

8 Special claims

Foods which claim to have special properties, for example "Rich in Vitamin C" should be labelled with extra information to support this claim.

9 Quantity or weight

Most foods are labelled with the weight in grams. An "e" after the weight indicates that the manufacturer is complying with the average system of weights and measures which is common throughout the European Community.

Is it good enough?

Many people feel that the information which is compulsory is not enough and that we should have more detailed information about the foods we eat. A nutrition report about heart disease (the COMA report) recommends that the percentage by weight of fat and the proportion of saturated and polyunsaturated fat should be shown on the label. This would help people to reduce the amount of fat eaten in their diet, which may help to reduce heart disease. Labels do not have to show the amounts of fat, sugar and fibre. Nutrition labels showing actual amounts of nutrients present might help people to plan healthy diets. They would also help people who have special diets for health reasons.

Many supermarkets and food manufacturers are giving us detailed nutrition labels, but this is voluntary. Here are some examples of voluntary nutrition labels:

NUTRITION
Sainsbury's Muesli is a good source of dietary fibre. This is the roughage in food and is needed for a healthy digestive system

	TYPICAL VALUES PER 100g (3½oz)	TYPICAL VALUES PER SERVING 60g/2oz
ENERGY	345 K/CALORIES 1465 K/JOULES	205 K/CALORIES 880 K/JOULES
PROTEIN	9.8g	5.9g
CARBOHYDRATE AVAILABLE	66.0g	39.6g
TOTAL FAT	6.5g	3.9g
DIETARY FIBRE	8.0g	4.8g
ADDED SUGAR	8.5g	5.1g
ADDED SALT	0.4g	0.2g

This pack contains approximately 8 servings

NUTRITION

Bran Flakes with Sultanas are a useful source of dietary fibre. They also contain significant amounts of the B vitamins, thiamin, riboflavin and niacin which the body needs every day to help turn the food we eat into energy and iron, which forms a vital part of red blood cells

CEREAL ONLY WITHOUT MILK OR SUGAR

AVERAGE COMPOSITION	PER 30g (1oz) serving	PER 100g (3½oz)
Energy	388kJ/ 93kcal	1293kJ/ 309kcal
Fat	0.5g	1.5
Protein	2.2g	7.3g
Available Carbohydrate	20.9g	69.6g
Fibre	3.9g	13.0g
Added Salt	0.4g	1.4g
Added Sugars	3.7g	12.4g
MINERALS/ VITAMINS	% RECOMMENDED DAILY AMOUNT	
Thiamin B$_1$	23%	0.9mg
Riboflavin B$_2$	23%	1.2mg
Niacin	20%	12.0mg
Vitamin D	24%	2.0µg
Iron	38%	15.0mg

THIS PACK CONTAINS APPROX. 12 SERVINGS

INFORMATION

Some supermarkets have also tried to make it easier for us to choose healthy products by providing us with simple nutritional information. Here are some examples:

HIGH FIBRE
LOW FAT

Workshop

1 Collect five empty food packets and examine the way that they are labelled. Make a checklist of the nine labels required on foods, and put a tick or a brief comment against each label as you identify it on the packet. Now write your conclusions about each label you have studied.

Your conclusions   Does the label contain all the legal requirements? Are these easy to find and easy to understand? Are the instructions for use easy to understand? Does the label or box contain any advertising? Does the picture on the label or box accurately depict the product?

2 a Collect a selection of empty breakfast cereal boxes with nutrition labels. Using the labels, make a consumer investigation into cereals. Make a chart for your results (see below).
   b From your results make conclusions about which cereals are best to form part of a healthy diet, and explain why.
   c Try similar investigations into yoghurt and bread.

	Name of product	Name of product	Add another column for each cereal
Values per 100 g			
Energy			
Protein			
Carbohydrate			
Fat			
Dietary fibre			
Added sugar			
Added salt			

The additives debate

Facts about additives

- Additives are substances that preserve food or change it in some way.
- There are approximately 3500 additives that food manufacturers use.
- Some additives are natural (found in nature). Lecithin (E322) is made from soya beans and is used to stop food separating.
- There are 280 E numbers.
- The 1990 Food Safety Act makes it illegal to add anything to food which would damage health.

What additives are used for

Additives can be put into four main groups, according to whether they affect the taste, texture, colour or shelf-life of foods.

1. Taste

Flavourings are the most common type of additive. There are about 3000 of them. Flavourings are not at present controlled by additive regulations. If flavouring has been used in food the label will say flavour or flavouring without giving its chemical name.

Flavour Enhancers are not flavourings, but substances that make existing flavours in the food seem stronger. The best known is monosodium glutamate (E621). Flavour enhancers are used in a wide range of savoury foods.

Artificial Sweeteners such as saccharin, and aspartame may be used in foods for slimmers and diabetics as well as other foods.

2. Texture

Emulsifiers and Stabilisers Emulsifiers mix together ingredients like oil and water, which would normally separate. Stabilisers prevent them from separating again. Both are used in low-fat spreads and many other sweet and savoury foods. For example, E407 (carrageenan, Irish moss) is a natural extract of seaweed and is used in quick-setting jelly mix, ice-creams and desserts.

Thickeners As the name suggests, thickeners act like flour or cornflour in a sauce. For example, E412 (guar gum) is used in packet soups and meringue mixes. Other popular thickeners seen on labels are modified starches.

Anticaking agents stop lumps forming in powdery foods. A common example is magnesium carbonate (E504) which is used to keep salt running freely.

Gelling agents are used to make jams, desserts and similar foods set. For example, E440 (pectin) is used in jams, jellies, marmalades, puddings and desserts.

Raising agents which, like baking powder, make food rise. For example, E500 (sodium bicarbonate).

3. Colour

There are 58 permitted natural and artificial colours. The commonest is caramel (E150) which is made by over-cooking sugar. Many colours are obtained from plants, for example, E140 (chlorophyll a green colour). There are 20 permitted artificial colours, for example, E102 (tartrazine – a yellow colour).

4. Shelf-life

Preservatives help food keep longer – they delay the spoilage of food by preventing the growth of microbes.

Antioxidants stop oils and fats from combining with oxygen and going rancid, for example E320, butylated hydroxyanisole (BHA), used in cheese spread, beef-stock cubes, biscuits and margarine.

E numbers

In order to have a system for listing additive ingredients, most of the permitted additives have been given a number. Of the permitted additives, 280 have been given an E number. This means that the additive has been approved by the European Community. Since 1986 additives must be listed by type and chemical name or number in the ingredients list, for example PRESERVATIVE SORBIC ACID or PRESERVATIVE E200. It is possible to look up E numbers and find out their chemical names and more details about them.

Find out more about E numbers

Send away for "Food Additives: The Balanced Approach", free from the Ministry of Agriculture, Fisheries and Food. A useful book is *E For Additives, The Complete E Number Guide*, by M. Hanssen and J. Marsden, published by Thorsons. Some supermarket chains have also produced free literature.

The problem with Es

There has recently been much public interest and concern about the additives used in our food, and E numbers have got a very bad name. There are advantages and disadvantages of the use of additives. The consumer needs to be aware of what additives are used in foods and why they are used, and foods need to be properly labelled so that anyone wishing to avoid any additives can do so. Many food manufacturers have reduced additives in their foods or have replaced artificial additives with natural additives.

For
- Food looks colourful and more appealing.
- Food lasts longer and food-poisoning may be prevented.
- Many processed foods would not be available, e.g. low-fat spreads.
- Their use is becoming more strictly regulated so that we do not consume more than is necessary.

Against
- Some additives cause allergies in some people.
- Many are used for cosmetic reasons only, e.g. colouring.

Workshop

1 Study each of the following ingredients lists. List the additives used in each product. Explain why each additive is used. Are all the additives in the four products necessary, in your opinion?

Instant mashed potato

> Potatoes (97%), Salt (2·3%), Emulsifier (E471), Acidity regulator (E450a), Vitamin C preservative (E222), Antioxidant (E321).

Low-fat spread

> Skimmed milk, Vegetable oil, Hydrogenated vegetable oil, Buttermilk, Caseinates, Salt, Acidity regulators (E325, E331, E339), Emulsifier (E471), Preservative (E202), Flavouring, Vitamins A and D, Colour (E160a).

Instant custard powder

> Sugar, Partially hydrogenated vegetable oil, Dried glucose syrup, Farina, Cornflour, Dried skimmed milk, Lactose, Stabilisers (E415, E340), Caseinates, Salt, Flavouring, Colours (E110, E102, E122, E124).

Sponge cake mix

> Flour, Sugar, Animal and vegetable fats with emulsifier (E471) and Antioxidant (E320), Raising agents (Glucono-delta lactone, Sodium bicarbonate), Cornflour, Salt, Dextrose, Flavourings, Stabiliser (xanthan gum), Colour (crocin extract).

2 Have a class discussion about the use of additives in food.

3 Name the four main categories of additives used in foods and give an example of an E number for each category.

4 Write about the advantages and disadvantages of food additives and give your own opinion on the subject.

Be label literate

There is now a wide range of labels giving information to the consumer. The information given on labels may help us to choose products by advising us of the quality, safety and construction of goods. Labels can also help us to care for goods when we have bought them. Some of the labels frequently found on goods and equipment are described here. Be label literate and be a better informed consumer!

1

2

3

The Kitemark

The Kitemark is the mark of the British Standards Institute. The BSI grants manufacturers a licence to use the Kitemark on a product if they can consistently make the product to standards laid down by the BSI. The number of the standard should appear beneath the Kitemark. The Kitemark is found on a wide range of goods.

The Safety Mark

This mark appears on a number of products which meet the safety requirements of particular British Standards. This mark is often found on portable lighting.

Double Insulation of Electrical Appliances

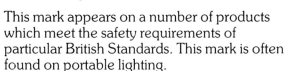

This mark is found on a particular class of electrical goods which are built in a special way – without any provision for earthing but with double insulation and/or reinforced insulation throughout. This mark is often found on hairdryers and vacuum cleaners. It may be seen beside the BEAB mark.

The BEAB Mark

Equipment bearing any of these three marks has been approved as safe by the British Electrotechnicals Approvals board. Each mark is slightly different.

1 This is the old BEAB mark which used to be found on a wide range of electrical equipment. It will now only be found on electric blankets.
2 This is the new safety mark, which will be found on most electrical appliances.
3 This mark means that the product has been tested and approved by another European Approvals Authority to a standard which is broadly equivalent to the British Standard.

Bar Codes

A bar code is a symbol printed on packages which identifies goods in a form which can be read electronically and transmitted to a computer. Computerized checkouts in supermarkets electronically read bar codes, and the scanner transmits the product number to an in-store computer. This relays the product's description and current price back to the checkout, where the information is displayed on a screen, and at the same time printed on the till receipt. The in-store computer then deducts the item from the stock list so that the store knows the quantities of all goods which need to be re-ordered.

Bar code

Part of a computerized till receipt

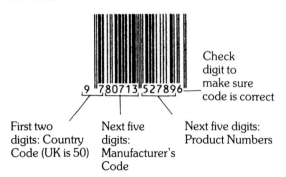

Check digit to make sure code is correct

First two digits: Country Code (UK is 50)

Next five digits: Manufacturer's Code

Next five digits: Product Numbers

MINCED BEEF   1.05
JS PLAICE FLLTS   2.12
STEWING BEEF   2.42
POTATOES 2KG   0.61
GROUND CINNAMON   0.67
TOMATOES IN JCE   0.30
JS YOGURTS X12   2.79
BEANS/SAUSAGE   0.37
JS ITAL LASAGNE   0.57

Flammability of furniture

This square green label means the fabric and filling meet the new regulations.

This label will be used until March 1993 on second-hand furniture which does NOT meet the 1988 regulations.

This label is found on furniture where the filling meets the new regulations. The cover does *not* pass the match test, so a fire-retardant interliner has been used instead.

As for the previous label, BUT a fire-retardant interliner has NOT been used.

Textile labelling

Regulations require that most textile products be labelled with the type of fibre used. If more than one fibre is used then the percentage of each fibre must be shown, for example 65% polyester 35% cotton. These regulations apply to clothes, household textiles, carpets and furniture.

WASH DEEP DYES SEPARATELY

65% POLYESTER 35% COTTON
WASH DEEP DYES BEFORE USE
ALWAYS WASH AND DRY SEPARATELY

MADE IN THE U.K.

TO FIT CHEST

33in

TOUR DE POITRINE

85cm

100% ACRYLIC/ACRYLIQUE

WARM

COLD RINSE
RESHAPE WHILE DAMP
DRY FLAT AWAY
FROM DIRECT HEAT
COOL IRON WHEN DRY
RINCER A L'EAU FROIDE
REMETTRE EN FORME
ENCORE HUMIDE
SECHER A PLAT LOIN D'UNE
SOURCE DE CHALEUR
REPASSER SEC A FER DOUX
H   CA 01295

Textile care labelling

The washing process

 White cotton and linen articles without special finishes

 Cotton, linen or viscose articles without special finishes where colours are fast at 60°C

 Nylon; polyester/cotton mixtures; polyester cotton and viscose articles with special finishes; cotton/acrylic mixtures

 Cotton, linen or viscose articles, where colours are fast at 40°C but not at 60°C·

 Acrylics, acetate and triacetate including mixtures with wool; polyester/wool blends

 Wool, wool mixed with other fibres; silk

 Handwash (Do not machine wash)

 Do not wash

The number in the wash tub indicates the maximum temperature in degrees C which should be used for washing. The bars below the wash tub refer to the amount of washing action which should be used.

No bar normal (maximum) machine action

Bar reduced (medium) machine action

Broken bar much reduced (minimum) machine action

Wash tubs should be labelled as follows:

 wash as cotton

 wash as synthetics

 wash as wool

Tumble drying after washing

A circle in a square indicates that a garment may be tumble dried.

 May be tumble dried

where dots appear –

 means high heat setting

 means low heat setting

 DO NOT TUMBLE DRY

Bleaching

CHLORINE BLEACH MAY BE USED   DO NOT USE CHLORINE BLEACH

Ironing

 WARM IRON
An iron with one dot (.) means cool
An iron with three dots (...) means hot

DO NOT IRON

163

Dry cleaning

The following symbols indicate that a garment should be dry cleaned. The circle may contain letters A, P or F, depending on the requirements or limitations of the article itself. If the circle has a bar beneath it, special treatment is required and advice should be sought from a professional dry cleaner.

 MAY BE DRY CLEANED

 DO NOT DRY CLEAN

The Woolmark

The Woolmark is the International Wool Secretariat's (IWS) certification mark for products made from pure new wool. Manufacturers may be licensed by the IWS to use the mark, providing they meet IWS standards of quality. The mark may be found on carpets, knitting yarns, blankets and clothes.

The Leather Mark

The International Leather Mark is the sign of real leather.

Workshop

1 Explain the importance of labels to the consumer. In what way do they help consumers in their choice of household products?

2 Labels (a) and (b) are from jumpers, and label (c) is from a shirt. Explain the information contained on each label. Labels (a) and (b) could contain another symbol – what is it?

3 Conduct a label survey. Copy the labels in this unit onto small cards, and give each label a number. Show people the cards one at a time and ask them if they know what the label means. Make a simple chart for recording your results. If each person in the class asks five to ten people, the total sample will be quite large and you will be able to make conclusions about how well-informed consumers are.

(a)

```
TO FIT BUST
TOUR DE POITRINE
86cm    34in
```
100% WOOL/LAINE

WARM HAND WASH WARM
DO NOT RUB OR WRING
COLD RINSE
DO NOT TUMBLE DRY
RESHAPE WHILE DAMP
DRY SUPPORTED

(b)
```
TO FIT BUST
TOUR DE POITRINE
81cm    32in
```
100% WOOL/LAINE

WOOL CYCLE
DO NOT TUMBLE DRY
RE-SHAPE WHILE DAMP
DRY SUPPORTED

(c)

MADE IN THE U.K.
100% COTTON/COTON

WARM
RE-SHAPE
WHILE DAMP

Safe as houses? (1)

Each year about 5000 people in Britain die in accidents, and a further 3 000 000 need medical attention after accidents in the home. Look at the charts *(below)*. Do more people die as a result of accidents in the home or accidents on the road? Do more people need hospital treatment after accidents at work or at home?

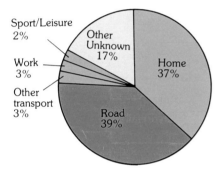

Fatal accidents

Figures for England and Wales.

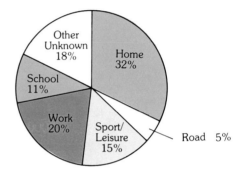

Accidents treated in hospital

Estimates for England and Wales.

What is meant by an accident?

An accident is an unintentional and unexpected injury. An accident may occur because a person is in a particular place and using a particular product, for example Simon (aged two) sees his favourite toy car on a shelf in the living room, climbs on a stool which overbalances, falls and breaks an arm.

Most accidents in the home are caused by human error and could be prevented. More accidents occur in the garden, yard, patio and garage areas in the summer than in the winter, and the opposite is true of the rooms indoors.

What kinds of injuries occur?

Injuries can be grouped under three main headings which make up about 92 per cent of all accidents in the home (see table on p. 167).

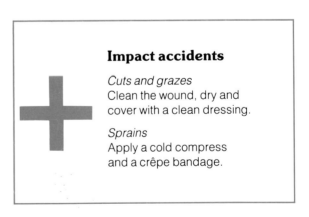

Impact accidents

Cuts and grazes
Clean the wound, dry and cover with a clean dressing.

Sprains
Apply a cold compress and a crêpe bandage.

These include falls, cuts, bumping into things and being hurt by falling objects. About 65 per cent of home accidents are of this kind. Young children and the elderly are particularly at risk.

Histogram showing
the location of
accidents in the home

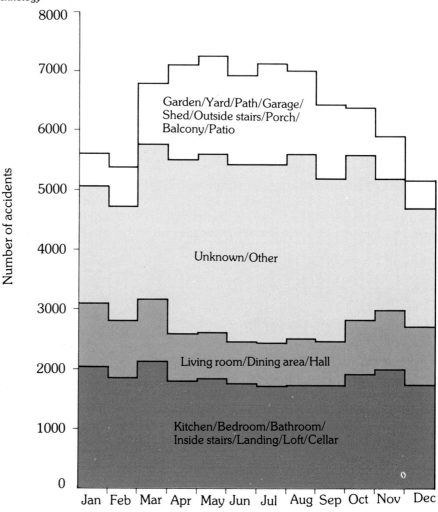

Number of accidents

Garden/Yard/Path/Garage/
Shed/Outside stairs/Porch/
Balcony/Patio

Unknown/Other

Living room/Dining area/Hall

Kitchen/Bedroom/Bathroom/
Inside stairs/Landing/Loft/Cellar

Jan Feb Mar Apr May Jun Jul Aug Sep Oct Nov Dec

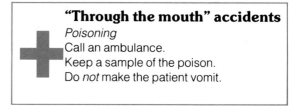

Heat accidents

Burns and scalds
Cool the site immediately and thoroughly –
hold under cold running water for ten
minutes. Get medical advice if the burn
covers a large area.

"Through the mouth" accidents

Poisoning
Call an ambulance.
Keep a sample of the poison.
Do *not* make the patient vomit.

These include burns and scalds. These
accidents occur less frequently, but can be
very serious.

Burns occur when the skin comes into
contact with dry heat (for example a hot pan),
or fire. Scalds are caused by hot liquid, such as
water or fat.

There are over 50 000 accidental fires per
year in which about 650 people die and over
6000 are injured.

These include accidental poisonings,
suffocation and choking. Young children are
particularly at risk as they put so many things
into their mouths and do not know the
difference between safe and poisonous liquids
in bottles.

Type of injury	%	
Cut/laceration	29.2	
Puncture wound	2.5	
Splinter	0.9	
Abrasion/graze	2.7	
Other open wound	0.2	
Dislocation	0.7	Impact accidents
Fracture	9.3	
Sprain/strain	4.1	
Bruise/contusion	11.6	
Concussion	0.7	
Tenderness/swelling	19.6	
Burn	2.4	Heat accidents
Scald	2.5	
Poisoning	1.7	Through the mouth accidents
Ingestion	0.7	
Foreign body	3.5	
Suffocation	0.2	
Other/unknown	7.5	

Workshop

1 Draw up a table with four columns headed Accident, Cause, Injury and Avoidance. In your table:
 a list four accidents which have happened in your home in the last year
 b note the cause of each accident
 c note the injury
 d suggest how the accidents could have been avoided.

2 Compare your table with others in your class and record the class results in another table, as shown in the example below.

 Compare the class results with the figures given in the table above.

3 Why do you think that some types of home accidents increase in the summer?

4 Explain why young children and the elderly are more likely to have accidents in the home.

5 a Carol, aged 12, has touched a hot iron and burned her hand a little. What should she do?
 b Your brother Peter, aged 4, has taken a drink from an unlabelled bottle he found in the garden shed. What should you do?
 c You cut your hand while slicing vegetables. How should you treat it?

Type of accident	Number of accidents	Number in class	% of total accidents
Fall	12	24	$12/24 \times 100 = 50$
Cut	7	24	$7/24 \times 100 = 29$
Burn	4	24	$4/24 \times 100 = 17$
Poisoning	1	24	$1/24 \times 100 = 4$

Safe as houses? (2)

The table on the right shows the percentage of accidents which occur in different areas in the home.

The kitchen

The most common accidents to occur in the kitchen are cuts, burns and scalds. To avoid cuts, sharp utensils should not be left lying around and should be stored out of reach of small children. Always cut food on a board, not in the hands. To avoid heat accidents, turn pan handles towards the back of the cooker to prevent the pans being knocked off. A hob guard can be fitted if there are young children in the family. Use oven gloves to remove hot containers from the oven, *never* a damp cloth. When frying, constant care is necessary as unattended pans may catch fire.

You should always clean up spills immediately, particularly if on the floor. Check that flexes do not trail across cookers or across the floor. Bleaches, disinfectants and cleaning agents should be stored well above the reach of children, in a secure cupboard. If they have been removed from the original container, the new container must be clearly labelled. Never touch switches, plugs or any electrical appliance with wet hands – you may get an electric shock. (See page 181) for more about safety of children in the kitchen.)

The living/dining room

Open fires should have a fire guard fixed firmly around them if there are children or elderly people in the family. Check that guards on other fires and heaters are suitable. Keep furniture, curtains etc. away from fires and heaters. Do not drape clothing over heaters.

Check floor coverings are in good condition – not frayed – and are properly fitted, particularly in doorways.

Do not overload electric sockets, and make sure appliances are fitted with the correct fuse.

You should be careful with hot drinks, particularly if there are small children around. Make sure there are no overhanging table-cloths for small children to tug at.

Location	%
Kitchen	9.0
Bathroom/toilet	2.2
Bedroom	5.6
Loft/attic	0.2
Living/dining room	9.7
Hall/lobby	1.5
Landing	0.6
Inside stairs	6.4
Cellar	0.1
Balcony/patio	0.3
Porch/threshold	1.2
Garden/grassed area	7.2
Yard/path/driveway	3.6
Outside stairs/steps	1.0
Garage/garden shed	1.6
Other	0.9
Unknown	48.9

The hall and stairs

Good lighting is essential here. Make sure there is a two-way switch so that lights can be operated at each end of the staircase. Avoid leaving any articles on the stairs and check that children's toys are removed.

Carpets should be firmly fixed – avoid highly polished surfaces and loose mats.

A smoke detector can be fitted at the top of the stairs as an additional safety precaution. Safety gates can be fitted at the top of the stairs if there are young children in the family.

The bedroom

Ensure that electric blankets are checked regularly and that electric underblankets are switched off before getting into bed. Check the seal on hot water bottles and do not overfill them.

A bedside light could prevent an accident. Smoking in bed can cause fires and should be avoided.

The bathroom

Water conducts electricity, so do not use portable electrical appliances in the bathroom. Heaters should be wall mounted and have a cord-pull switch. Lights should also have cord-pull switches.

Medicines should be stored in a cabinet with a safety catch.

Fitted hand rails help elderly people getting in and out of the bath. A mat in the bath will prevent slipping.

Do not leave young children alone in the bath. Always run the cold water into the bath first.

The garden

Electrical appliances can be dangerous. Sockets should be fitted with a residual current earth leakage circuit breaker (an RCB) to reduce the risk of electric shocks. Switch off and remove the plug before adjusting or cleaning any appliance.

When using a mower, wear strong shoes, not sandals. Do not leave hand tools lying on the ground, particularly rakes and forks as the tines can cause a nasty wound.

Label garden chemicals clearly and store them out of the reach of children.

Ponds and swimming pools should be covered if there are very young children about. A garden gate can prevent children running on to roads.

The garage

If the garage is also used as a workshop, ensure that lighting and ventilation is good. Tools should be securely stored on racks or shelves. Flammable substances such as paints, petrol and paraffin should be stored in sealed containers away from heat.

Workshop

1 Look at the table on page 168.
   List the four places in the home where accidents happen most often and the percentage of accidents occurring in each of these places.

2 Suggest six ways of avoiding impact injuries in the home.

3 Heat injuries often occur in the kitchen. State four ways in which they could be avoided.

4 Is your home safe? How could the safety of your living room be improved?

5 Look at the drawing and list seven possible dangers.

Ergonomics in the kitchen

Before you begin to design a kitchen it is important to know a little about **ergonomics**. Ergonomics is the study of work and its environment in order to achieve maximum efficiency. In relation to kitchen design this means designing and planning a kitchen so that it is safe, efficient and easy to work in. We are going to look at three aspects of ergonomics in kitchens.

1 The work triangle

Most of the work done in the kitchen involves walking between three essential pieces of equipment: the cooker, sink and fridge. You can't even boil an egg without visiting the cooker, sink and fridge! For maximum efficiency the cooker, sink and fridge need to be placed conveniently close, but with work surfaces in-between. There are several basic kitchen layouts, depending on the shape and size of the room and the position of the doors and windows.

If we take each of these layouts and position the essential pieces of equipment with work surfaces in between, we have what is known as the work triangle.

Most of the walking done in a kitchen will be in this triangle. In a large kitchen, if the triangle is also large, you will spend unnecessary time and energy walking around. This is poor ergonomic design. If the work triangle is very small with insufficient work surfaces it is inconvenient and could be dangerous. It is also poor ergonomic design. Once the work triangle has been planned it must not be obstructed by tables and chairs or other objects.

Basic kitchen shapes

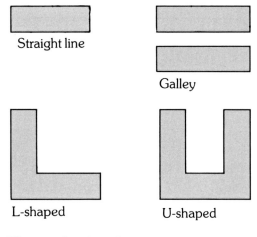

Straight line

Galley

L-shaped

U-shaped

The work triangle

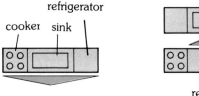

cooker   sink   refrigerator

refrigerator

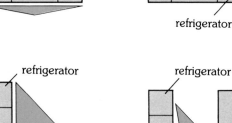

refrigerator   refrigerator

L-shaped   U-shaped

2 Working heights

It is essential that the work surfaces in a kitchen are at the correct height. Working at

Correct working height: 75 mm below elbow

working surface

75 mm

surfaces which are either too high or too low can be tiring. Bending and stretching to reach equipment in cupboards is also tiring, inefficient and could be dangerous. Factory-made kitchen units are a standard 900 mm height, suitable for someone approximately 165 cms tall (5'5"). To find a person's correct working height, measure from the floor to 75 mm below their elbow.

How to get units of the right height

Some kitchen design companies make custom designed kitchens exactly the right height for the customer, but this is usually very expensive. The height of factory-made units can be adjusted by raising or lowering the plinth.

Changing the height of factory-made units

Plinth section can be raised or lowered.

Height of legs can be adjusted before adding plinth.

Wall units can be bought in different heights and can be fixed at different heights on the wall. For a tall person the taller wall units can be bought and can be fixed higher up the wall. For a shorter person it would be better to have the smaller wall units fixed lower down.

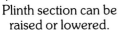

60 mm wall unit

90 mm wall unit

3 Storage

An ergonomically designed kitchen has all the equipment stored in safe and convenient positions. Equipment which is not used very often can be placed in less accessible places such as top shelves. Heavy equipment should be stored in base cupboards or in pull-out units where it is easy to get at. Equipment can be grouped and placed where it is likely to be used, for example mugs and coffee can be stored in a cupboard above the unit where the kettle is kept. Cleaning materials are usually stored near the sink. This is convenient, but if there are any small children in the house a child-proof catch should be fitted to the door.

Workshop

1 Draw two basic kitchen layouts. Show the positions of the cooker, sink and fridge on each plan and draw in the work triangle. Explain the importance of a convenient work triangle.

2 What is meant by the term *ergonomics*? Why is it important to get work-surface and cupboard heights correct? Work out your own most convenient work-surface height.

3 Conduct your own workstudy exercice.

   Work in pairs. One person does the cooking, the other is the workstudy analyst.

   a Using graph paper, make a scale plan of an area of your home-economics room, including a cooker, sink and refrigerator. (If there is not a refrigerator nearby, use a cupboard to represent one.) Every 1 cm on your graph paper should represent 25 cm in the home-economics room.

   b Attach your scale plan to a cork or polystyrene tile. Place pins in the plan to mark the cooker, sink and refrigerator.

   c The cook makes a snack e.g. an omelette.

   d The workstudy analyst plots the cook's movements on the graph by wrapping string round the pins. The analyst should also note any bending, stretching and unnecessary movement, and should time the cook.

   e When the task is complete, measure the string and scale it up to see how many metres were walked.

   f Discuss the findings. Repeat the task. How much time and effort can be saved?

Design a kitchen

Make a kitchen design file by following this step-by-step guide.

1 **Study the floor plan and diagrams**
   The grid on page 173 represents the floor plan of a kitchen 3 m by 4 m. Trace round the grid, and all the units on page 174. You can alter the grid if you want your kitchen to be larger or smaller. Stick the grid onto a piece of plain A4 paper.

2 **Doors and windows**
   Mark the position of the doors and windows on your floor plan. A kitchen usually has two doors, one connecting with the rest of the house and one leading to the garden.

3 **Work triangle**
   Start your plan by positioning the cooker, sink and fridge. It is usual (though not essential) to place the sink under the window. This is the most convenient place because of the plumbing. Most people also like to have a pleasant view to look at when they are working at the sink. Remember to have a convenient work triangle.

4 **Appliances**
   Decide which other appliances you need in the kitchen, and position them on the plan.

5 **Base units**
   Now position all the base units. Base units can be drawn round and used more than once. When the floor plan is complete and you are sure that your design is safe and convenient, stick all the pieces to the plan.

6 **Wall units**
   Position wall units above the base units.

7 **What does it look like?**
   Now that you have completed your floor plan, make drawings of each wall in the kitchen.

8 **Finishing touches**
   Using catalogues, magazines and your imagination, give details of the type, colour and design of the following. Include drawings and samples in your file.
   Base and wall units
   Work surfaces   Heating
   Floor covering   Lighting
   Wall covering   Ventilation

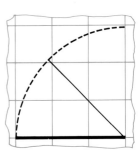

A door is shown like this to indicate the path it takes when opened.

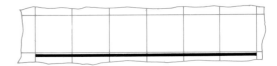

1½ metre window

Mark windows with a heavy line on the outside of the plan.

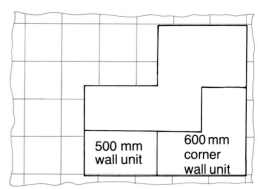

500 mm wall unit

600 mm corner wall unit

Position wall units above base units.

9 **Cost your plan**
   The cost of medium-priced units is included. Remember that for a more detailed costing you need to find out the cost of work surfaces, appliances, floor covering, wall covering, heating, lighting ventilation and perhaps the cost of installation.

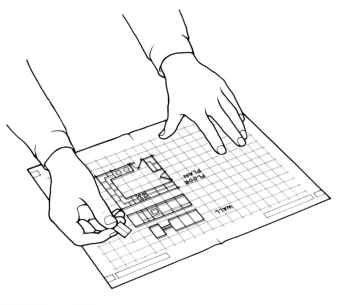

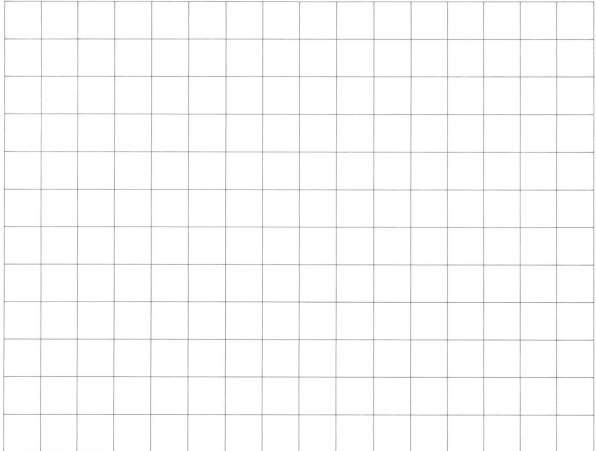

Grid represents a kitchen 3 m by 4 m.　　　　**SCALE: 1 square (10 mm) = 250 mm**

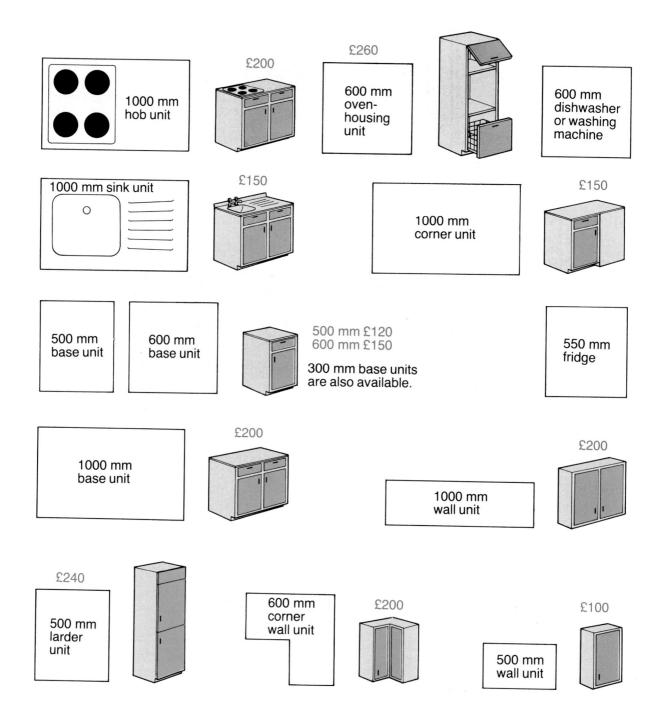

1000 mm hob unit

£200

£260

600 mm oven-housing unit

600 mm dishwasher or washing machine

1000 mm sink unit

£150

1000 mm corner unit

£150

500 mm base unit

600 mm base unit

500 mm £120
600 mm £150

300 mm base units are also available.

550 mm fridge

1000 mm base unit

£200

1000 mm wall unit

£200

£240

500 mm larder unit

600 mm corner wall unit

£200

£100

500 mm wall unit

A practical kitchen

When the basic layout of a kitchen has been decided, other important aspects need to be planned before the kitchen is fitted. We will now look at these.

Lighting

A single centre light is usually not adequate in a kitchen, especially a large kitchen. Good lighting makes work easier and is essential for safety. Interesting decorative effects can also be achieved with lighting.

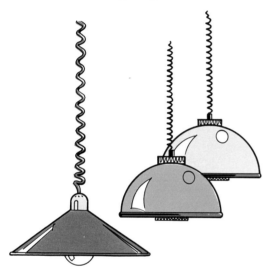

Adjustable rise-and-fall pendant lights can be fitted over dining areas.

Some lighting ideas for kitchens

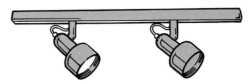

Spotlights can be fixed on walls or ceilings and can then be individually angled to direct light where it is required.

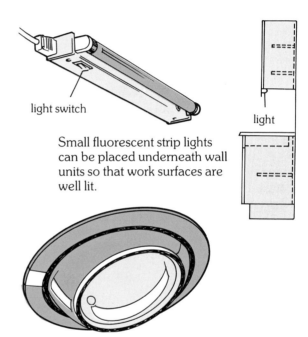

light switch

light

Small fluorescent strip lights can be placed underneath wall units so that work surfaces are well lit.

Downlights can be fixed into ceilings and angled to give light where it is needed.

Heating

Safety is the most important consideration when planning heating for a kitchen. Portable heating appliances should not be used in a kitchen. Radiators are the best type of heating for a kitchen. If other heaters are used, they should be fixed to the wall.

Ventilation

Adequate ventilation is important in a kitchen.

Moisture, heat, grease and fumes all need to be removed from time to time. If a kitchen is not well ventilated it can be very hot and uncomfortable to work in and a build-up of steam can lead to condensation and damp, which can spoil the decor. Windows can be used for ventilation, but having windows open in winter can cause draughts and make the kitchen cold. If possible, it is better to incorporate some type of ventilation when the kitchen is being planned.

Extractor fans can be fitted into external walls and windows.

Cooker hoods with extractor fans can be fitted above cookers. Some have matching unit trims and some incorporate lights.

Surfaces

Work surfaces need to be

- easy to clean
- heat resistant
- hardwearing
- scratch proof

The most common type of work surface used in the kitchen is laminated plastic. (Formica is a trade name for laminated plastic.) This type of work surface is hardwearing and reasonably priced. It can be scratched, so chopping boards should always be used. If can also be charred by excessive heat and so very hot saucepans should not be placed directly on it.

Ceramic tiles can also be used for work surfaces. They are decorative and hardwearing but expensive, and can crack or chip if heavy objects are dropped on them.

Wall coverings

Walls in a kitchen need to be

- easy to clean
- water resistant
- hardwearing

Vinyl emulsion paints and wallpapers are practical and inexpensive. Ceramic tiles are also practical and hardwearing, and can add interesting decorative effects to a kitchen with plain units. The main disadvantages of tiles is that they can be expensive.

Floor covering

Floor covering in a kitchen needs to be

- slip resistant
- hardwearing
- waterproof
- easy to clean
- heat resistant

Vinyl floor covering is economical, fairly hardwearing, easy to clean, waterproof, and is slip resistant if it has a textured surface. It can be damaged by heat. A wide variety of colours and patterns is available.

Carpets which are stain and water resistant can be used in kitchens. Other types of carpet are not suitable.

Ceramic floor tiles are very hardwearing and are decorative, but they are expensive.

Workshop

1 Where would you position the lighting in this kitchen? Explain the type(s) of lighting you would use and give reasons for your choice.

2 You have decided to have laminated plastic work surfaces in your kitchen. Write a few sentences about their advantages and disadvantages and explain how to care for them.

3 You have chosen plain cream kitchen units for reasons of economy but you want to add interesting colour and texture to the kitchen. Explain how you can achieve this with wall coverings and floor coverings.

4 Why is efficient ventilation in a kitchen important? Suggest ways of ventilating
a an existing kitchen economically
b a new kitchen being planned.

How green is your kitchen?

Every day of the week, as we shop for food, cook food and dispose of waste we make choices that can affect the environment of the world we live in. It is possible to be a 'green' cook and consumer , and to make choices and act in ways that will help to conserve our world.

Why be green?

For many years the developed nations of the world have improved their lifestyles at the expense of the environment. Earth's resources have been exploited without much thought and have therefore been used up at a much faster rate than they can be replaced. Our modern way of life has also caused immense pollution. Most scientists now believe that damage to our environment will cause major problems unless there is collective action by governments, industries and individuals worldwide. We can all do our bit to help.

What are the problems?

Some of the main problems that we can do something about are described below.

1. Global warming

This is also known as 'the greenhouse effect'. The Earth's atmosphere is being made warmer as a result of the blanketing effect of sulphur, carbon dioxide, chlorofluorocarbons (CFCs) and other polluting gases. These gases act like a blanket around the Earth, keeping solar radiation close to the surface instead of allowing it to escape into space. The main ways by which man has created this warmer climate are by burning fossil fuels (coal, gas, oil and wood) which produce carbon dioxide; using aerosols containing CFCs; and using CFCs in manufacturing processes and in refrigerators and freezers. A warmer climate might seem like a good idea, but it would

cause devastating problems. Some parts of the world would become flooded while other parts would become very dry and arid, affecting world food resources.

What can we do to help?

- Save fuel whenever possible (see p. 94). Saving fuel also saves money.
- Don't buy aerosols that contain CFCs. It would be better still to avoid aerosols altogether as they are *not* environmentally friendly. They are also expensive to produce and difficult to dispose of.
- When you buy new appliances check their fuel consumption and choose the ones that use the least fuel.
- When you buy a new refrigerator choose one which contains a low amount of CFCs. Dispose of old refrigerators carefully. You can contact the local authority for help.

2. Water pollution

Detergents, fertilisers and other manufactured products contain a group of chemicals called phosphates which can find their way into our water supply and can be released into rivers and lakes. Phosphates encourage excessive growth of algae which causes a solid green mat to form across the surface of the water. This blocks out the sun so that there is a reduced level of oxygen in the water below and fish and plant life may be killed.

What can we do to help?

- Use all cleaning products sparingly. This will also save money.
- Use phosphate-free cleaning products.
- Try to avoid using harmful chemicals in the home, for example caustic soda oven cleaners and chlorine bleach.

3. Depletion of the Earth's resources

Every day we waste valuable raw materials and fuel in the manufacture of packaging and containers. It then costs a lot of money to dispose of them.

The life of a jam-jar

Fuel and raw materials go into the manufacture of the jam-jar.

Consumer buys jam, cost of jar is included in the price.

Consumer throws jar in dustbin.

Consumer pays money, through the poll tax, to have jar disposed of. Jar dumped in landfill site.

Consumer buys new jar of jam after paying for the old jar to be disposed of.

It has been estimated that 55 to 60 per cent of domestic rubbish could be reclaimed. Much of our waste is dumped in large holes in the ground called landfill sites. The rotting waste causes pollution and may also leak methane gas (a greenhouse gas) into the atmosphere. Millions of trees are chopped down every year to produce paper, much of which is thrown away.

Before you throw anything away you should stop to think where it will go to. Everything comes from somewhere, costing money and resources. Everything must go somewhere, possibly causing pollution and costing money.

What can we do to conserve the environment?

- Avoid using 'disposable' paper products such as kitchen paper and paper plates.
- Buy products which have the minimum of packaging.
- Find products which come in containers that can be re-used or recycled.
- Re-use plastic carrier bags.
- Find out if a local charity collects empty aluminium cans for recycling.
- Buy biodegradable plastics which rot in the ground.
- Look for PET plastic which can be recycled.
- Always return milk bottles.
- Take empty glass bottles to a bottle bank.
- Find out if the local authority or a local charity collects paper for recycling.
- Buy recycled paper products.

Ecover is a company that produces environmentally-friendly products such as phosphate-free washing powder and chlorine-free bleach. Ecover also organises nationwide campaigns to make people aware of the pollution caused by many cleaning products and detergents.

Green food – not just cabbages!

Some foods are more environmentally friendly than others. For example, it is more cost effective in terms of land use to grow crops to feed *directly* to people, rather than to grow crops to feed to animals and then to feed the animals to people.

Many environmental groups are concerned about factory-farming processes such as the intensive rearing of poultry and battery egg production. There is also concern that the huge increase in the consumption of processed foods may be harmful to our health, and that many of our foods contain too many additives. Many people believe that too many fertilisers and pesticides are used in the production of food crops. These issues are debatable and so it is up to the individual to learn about these issues and to make his or her own choices. Those interested in eating more natural foods might consider taking some of the following steps.

- Eating fresh foods where possible, especially fruit and vegetables.
- Eating less meat.
- Eating organic fruit and vegetables which are produced without chemical fertilisers.
- Eating free-range eggs and free-range poultry.
- Reading food labels and avoiding foods with large numbers of unnecessary additives.
- Learning more about where foods come from and how they are produced. Being better informed about food will help you to make sensible choices and to eat healthily.

Being a deep shade of green may be difficult, but if we were all just a shade greener the world would be a better place.

Workshop

1 Conduct an energy audit of your home. Draw up a list of recommendations for saving fuel. This could make you very popular with your parents! Try to put your recommendations into practice and compare fuel bills to see if you have managed to save fuel.

2 Make a chart which lists aerosol products and gives alternatives to them.

Aerosol product	Alternatives
Spray polish	Polish in tin
Spray anti-perspirant	Solid anti-perspirant

Give reasons for finding alternatives to aerosol products.

3 Encourage your school to become green. As a class exercise, make a noticeboard display of the green issues and produce a leaflet called *How we can all help to improve our world*.

4 Explain why the large amount of waste produced by homes every week is a waste of money, fuel and resources. Suggest a list of ways of reducing domestic waste.

Design Project 1

A kitchen dining room for a young family

Mr and Mrs Lee have two small children aged six and three. They need more space for their family and so they have decided to build a new garage on to the side of their house and convert the present garage into a kitchen/dining room. The present kitchen will become a utility room.

Present plan of house

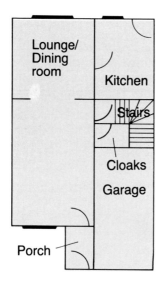

Plan showing proposed alterations

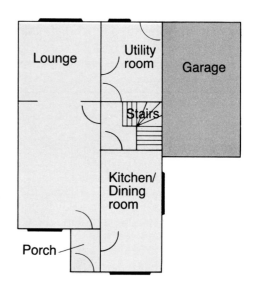

Essential information

- The proposed kitchen measures 2.5 m by 5.25 m.
- There will be two windows (see plan above).
- There will be two doors (see plan).
- The washing machine and freezer will be in the utility room. Appliances needed in the kitchen are a cooker, fridge and dishwasher. Mr and Mrs Lee intend to keep their present free-standing cooker and fridge. Both measure 550 mm wide.

- A small dining area is needed for a table and four chairs. The dining area needs to be very easy to clean so that the children can use it as a play area for painting and using Play Dough etc.
- With two small children in the house, safety must be considered.
- Mr and Mrs Lee are using medium-priced self-assembly units which they intend to fit themselves. They will also do the decorating to keep the cost down but will get professional help with the plumbing and electrics.

How to do Design Project I

A Adapt the grid on p. 173 to make it the correct size for the Lee's kitchen/dining room. Make a scale plan for the table and chairs.

B Follow the steps on the basic plan, but keep in mind the Lee family and their requirements.

C Give details of all the surfaces used in the dining area, including wall and floor coverings. Have you achieved a practical, easy-to-clean area?

D Suggest ways in which accidents in the kitchen involving children may be prevented.

E How can Mr and Mrs Lee ensure that the children stay safely in the dining area while they work in the kitchen?

Children in the kitchen

Fit a cooker guard to prevent children pulling saucepans off the top. Keep children away from cookers – the outside of an oven can become very hot.

Use a safety gate or barrier across the door to stop children getting into the kitchen.

Cover electrical sockets with socket covers to prevent children putting their fingers or objects into the pinholes.

Put child-resistant catches on the inside of cupboard doors. Especially useful for cupboards containing cleaning materials or heavy equipment.

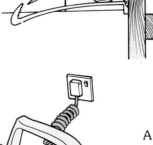

A coiled kettle flex will help to prevent children pulling the kettle off the work surface.

Put babies in playpens in a safe corner of the kitchen.

NEVER LEAVE BABIES AND SMALL CHILDREN UNSUPERVISED IN A KITCHEN

Design Project 2

A kitchen for a retired couple

Mr and Mrs Wright have recently retired. Now that they have plenty of time, they have decided to re-fit their kitchen. Both are fit and well but they intend to plan their kitchen with the future in mind and take into consideration that there may come a time when they are far less fit and active.

Essential information

- Their kitchen is fairly small, measuring 3 m by 3 m. There is a small utility room adjoining the kitchen which houses the washing machine and tumble dryer.
- Mrs Wright enjoys cooking and will be doing most of the work in the kitchen. She is 155 cm (5 ft 1 in) tall and wants the units to be suitable for her height.
- Mr and Mrs Wright intend to buy the following appliances for their kitchen: a dishwasher, refrigerator and a split-level cooker.
- They have decided to have a luxury kitchen with good quality units and decoration.

Designing kitchens for elderly people

People are now living longer and often enjoying many years of retirement. This means that planning for old age is important. Birmingham University has a centre for Applied Gerontology which studies ways of making life easier for the elderly. Its motto is

> "Design for the young and you exclude the old. Design for the old and you include the young."

So when you design a kitchen for the elderly it will not look out of the ordinary, but it will be very safe, efficient and easy to work in – a good kitchen from an ergonomic point of view. You need to bear in mind the following points when producing a design.

- Have work surfaces at the correct height (see page 171).
- Choose surfaces which are easy to clean.
- The floor should be easy to clean and non-slip.
- Design a layout which is safe and well lit.
- Choose cupboard door handles and taps which are easy to open and turn.

Easy-to-turn lever tap

- Cookers and fridges can be set at waist height to eliminate bending. Cookers can have drop-down doors to rest dishes on.
- Make use of modern technology to reduce work in the kitchen, especially work which involves standing for any length of time. Consider incorporating a dishwasher and microwave oven into the plan.
- Arrange storage so that everything is easily accessible to avoid bending, stretching and reaching into corners. For convenient storage have carousel corner units, deep, pull-out drawers for saucepans, baskets on the backs of doors, tall larder units and pull-out larder units.

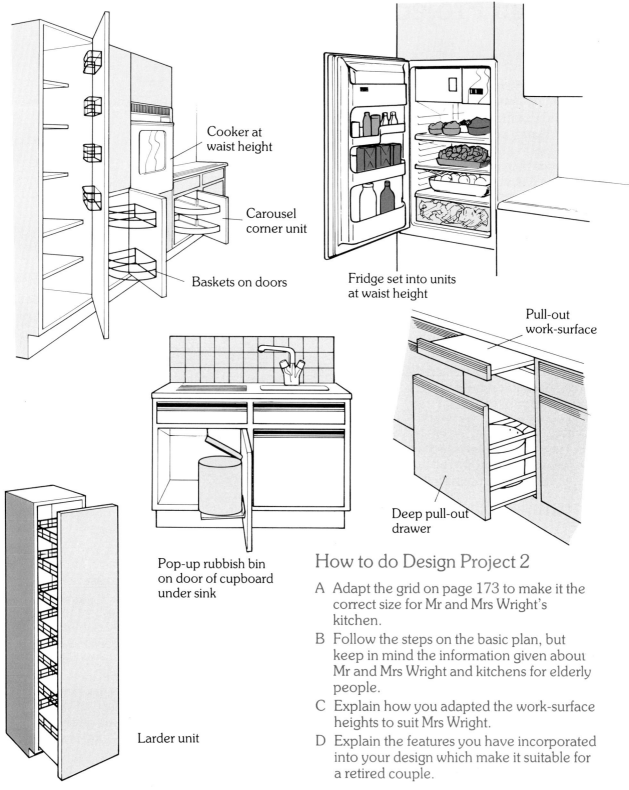

Cooker at
waist height

Carousel
corner unit

Baskets on doors

Fridge set into units
at waist height

Pull-out
work-surface

Deep pull-out
drawer

Pop-up rubbish bin
on door of cupboard
under sink

Larder unit

How to do Design Project 2

A Adapt the grid on page 173 to make it the
   correct size for Mr and Mrs Wright's
   kitchen.

B Follow the steps on the basic plan, but
   keep in mind the information given about
   Mr and Mrs Wright and kitchens for elderly
   people.

C Explain how you adapted the work-surface
   heights to suit Mrs Wright.

D Explain the features you have incorporated
   into your design which make it suitable for
   a retired couple.

Design Project 3

A kitchen for a disabled person

Mark is 25. He has been paralysed from the waist down since the age of 19, when he was involved in a motor bike accident. He works as a computer operator for the local council. He has his own car and drives himself to work. He enjoys playing basketball in his spare time. Mark has been living with his parents but will soon move into a bungalow which is being built at the moment. He must be able to cook for himself and for friends and family when they visit and so wants a kitchen which is adapted to his needs.

Essential information

- The kitchen measures 3 m by 4 m.
- Equipment needed: hob, oven, fridge and washer-dryer.
- There are two doors, both 800 mm wide, and one window 1.5 m wide.

Points to note

1 There should be enough floor space after the units are fitted to allow for a wheelchair to move around.

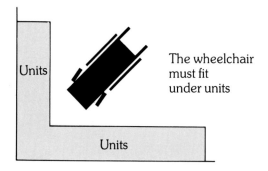

The wheelchair must fit under units

2 Space needs to be left under the hob, sink and work-surface for the wheelchair to go underneath.

3 Units need to be set a little lower than standard height (800 mm rather than 900 mm) so that it is easy to work at the work surfaces from a wheelchair.

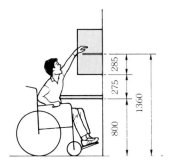

Suggested heights in mm for units used from a wheelchair

4 A small work triangle means that moving around is kept to a minimum. Ideally the cooker, sink and fridge should be in a continuous sequence.

5 The fridge and cooker need to be housed in units at the correct height (see diagram).

6 Mobile storage trolleys are useful. They can be used as an extra work surface and stored under the sink or hob when not in use.

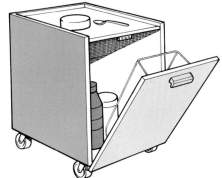

Mobile storage trolley

7 The sink needs to be shallow enough for Mark to reach into and the piping needs to be set back far enough to allow the wheelchair to go underneath.

8 Storage needs to be easily accessible. Units can be fitted with carousel shelves, pull-out baskets and baskets on the doors.

9 The floor needs to be non-slip.

10 If the window is difficult to reach, an extractor fan is needed for ventilation.

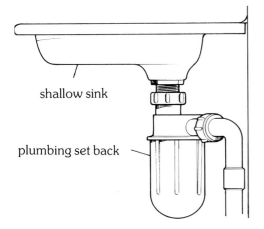

shallow sink

plumbing set back

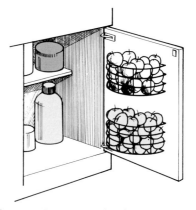

Accessible storage: baskets on doors

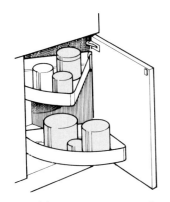

Accessible storage: carousel unit

How to do Design Project 3

A Use the grid on page 187. It is the correct size for Mark's kitchen (3 m by 4 m). Mark the position of the doors and window.

B Study the photograph for ideas. An L-shaped kitchen would give a continuous work sequence and would also leave enough floor space.

C Plan the layout using the scale units overleaf.

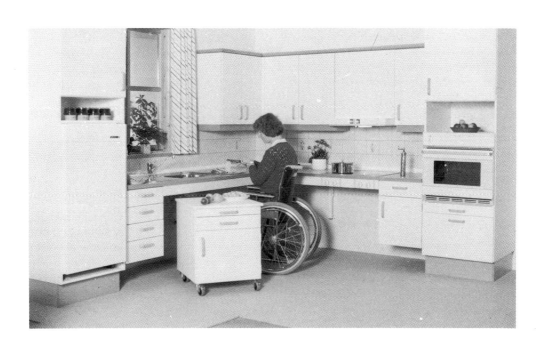

When you have completed the plan draw each wall with its units in position to give a clearer idea of what your kitchen looks like. Your drawings could be done to scale using graph paper. Give details of all equipment and materials used in the kitchen and explain how you have made the kitchen suitable for Mark.

Advice about adapting or planning a kitchen for a disabled person can be obtained from The Disabled Living Foundation, local Social Services Departments and occupational therapists.

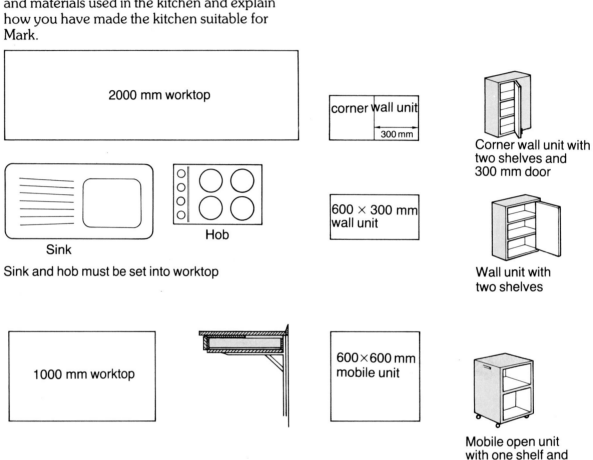

2000 mm worktop

Sink

Hob

Sink and hob must be set into worktop

1000 mm worktop

600 mm cupboard

corner wall unit
300 mm

600 × 300 mm wall unit

600 × 600 mm mobile unit

600 mm drawer unit

Corner wall unit with two shelves and 300 mm door

Wall unit with two shelves

Mobile open unit with one shelf and a worktop (2 brake castors)

Unit with pull-out worktop and one wire tray

Unit with two deep drawers and one shallow drawer

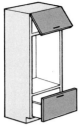

600 mm
fridge-
housing
unit

Fridge-housing unit
with drawer and
cupboard

600 mm
oven-
housing
unit

600 mm
washer/
dryer

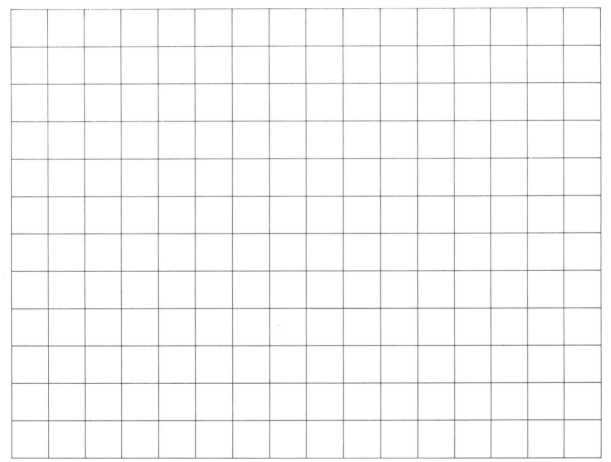

Grid for a kitchen 3 m by 4 m.   SCALE: 1 square (10 mm) = 250 mm

Tables to show the recommended daily amounts of nutrients for population groups in the UK

Recommended daily amounts of nutrients for population groups

Age ranges	Energy		Protein	Calcium	Iron	Vitamin A (retinol equivalent)	Thiamin	Riboflavin	Niacin equivalent	Vitamin C	Vitamin D*
	MJ	kcal	g	mg	mg	µg	mg	mg	mg	mg	µg
Boys											
15–17	12.0	2,880	72	600	12	750	1.2	1.7	19	30	–
Girls											
15–17	9.0	2,150	53	600	12	750	0.9	1.7	19	30	–
Men											
18–34	12.0	2,900	72	500	10	750	1.2	1.6	18	30	–
35–64	11.5	2,750	69	500	10	750	1.1	1.6	18	30	–
65–74	10.0	2,400	60	500	10	750	1.0	1.6	18	30	–
75 and over	9.0	2,150	54	500	10	750	0.9	1.6	18	30	–
Women											
18–54	9.0	2,150	54	500	12	750	0.9	1.3	15	30	–
55–74	8.0	1,900	47	500	10	750	0.8	1.3	15	30	–
75 and over	7.0	1,680	42	500	10	750	0.7	1.3	15	30	–

*Most people who go out in the sun need no dietary source of vitamin D, but children and adolescents in winter, and housebound adults, are recommended to take 10 µg of vitamin D daily.

(See pages 51 and 67)

Recommended daily amounts of nutrients for women aged 18–54

	Energy		Protein	Calcium	Iron	Vitamin A (retinol equivalent)	Thiamin	Riboflavin	Niacin equivalent	Vitamin C	Vitamin D
	MJ	kcal	g	mg	mg	µg	mg	mg	mg	mg	µg
Most occupations	9.0	2,150	54	500	12	750	0.9	1.3	15	30	–
Very active	10.5	2,500	62	500	12	750	1.0	1.3	15	30	–
Pregnant	10.0	2,400	60	1,200	13	750	1.0	1.6	18	60	10
Lactating	11.5	2,750	69	1,200	15	1,200	1.1	1.8	21	60	10

(See page 58)

Recommended daily amounts of nutrients for girls aged 3–17

Age	Energy		Protein	Calcium	Iron	Vitamin A (retinol equivalent)	Thiamin	Riboflavin	Niacin equivalent	Vitamin C
	MJ	kcal	g	mg	mg	µg	mg	mg	mg	mg
3–4	6.25	1,500	37	600	8	300	0.6	0.8	9	20
5–6	7.0	1,680	42	600	10	300	0.7	0.9	10	20
7–8	8.0	1,900	48	600	10	400	0.8	1.0	11	20
9–11	8.5	2,050	51	700	12	575	0.8	1.2	14	25
12–14	9.0	2,150	53	700	12	725	0.9	1.4	16	25
15–17	9.0	2,150	53	600	12	750	0.9	1.7	19	30

(See page 62)

Index

Acknowledgements

The authors and publisher would like to thank the following for permission to reproduce photographs, illustrations and charts:

Amberley Chalk Pits Museum 42; American Express Europe Ltd 149; Australian Nutrition Foundation 53; British Dietetic Association 52; British Gas North Thames 95; Brogdale Experimental Horticulture Station 133; Care Design 185; Cheeky Design Products 70; Churchill Livingstone Ltd from *Human Nutrition and Dietetics* by Davidson, Passmore, Brock and Truswell 37; Creda Ltd for fan-assisted oven 122; Department of Trade and Industry from *Home and Leisure Accident Research* 166; Eastern Electricity 95; Ecover 178; Health Education Authority from *Guide to Healthy Eating* 14; David Hoffman 67; Imperial War Museum for World War II ration book and coupons 43; Kenwood Ltd 112, 113, 116; Marks and Spencer Plc 149; Midland Bank Plc 147, 149; Ministry of Agriculture Fisheries and Food for Wartime Advice Leaflets from the Imperial War Museum 43 and Changes in the consumption of bread in Britain over the past 40 years from the National Food Survey reports 44; Panasonic Consumer Electronics UK for microwave combination oven 122; Tesco Stores Ltd 157; Understanding Electricity, Electricity Association, 30 Millbank, London SW1P 4RD for Microwave energy patterns 99, 106; Variable power control panel 107; Contact grill, Grill (lift and lock hinge) and Detachable plates 108; Slow cookers and Slow cooker (removable type) 110; Slow cooker (fixed pot) 111; Food processor (belt driven) 115; Structure of refrigerator 117; Refrigerator interior 118; HLCC symbols 163; Kitchen planning 173, 187.

The authors and publisher would like to thank the following for permission to reproduce extracts, charts and figures:

British Nutrition Foundation and Health Education Council for questions from JACNE Quiz Pages 4 & 5 25, 27, 31; Daily Mail for 'Slimmers in danger' from the *Daily Mail* 2/2/89 66; HASS Location of accidents survey for 1987 sample hospitals for figures of pie chart Accidents treated in hospital 165; HMSO for Average energy expenditure figures from *Manual of Nutrition* (1985) 37 and Tables to show the recommended daily amounts of nutrients for population groups in the UK (HMSO 1979) 51, 58, 62, 67, 188; Kelloggs Ltd for nutrition label for Bran Flakes with Sultanas 157; Ministry of Agriculture Fisheries and Food for figures for Average amount of household sugar purchased, from National Food Survey reports 26; Methuen Children's Books for extract from *When We Were Very Young* by A A Milne 62; Dr Anne Miller for information from her article in *Housecraft*, January 1982, for the Unit Testing, testing 104–5; OPCS mortality statistics 1986 for figures of pie chart Fatal accidents 165; ROSPA for accident categories used in table 167; Sainsbury's for nutrition label for Sainsbury's Muesli 157; Vegetarian Society for one week's menus for an ovo-lacto vegetarian 72, 73; World Health Organisation for figures for table Death rates from diseases of the circulatory system 13.